CREATING STRATEGIC READERS

Techniques for Supporting Rigorous Literacy Instruction

Author
Valerie Ellery, M.A.Ed., NBCT

Foreword
Lori Oczkus, M.A.

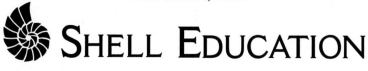

SHELL EDUCATION

Publishing Credits

Robin Erickson, *Production Director*; Lee Aucoin, *Creative Director*;
Timothy J. Bradley, *Illustration Manager*; Sara Johnson, M.S.Ed., *Editorial Director*;
Maribel Rendón, M.A.Ed., *Editor*; Sara Sciuto, *Assistant Editor*;
Grace Alba Le, *Designer*; Corinne Burton, M.A.Ed., *Publisher*

Image Credits

Cover illustration, Kristi Valiant; p. 4, 31, 105, 179, 225 Valerie Ellery

Standards

© 2007 Teachers of English to Speakers of Other Languages, Inc. (TESOL)

© 2007 Board of Regents of the University of Wisconsin System. World-Class Instructional Design and Assessment (WIDA). For more information on using the WIDA ELP Standards, please visit the WIDA website at www.wida.us.

© Copyright 2010. National Governors Association Center for Best Practices and Council of Chief State School Officers. All rights reserved.

Shell Education

5301 Oceanus Drive
Huntington Beach, CA 92649-1030
http://www.shelleducation.com

ISBN 978-1-4258-1185-3

© 2014 Shell Educational Publishing, Inc.

CREATING STRATEGIC READERS

Table of Contents

Dedication and Acknowledgments

Dedicated in loving memory to Velma, my grandma, who believed in me, and encouraged me to become a teacher. It was through her love for writing and inspiring words that the seed for writing was planted in my heart.

The legacy of love continues through my son, Nick, whose story has inspired thousands of educators globally to believe in their students.

Velma, excited about receiving her copy of *Creating Strategic Readers*.

Nick continues to leave a legacy of love and learning to his daughter, Evelyn.

There are always those special people in your life to whom you are forever grateful. I am so fortunate to have so many who believe in me and inspire me to be all that God has called me to be, and to live a life of integrity.

I am grateful for:

- my loving husband, Gregg, who is my true north and continues to be there through it all

- my children—Nick, Derek, Jacey, and Brooke—who are my priceless treasures

- my granddaughter, Evelyn Marie, who is one of the main reasons why I stay passionate about creating strategic readers. She will always be my "Princess Evie."

- my mother, Laurie, who never stops believing in me, and my father, Roger, who always was there cheering me on and is now watching over me from heaven

- my sisters, Connie and Christy, who are also my friends, and are always there for me

- my dear friends, Lisa Hanna, Tammy Thompson, and Michele Howard, who continue to encourage me with their genuine hearts and true friendship

- my church family, Bayside Community, who never stops praying for me

- my colleagues and friends, Amy Gaston, Mary Garced, Sue Gore, Shannon McCoy, and Nancy Roever, who never cease to amaze me with their support and love for education, as well as bringing laughter through this process

- my Teacher Created Materials/Shell Education and International Reading Association team, Sara Johnson, Maribel Rendón, and Tori Bachman, who bring an expertise to their profession and have inspired me more than they will ever know

About the Author

Valerie Ellery has dedicated 25 years to the field of literacy in various roles as a National Board Certified Teacher, a curriculum specialist, a mentor, a reading coach, a national consultant, and an international author. After acquiring her master's in reading K–12 from the University of South Florida, she became a district curriculum specialist. This new role gave her the opportunity to model reading strategies, mentor teachers, and construct a road map for creating strategic readers. In 2005, her first book, *Creating Strategic Readers: Techniques for Developing Competency in Phonemic Awareness, Phonics, Fluency, Vocabulary, and Comprehension* was published by the International Reading Association (IRA). The book has been used internationally in universities as an undergraduate course text, helping to propel the reading process into the forefront of education. She also published a staff-development video series titled "Creating Strategic Readers: Teaching Techniques for the Primary and Intermediate Grades." In 2009, the second edition of *Creating Strategic Readers* was written and once again chosen as the IRA's Book Club Selection and soared as one of their best sellers.

Valerie's coauthored titles include *The Facilitator's Guide to What Research Has to Say About Reading Instruction*, 3rd edition (IRA 2009); *Sustaining Strategic Readers: Techniques for Supporting Content Literacy in Grades 6-12* (IRA 2010); and *Strategic Reading Resource* (Saint Mary's Press 2013). Additionally, she coauthored two secondary curriculums in the area of self-worth and human trafficking: *Bodies Are Not Commodities* (A21 2014) and *ShineHOPE* (Hillsong 2014), which will impact young adults in 37 nations.

Currently, Valerie is working internationally in Zimbabwe, Africa, and Honduras to empower and enrich educators to create literacy reform. She offers innovative, interactive, and motivating techniques with relevant and practical application. She is truly passionate about creating strategic readers and leaders. Valerie carries that same passion into her home in Bradenton, Florida. She is a devoted wife to Gregg, mother to four—Nick, Derek, Jacey, and Brooke—and grandmother to Evelyn Marie. She is also an international inspirational speaker and author. Through her book *Warrior Woman: Strategies to Awaken Your Purpose, Strength, and Confidence* (Deep River 2010), she has inspired thousands.

Foreword

Creating Strategic Readers fits into a rare category of resources that are so valuable to educators they warrant a third edition. Tens of thousands of teachers around the world rely on Valerie Ellery's research-based, accessible, best-selling book for powerful literacy ideas. Trends in education, much like fashion, come and go. Just like on the runway, in education some classics remain true and worthy of reinvention. Whether you are new to Valerie's work or a devoted fan already, you'll find that the third edition of her classic text is loaded with dozens of new, proven ideas and solutions for improving literacy in the classroom and across the school.

Fortunately, Valerie has updated her work just in time as educators face the challenges of implementing new standards in their classrooms. Veteran and new teachers alike will find that this edition equips educators with the foundations necessary for designing effective, rigorous instruction. After listening to her readers and relying on her work in classrooms, Valerie incorporated solutions for the most up-to-the-minute needs of today's classroom.

The goal of Valerie's work remains consistent and true: to promote strategic reading with the five components of a comprehensive literacy approach (phonemic awareness, phonics, fluency, vocabulary, and comprehension) in an authentic learning environment. Ellery shows us how to teach the whole child to prepare students to become truly college- and career-ready. The proven CAI model—curriculum, assessment, and instruction—permeates the book. By skillfully weaving curriculum, assessment, and instruction throughout the day, teachers meet the needs of students and advance their literacy learning.

What makes this resource really stand out are three essential foundations included in every technique: the gradual release model, critical thinking, and multiple intelligences. Every technique in the book includes a solid, research-based reason for teaching the strategies and skills involved. The techniques also include Ellery's famous "teacher talk" feature so you'll be ready with just the right language to promote critical thinking *every step of the way*.

Creating Strategic Readers includes exciting and varied hands-on ways to teach reading. Students will be moving, interacting, and engaging as they learn the essential strategies for literacy development. Every technique includes a mix of ways to teach the concepts so students are listening, speaking, reading, and writing with the teacher, each other, and independently and are also provided opportunities for purposeful use of technology.

Please join me in applauding Valerie Ellery for her new fabulous edition of the classic hit *Creating Strategic Readers*! The saying "the third time is a charm" certainly applies to this useful resource that belongs on the desk of any educator who desires to teach literacy with rigor in the age of standards.

—Lori Oczkus, M.A.
Literacy Consultant and Author

Introduction

Since the publication of the first edition of *Creating Strategic Readers* in 2005, and the second edition in 2009, I have had the opportunity to travel nationally and internationally to meet firsthand with teachers who have read and applied the strategies. *Creating Strategic Readers* has been overwhelmingly received by educators globally and has been making an impact on the next generation of readers. It is inspiring to know that teachers are using this resource to support their learners to think strategically.

Prior to the first edition of *Creating Strategic Readers*, research was proving—and is still proving—that teachers need to modify some of their traditional practices of teaching skills in isolation (Duffy and Roehler 1986; Loughran 2013; Pressley et al. 1992; Pressley et al. 1989). I wrote *Creating Strategic Readers* to support teachers who knew they wanted a comprehensive literacy approach and did not want to teach skills in isolation. These educators know that our *goal* is to teach reading as a strategic decision-making process that allows readers to use basic reading skills automatically and apply strategies independently to comprehend what they read.

At the birth of *Creating Strategic Readers*, reading initiatives were leaning towards explicit, direct instruction, and my trepidation was that reading would be viewed as very skill-driven without the emphasis being on why readers are doing what they are doing to read. During that time, federal mandates reflected on embedding the five reading components (phonemic awareness, phonics, fluency, vocabulary, and comprehension) in a segmented literacy block of instruction, as identified by the National Reading Panel (NRP) report (National Institute of Child Health and Human Development [NICHD] 2000). This fragmented framework caused a deep concern within the literacy world. It was my desire to equip educators with techniques that concentrate on effective instruction within these five components, promoting strategic reading in an authentic learning environment.

Looking Back to Go Forward: A Focus on the Whole Child

As we continue to strive to help create these strategic learners, it is imperative that we assess the multitude of theories and initiatives that educators have researched and applied over generations in the name, and sometimes *game*, of education. We continue to revisit what has worked and what has not within educational mandates, and bring forth a secure and steady system that will globally prepare learners for success. We need to consistently analyze the art and science of how to support, rather than suppress, critical and creative thinking.

Prior to the No Child Left Behind (NCLB) Act, the Goals 2000: Educate America Act of 1994 focused on preparing students for "a technologically sophisticated and competitive job market" (Short and Talley 1997, 234). Standards embedded in this act focused more than NCLB on the whole child: critical thinker, creative learner, effective communicator, and cooperative worker, to name a few. As we continue to take the cognitive, scientifically-based knowledge and questions that surfaced from NCLB and interweave it with the artistic standards incorporated in past educational acts, our focus will remain on educating the whole child to become college and career ready. It is a crucial time for all of us to support the education system in teaching the minds of tomorrow to empower them to lead the way. To be able to scaffold their instruction authentically and systematically, it is necessary for today's educators to have cognitive knowledge and artistic design as they construct effective instruction. In order for students to become responsible for their learning, educators will need to cultivate them to be intrinsically motivated, engaged, strategic, and able to direct their own learning.

When working with teachers who were using the first and second editions, I found that many wanted to discuss and reflect on ways to motivate and engage their readers while focusing on the strategies. The first and second editions presented timeless strategies that proficient readers apply, and these strategies continue to stand the test of time. In this updated edition, new research to support each of these strategies and to show why they are widely successful with literacy learners has been included.

This third edition will empower and equip educators to have a solid command of designing effective, rigorous instruction. All 126 techniques within *Creating Strategic Readers, 3rd edition*, has woven the Gradual Release of Responsibility (GRR) model (Pearson and Gallagher 1983) as one of the strong cords throughout the fabric of each strategy. This approach should include scaffolding: modeling for the students, interacting with the students, gradually guiding the students, and allowing ample time for independent application of skills and strategies by the students. This scaffolding, or Gradual Release of Responsibility (Pearson and Gallagher 1983), should occur repeatedly throughout teaching and learning opportunities. Scaffolding instruction, according to the individual needs of readers, will help students to become independent, strategic readers.

The second cord that has been woven within each strategy is a combination of Bloom's Taxonomy (Bloom 1956; Anderson and Krathwohl 2001) and Webb's Depth of Knowledge (Webb 2002) to continue to elevate the level of Teacher Talk to increase critical thinking. The final strong cord in this trio of strength is Multiple Intelligences (Gardner 1983), which have been enhanced and magnified to ensure that instruction focuses on reaching and teaching the whole learner.

Literacy *needs* to be at the forefront of all content-area learning. This interaction between the reader and the text generates critical thinking and problem solving while the reader is engaging in the reading process, allowing readers to be active thinkers rather than passive ones. Currently, the United States has embarked on providing Common Core State Standards for all. The Common Core's mission statement includes that "the standards are designed to be robust and relevant to the real world, reflecting the knowledge and skills that our young people need for success in colleges and careers" (2010). The days of stressing the acquisition of reading skills *in isolation* are in the past. Skills are valuable if it is understood how to apply them strategically. Self-regulated readers apply their reading skills automatically, concentrating on the strategies rather than the skills. This form of self-regulation is the ultimate design of strategic readers (Bjork, Dunlosky, and Kornell 2013; Hilden and Pressley 2007; Paris, Wasik, and Turner 1991; Parsons 2008).

Educators may utilize this book as a source to better equip themselves in the craft of teaching reading throughout the entire curriculum and in all content areas. The three cords of Gradual Release of Responsibility, Critical Thinking, and Multiple Intelligences have been embedded with this third edition to empower educators to be confident, dedicated, and determined to reach todays' global learners. To move forward successfully, teachers need a plethora of research-based reading strategies at their disposal. That continues to be the heartbeat of *Creating Strategic Readers, 3rd Edition*.

Overview of This Book

A Curriculum, Assessment, and Instruction (CAI) framework, guided by addressing the whole child, is presented in Chapter 1 of this book. **Chapter 1** explores the comprehensive literacy classroom with emphasis on effective, rigorous instruction; the developmental stages of reading with component indicators; a model of text complexity; conditions of optimal learning; and scaffolding instruction. The CAI icon is located throughout the book to identify each designated framework area. The shaded area of the triple Venn diagram corresponds with each identified section (i.e., curriculum, assessment, and instruction).

Chapters 2–5 focus on word study, vocabulary, fluency, and comprehension. Each chapter focuses on a specific-reading component, beginning with an overview of the essence of the component and current evidence-based research. The CAI framework is formatted and demonstrated in each chapter.

The *curriculum* section in each chapter is identified as the reading component with 32 strategies within the chapters (i.e., what you want your students to know about a specific reading component, and what strategies you want them to apply to that component). Each strategy is defined and then followed by instructional techniques that support the application of the strategy. These strategies are aligned with supporting skills and additional reading strategies for reciprocal flow between skills and strategies in a synchronized way, which results in making meaning while reading a text. It is important to remember that the strategies do not need to be taught in a specific order; the order should be based on individual students' needs.

Strategy *assessments* are embedded within each chapter for educators to evaluate students' strengths and weaknesses (behavior indicators) within a particular strategy. These assessments are guides to help keep the end results in mind as educators implement the various techniques that support the strategies. A review of appropriate Teacher Talk (e.g., statements, questions, and prompts) is provided at the beginning of each strategy section and within each technique. The Teacher Talk is hierarchically aligned with Bloom's Taxonomy and Webb's Depth of Knowledge, asking students to stay in the realm of "why" they are learning a specific content at a deeper level of understanding that relies more on complexity than difficulty. Try using some of these statements, questions, and prompts with students as you work through the techniques in the Rhyming section. It is imperative to scaffold the implementation of teacher talk and concept of application, beginning with the simple taxonomy of "Remembering" assisting to the more complex taxonomy of "Creating", to effectively implement rigorous instruction for academic success. Using this form of conversational coaching encourages readers to think strategically as they employ the given skills and strategies.

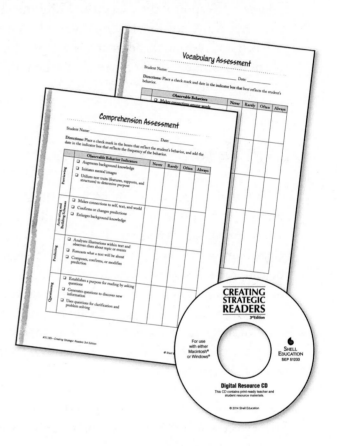

The techniques in this book are aligned to the Common Core State Standards. The standards are provided on the Digital Resource CD (standards.pdf). Many of the techniques have accompanying resources that can be used for assessment purposes, if desired. These can be found on the Digital Resource CD. Also included is an assessment rubric for each chapter. (See Appendix B for a complete list of materials included on the Digital Resource CD.) These assessments include all of the strategy behavior indicators from each chapter in one comprehensive format. They can be used in many ways, such as:

- formative assessments

- summative assessments

- parent and/or student conferences

- instructional grouping

- student goal setting

- differentiation

- process monitoring

This is by no means an exhaustive list; it is only meant to support educators and can be used as a springboard to inform instruction.

The *instructional* techniques support the strategies and are designed to help the whole child become a sophisticated learner. These chapters include 126 techniques to support teaching the necessary strategies for self-regulated reading. The procedure for each technique should begin with the teacher modeling the entire technique, using appropriate text, and then be followed by ample time for students to work toward independent use of the strategy. A scaffolding, or Gradual Release of Responsibility (GRR) model (Pearson and Gallagher 1983), should occur repeatedly throughout teaching and learning opportunities. Within the instructional steps of each technique, the GRR model is embedded to present a consistent picture of how this looks in the classroom. The first step correlates with the teacher modeling the "I do" phase, the second and third steps correlate with the "we do" and "with you" phase of collaboration, and the final step correlates with the "by you" phase of self-sufficiency. Scaffolding instruction according to the individual needs of readers will help students to become independent, strategic readers.

In this third edition, I also include additional ways to differentiate learning and extend instruction to motivate and engage students. I felt it was important to include techniques that best support English language learners (ELLs) as well; applicable techniques are identified in Chapters 2–5 for these learners. However, it is important to note that the Center for the Improvement of Early Reading Achievement (CIERA) recommends that English language learners learn to read in their first language before being taught to read English (Hiebert et al. 1998).

My life's mission has always been to inspire, encourage, and transform lives. As a classroom teacher, I wanted my students to leave my doors *confident* in who they were, *dedicated* to being lifelong learners, and *determined* to apply their newfound knowledge. More than ever, the time has come for all of us to rise above the challenges that are all around and become *confident*, *dedicated*, and *determined* educators who believe that their students can achieve! The students in today's classrooms are tomorrow's future. It is time for all of us to believe that these students can be lifelong, self-regulated, strategic literacy learners. Do you believe that the children are our future? A well-known song by Whitney Houston says for us to "teach them well and let them lead the way." I do believe we need to provide opportunities for these young minds to fully develop so that they are equipped to be *confident*, *dedicated*, and *determined* as strong, literate individuals.

Use this book as an artist's palette. Dip your brushes into the colorful ways (strategies and techniques) to create on your canvases (your students' minds) a masterpiece of learning that completes the whole picture—strategic readers!

A Comprehensive Literacy Classroom

The basis for a comprehensive literacy classroom is a solid command of Curriculum, Assessment, and Instruction (CAI). These three essentials are the infrastructure that gives educators a sound foundation upon which to build comprehensive literacy teaching. A comprehensive literacy classroom ensures that this infrastructure is inclusive, extensive, far reaching, and wide ranging in the content of literacy and throughout all other content areas. Literacy involves all aspects of the strands of reading, writing, listening, speaking, and language. It is the thread within all content areas. Weaving curriculum, assessment, and instruction daily into a comprehensive literacy classroom is crucial for student achievement. If our ultimate goal, as educators, is for students to exhibit a wide mental grasp of all aspects of literacy, then we must be knowledgeable about how to teach and reach the "whole child." By *whole child*, I am referring to the developmental domains of the student's cognitive growth, mental and physical health, social and emotional welfare, and their multiple intelligences. Finland's education system has ranked among the top in the world consistently. Its success has been through empowerment of the whole child, where the focus is on collaboration, not competition or accountability of high-stakes testing. In a comprehensive literacy classroom, the whole child, or comprehensive learner, is at the center of all areas of curriculum, assessment, and instruction. In this chapter, I provide an overview of the CAI cycle, and provide details on how to best meet the needs of comprehensive learners.

C = Curriculum

The first aspect of the CAI comprehensive literacy classroom is curriculum. The word *curriculum* in its early Latin origin means "a course of action," sometimes referred to as "a course for racing." In this fast-paced world we live in today, educators do feel like they are on a track, doing sprint intervals all day with the curriculum. A comprehensive literacy classroom allows the curriculum to be more of a course of action, with stamina and ambition being the critical ingredients. It is time for schools to be able to "go the distance strategically." Using a standards-based curriculum is the initial step for teachers to be aware of what they want their students to know and be able to do. "Do" is an action to perform or execute. A form of curriculum is found in many shapes and sizes (e.g., supplemental resources, motivating materials, and promising programs). These forms should be founded on solid standards, with evidence-based strategies designed to elevate knowledge and application. By aligning instruction with current standards, teachers can express a specific purpose for what they want students to learn (know) and apply (do). Standards are meant to be cohesive with other standards for an authentic learning experience and real-time application. They are to spiral through the fabric of what learners "wear" every day to add depth of understanding. The authors of the Common Core State Standards in English Language Arts (2010) recognize the value of cohesive standards: "While the standards delineate specific expectations in reading, writing, speaking, listening, and language, each standard need not be a separate focus for instruction and assessment. Often, several standards can be addressed by a single rich task" (5). Within these standards are many overarching strategies. The word *strategy* is defined as "an adaptation or complex of adaptations that serves or appears to serve an important function in achieving evolutionary success" (Merriam-Webster 2013). To unpack this concept one step further, we need to grasp the meaning of "evolutionary success." A comprehensive literacy classroom development is a process of ongoing change toward enduring academic success. This development is founded on strategic thinking. Strategies represent the whole, while skills represent part of the whole. In a skill-drill world, many students are left for "kill." They are "spent" at the close of their school day, not truly understanding the why of what they were doing.

The strategies highlighted in Chapters 2–5 incorporate specific-supporting skills (parts) needed to accomplish the strategy (whole). For example, some skills necessary to support the strategy of summarizing are to organize information, recognize story elements, and deconstruct a text. There are also supporting strategies that align to each highlighted strategy to demonstrate spiraled authentic application. For example, a few strategies that support the strategy of summarizing are contextualizing (vocabulary), rereading (fluency), and determining importance (comprehension). According to Lucy Calkins, students "will need a repertoire of strategies that undergird these reading skills" (2012, 29). Stephanie Harvey and Anne Goudvis have been advocates for strategic thinking. They state, "We teach our kids to think strategically, so they can better understand the world around them and have some control over it. We teach them to ask questions, to delve into a text, to clarify confusion, to connect the new to the known to build knowledge, and to sift out the most important information to make decisions" (2013, 433). We salute their valiant efforts to guide all of us educators into the world of strategic thinking to ultimately accomplish the goal of creating strategic readers. It is imperative that teachers and students gain a firm understanding of the essential reading components and their corresponding strategies, which represent what strategic readers "do."

Figure 1.1 identifies the evidenced-based strategies within solid reading components highlighted in Chapters 2–5. Applying strategies in a standards-based curriculum involves bringing students to a metacognitive level within the curriculum. When students reflect on the purpose of the lesson by answering the question *Why are we doing this?* they begin to regulate, evaluate, and monitor their thinking. Effective learners can describe what they are learning, not just what they are doing (Marzano 2007). Metacognitive thinking causes students to be conscious of their learning processes and reinforces their understanding of the purpose of the lesson. They are then able to make conscious choices about what they need to do to learn the standards, and they are able to effectively apply strategies to achieve a level of success as readers and writers. Knowing which strategy to use provides students with the control to comprehend—and demonstrate their wide mental grasp of—the curriculum. Chapters 2–5 outline the strategies proficient readers apply independently and at times simultaneously, as needed, to acquire meaning from the text and provide specific techniques that directly support these strategies to use in the classroom.

Figure 1.1 Strategies Within the Essential Reading Components

Word Study: Phonological Awareness and Phonics	Word Power: Vocabulary	Finding the Flow: Fluency	All Roads Lead to: Comprehension
• Rhyming • Isolating and Identifying Sounds • Blending and Segmenting Sounds • Synthesizing Sounds • Analyzing Sounds • Embedding • Spelling • Recognizing	• Associating • Contextualizing • Categorizing • Visual Imaging • Analyzing Words • Word Awareness • Wide Reading • Referencing	• Phrasing • Assisted Reading • Rereading • Expressing • Pacing • Wide Reading • Accuracy	• Previewing • Activating and Building Schemas • Predicting • Questioning • Visualizing and Sensory Imaging • Inferring and Drawing Conclusions • Determining Importance • Summarizing • Synthesizing

Literacy is the basis for all other content-area learning. If students cannot read and write proficiently through various modes of meaning, their resulting inability to acquire necessary academic achievements in other areas becomes a deficit for learning. Content-area literacy involves students reading and writing about multiple forms of texts (Readence, Bean, and Baldwin 2007). The literacy communalities of reading, writing, and thinking still underpin these content areas, even with a variety of text formats. Multimodal learning is necessary in helping students meet the challenges of multiple forms of text in today's society across content areas (Jewitt and Kress 2003; Shanahan and Shanahan 2008; Thompson 2008; Unsworth and Heberle 2009). These various modes of text representations (e.g., digital media, artistic designs, symbols, and images) support the learners' meaning-making processes. Teachers who are serious about their commitment to developing a comprehensive literacy classroom must put this commitment into practice with a daily schedule that devotes ongoing literacy development throughout the entire day, throughout all content areas. Integrating with the content areas of science, social studies, and mathematics is the key to sound and relevant learning. Several important factors that support high-quality literacy learning instruction while implementing the standards, include maximizing the time students spend on reading, blending reading and writing into every subject area, explicitly instructing students about how to construct meaning from texts, applying critical literacy, incorporating inquiry-based learning, reading closely to use text evidence to support reasoning of understanding, and providing students with many opportunities to discuss what they are reading and share from different points of view (Behrman 2006; Hall and Piazza 2008; Knapp 1995; Lenz 2006; CCSS 2010).

Teachers' ultimate goal should be to provide real- and relevant-learning opportunities for students to apply the curriculum, make connections, and explore meaning before, during, and after reading strategically.

A = Assessment

The next component of the CAI comprehensive-literacy classroom is assessment. Assessments are windows into the learner's knowledge, beliefs, and attitudes. There are numerous purposes for gathering information about students. Educators assess to determine the progress of students' cognitive development, inform instruction, demonstrate teacher and school accountability, motivate and encourage students, and aid in educating and assessing the whole child. "Teachers use assessment to determine and address students' individual needs and best match each student with instruction" (Afflerbach 2010, 297). Students and teachers should utilize a variety of assessment tools such as oral-reading records, observations through behavior indicators, surveys, interviews, conferences, digital portfolios, anecdotal notes, developmental checklists, rich and authentic tasks, and commercial assessments to accommodate these assessment purposes (Afflerbach 2007; Beaver 2006; Edwards, Turner, and Mokhtari 2008). As teachers collect these artifacts, it is imperative that the assessments are used for learning about the whole child and to inform and guide future instruction.

Assessment for Learning and Evaluation for Informing

Assessment results reveal the students' current knowledge base and strengths and their need for future growth (e.g., areas of growth, possible weaknesses). Once the evidence is formulated, it is recorded as raw-score data. If educators just record this data and continue to cover the curriculum without feedback or using the data to inform instruction, students may fall into a cycle of failure (Stanovich 1986; Malloy, Marinak, and Gambrell 2010). With this method, teachers are assessing for recording, not for learning. Ultimately, assessment for learning "keeps students and their teachers in touch with understanding and achievement on a continuous basis, allowing them to know what specific actions they can take to improve learning every day" (Stiggins and Chappuis 2008, 44). Assessment collaboration between student and teacher allows students to know themselves and gives voice to their learning, increasing the way they think about their thinking through enhancing their metacognition for successful outcomes.

Data from these assessments must then be evaluated, which means, "making judgments about the effectiveness of teaching for learning on the basis of credible objective assessment" (Traill 1995, 5). Once the teacher evaluates the assessment, he or she must map out any changes in students' behavior as they develop as readers, collaborating and planning instruction with students accordingly (Davis 2003; Fountas and Pinnell 1999; Stiggins and Chappuis 2008). Teachers can be reflective and differentiate instruction based on the specific needs of students.

Types of Assessments

In the world of assessment, there are two major assessment classifications: formative assessment and summative assessment. Formative assessment guides instruction by providing key information about students' academic needs at a particular moment in time. By analyzing this information, educators reflect on their teaching practice and adjust instruction as needed. "The information formative assessment yields is central to this reflective practice" (Afflerbach 2010, 298). Summative assessment determines student learning following instruction and includes a specific product.

Teachers use a screening assessment to determine students' academic accomplishments and further educational needs. Literacy screening assessments are brief, informal, or formal assessments that identify students who are likely to need extra or alternative forms of instruction. If screening results indicate proficiency, then initial instruction continues. However, if concerns arise based on the evaluation from the screening results, further diagnosis is necessary. The teacher then administers a diagnostic assessment to determine students' strengths and weaknesses. In the classroom, teachers need to select a diagnostic that best assesses the problem area identified through the screening. The results of the diagnostic assessment will then indicate the type of rigorous instruction needed for immediate intervention (e.g., Response to Intervention—RTI). Teachers must give periodic, ongoing monitoring assessments for all students to evaluate student progress after instruction. This helps to decide whether instruction has been effective and should continue, or if it should be revised. The assessment data determines what instruction is appropriate to meet differing student needs. Instruction should be guided by the appropriate data. This data can range from very specific objectives to a wide range of information that informs classroom practice and leads to better application of materials and curriculum goals, making student success possible and pursuable rather than impossible and improbable (Tierney and Readence 2005).

With common standards at the forefront of education, consortia has been searching for innovative ways to design effective assessments while problem solving the current limitations of large-scale testing. The challenge is to develop an assessment that can be balanced—both summative and formative. This assessment must integrate the infrastructure of curriculum, assessment, and instruction; utilize advanced technology to effectively design computer-based tasks that are relevant, fair, and measurable; and focus on diagnostic measures while keeping the whole child in mind at all times. While addressing this challenge, we all need to keep students as the heartbeat of why we assess. We assess for understanding what students know and still need to know. We assess to inform instruction. An old Chinese proverb sums it up this way "You don't fatten a sheep by measuring it."

Developmental Stages or Levels of Reading

Knowing students' reading abilities is essential for teachers. Skillful teachers strategically observe their students' reading and writing behaviors and identify the specific characteristics each student is exhibiting as a literacy learner. As students develop into strategic readers, they gradually move through four stages or levels of reading: emergent, early, transitional, and fluent. Teachers can identify points along this gradual process toward strategic reading through the behaviors the readers demonstrate. Observation of learners at work provides "information needed to design sound instruction" (Clay 2002, 11). Today's classrooms have a variety of these leveled learners regardless of the grade. Therefore, it is important for teachers to be familiar with the characteristics within all of the levels to reach all readers. When teachers are able to see their students in light of their individual reading behaviors, they begin to recognize how they can support their students as readers. For example, if a student has the characteristics of an early reader, the teacher can then decide how to best support that student's further developmental progress in reading. The teacher uses this interaction to help propel the student into the next stage, that of a transitional reader. Therefore, it is vital that teachers gain a keen insight into these stages. This knowledge will assist educators in deciding what types of assessments and instructional strategies and techniques are suitable for their students' specific reading needs. Figure 1.2 aligns the developmental stages with sample indicators within the essential components of reading.

Figure 1.2 Developmental Stages with Sample Reading Component Indicators

Stages	Word Study	Vocabulary	Fluency	Comprehension
Emergent	Recognizes and continues patterns; isolates and identifies phonemes; blends phonemes; identifies letter names and sounds; demonstrates one-to-one correspondence; recognizes some high-frequency words	Expresses an awareness of word meaning	Follows an assisted reader as an echo	Makes meaningful predictions based on illustrations; understands that print conveys a message; participates in book discussions
Early	Segments and manipulates phonemes; uses letter-sound correspondence; recognizes high-frequency words	Expresses an awareness of word meaning; uses new words in conversations	Recognizes basic punctuation marks and adjusts voice while reading; reads word by word; begins to use tone to convey meaning	Begins to self-monitor reading behaviors (uses cueing system); uses text and illustrations to predict, check, and confirm meaning through close reading; participates in book discussions and makes connections; recognizes and retells story elements

Stages	Word Study	Vocabulary	Fluency	Comprehension
Transitional	Demonstrates a variety of decoding strategies independently; recognizes many high-frequency words with ease	Demonstrates an increased vocabulary through word relationships; recognizes meaning of affixes and inflectional endings	Reads with fluent phrasing; begins to pace reading; uses proper tone to convey meaning	Participates in discussion about literary elements; retells beginning, middle, and end of story; summarizes a story using references to text evidence; uses inferences to bring meaning to text
Fluent	Demonstrates complex word analysis; integrates and cross-checks cueing systems	Uses context vocabulary with confidence; analyzes words to determine meaning/uses and structural analysis (prefix, suffix, multiple meaning)	Demonstrates pacing, expression, and accuracy in oral reading	Summarizes and synthesizes text; distinguishes between significant and supporting details of text; evaluates, interprets, and analyzes literary elements; contributes in complex literary discussions and uses text evidence to support thinking

Assessing the Whole Child = Creating a Strategic Reader

Howard Gardner's prophetic message declares that "it's not how smart you are, it's how you are smart." As educators strive toward creating strategic readers, it is important to get to know the whole child. Effective whole-child assessments are interdependent and can occur simultaneously as they address the developmental domains of students' cognitive growth, mental health and physical well-being, social and emotional welfare, and learning approaches (Coffield et al. 2004; Gardner 1993; Hodgkinson 2006; Kohn 2005; Levine 2002; Maslow 1943; O'Connor and Jackson 2008; Zigler and Finn-Stevenson 2007; Zigler, Singer, and Bishop-Josef 2004). There is not one magical assessment that will evaluate the whole child; it is important to recognize that different learners learn best at different times with different contents and in different contexts. *Different* is the common thread here. Therefore, a one-size-fits-all, "high-stakes" achievement test may still leave educators and students motivated by the score and not the process of learning.

With each educational initiative, we should be able to gain clearer insight into how to reach and teach students. We should be evaluating what was effective within the initiative and what did not have a major impact on student achievement. Over the last two decades, we have seen education go through many changes toward teaching the "whole child." Although No Child Left Behind had its challenges, we still need to continue using the cognitive, scientifically-based knowledge gleaned from NCLB, along with the focus on the artistic standards incorporated in Goals Blueprint 2000, and the multitude of current theories available that strive to successfully propel our learners to be college, career, and civic ready for anything! Collaboration and coordination of teaching to the whole child is our best approach at long-term success. It is possible "to learn by making sense of experience, gain deep understanding, pick things up from the context, get a feel for things, engage in creative problem solving, master self-regulation, and take charge of one's own learning" (Caine and Caine 2007, 2). Assessments are a window into the learner's knowledge, beliefs, and attitudes. Assessment through rich tasks can demonstrate students' ability to address multiple standards across content areas and provide feedback on a deeper level of learning. Figure 1.3 illustrates the composition of a comprehensive learner that helps to shape the whole child.

Research in learning styles and intelligences indicates that there are multiple individual styles that teachers can identify and use to select specific instructional strategies to support students' strengths (Gardner 1983; Levine 2002). Gardner's (1983, 1993) theory of multiple intelligences suggests that there are a number of distinct forms of intelligence that each individual possesses to some degree. There are many *different* ways to be and "show" *smart*. These intelligences are included as indicators to consider when assessing and informing instruction that is individualized to meet the needs of the learners. A whole child can operate in all the intelligences. We believe that in order to be successful in today's fast and changing world, it will require the intelligences to overlap continually.

There is a common saying to remember as we try to keep the flow of learning happening, "There is no learning in the comfort zone and no comfort in the learning zone." Figure 1.4 aligns the multiple intelligences and whole-child standards to ways a college- and career-ready student experiences learning, types of techniques, levels of Teacher Talk, and alternative forms of assessments to support students in all zones of life.

Figure 1.3 The Whole Child

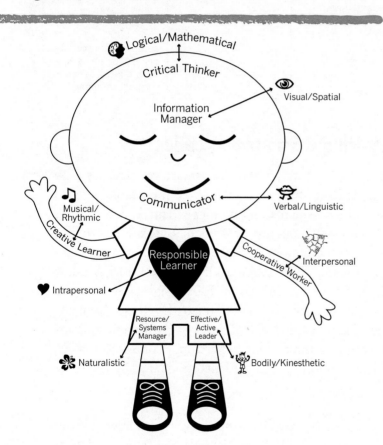

Figure 1.4 Comprehensive Learner Matrix

Whole Child/ Comprehensive Learners	Abilities: What they are able to do	Interests: What they like to do	Motivation Tools: How to enthuse them	Cognition: How they actively think	Teacher Talk: How to communicate with them	Assessment Tools: How to know if they can do it
Visual/Spatial (Information Managers)	Perceive the visual, locate and organize relevant information, relate to size, area, or position, directional	Design Draw Observe Doodle Paint Puzzles	Cartoons Images Multimedia Visual aids Virtual reality games Collages	In pictures: Mental images Graphic organizers Spatial orientation Digital video Color and design	Visualizing in their mind's eye Illustrating Interpreting Representing	Visual metaphors and analogies Checklists Graphs Rubrics Digital video Infographics
Verbal/Linguistic (Communicators)	Communicate for a given purpose, subject matter, and audience; story teller, wordsmith	Read and write Word processing Format stories Write in a diary Debate Tell stories	Bestselling books Word games Technology and digital media (Wikis/Blogs) Peer counseling Humor Dialogue	With words: Elaborative Expressive Symbolism	Convincing Describing Explaining Translating Identifying Listing	Surveys Interviews Spreadsheets Search tools Word associations Linguistic humor
Logical/ Mathematical (Critical Thinkers/ Evaluators)	Use reason and identify problems that need new and different solutions, (value evidence).	Experiments Puzzles Brain teasers Analyze abstract relationships	Graphing Evaluation Calculating Exploring Research	Reasoning, inductive and deductive Quantifying Critically Logically	Analyzing Calculating Distinguishing Verifying Comparing and contrasting	Strategic games Matrices Mnemonics Spreadsheets Web designs Problem solving Cite evidence
Musical/Rhythmic (Creative Learners)	Create, understand, and communicate intuitively	Sing and hum Listen to music Jingles and raps Improvise Compose	Audiotaping Rhythms Choral reading Musical instruments	By melody or rhythm patterns	Creating Demonstrating Expressing Performing	Tonal patterns Musical performances Checklists Compositions
Bodily/Kinesthetic (Effective/Active Leaders)	Control body movements, handle objects, multitask	Sports Dance Work with hands Create things	Acting Field trips Active learning Role-playing Digital probe	Movement sensations Global collaborators	Acting out Constructing Creating Dramatizing	Projects Interviews Dramatizations
Interpersonal (Cooperative Workers)	Recognize and respond to others' perspectives and cultures, moods, motivations, and desires	Spend time helping others E-mail, texting Community events	Reporting Dialogue Debate Peer teaching Chats	Communicating Self-reflecting Metacognitively Simulations	Brainstorming Role-playing Sharing Collaborating	Group projects Discussions Paraphrasing Video conferencing Buzz sessions
Intrapersonal (Responsible Learners)	Self-reflect and have awareness of one's own strengths and weaknesses, self-directed learners	Plan Imagine Think time Problem-solve	Journaling Learning logs Independent learning Goal setting Real-time projects	In relation to their self Reflection Imagery Responsibility	Concentrating Imagining Self-reflecting Rehearsing "I can" statements	Self-assessments Independent contracts Online surveys Digital portfolios
Naturalist/ Environmentalist (Resource/System Managers)	Distinguish among features of environment	Backpack Nature walks Visit zoos Digital media	Interacting with plants, animals, and other objects of nature Digital scrapbook	Systematic Orderly Environmental	Classifying Analyzing Investigating	Charts Graphs Systems Scavenger hunt lists Classification graphic organizers Database

Gardner's designation of *naturalist* has been adapted to also include *environmentalist*; this term helps to reflect a focus on conservation and improving the environment.

The techniques in this book incorporate and embed these intelligences to effectively motivate and engage the learners. Aligning the multiple-individual styles that focus on proven research-based practices with instructional techniques ensures success for both educators and comprehensive learners. Research suggests that the brain is a pattern detector and needs multiple experiences and instructional methods that are congruent, in order for the brain to seek and make connections for understanding (Jensen 2005; Lyons 2003; Willis 2010). Neurophysiologist Carla Hannaford authored *Smart Moves: Why Learning Is Not All in Your Head* (2007), which recognizes that the more parts of the child's brain we can engage, the more likely the material will be retained and internalized. It is our job as educators to open up the window of thinking and allow fresh air to flow through so learning does not stagnate. For this reason, it is necessary for you to *know* your students as readers and writers and to know the strategies, techniques, and Teacher Talk that are important for students' success as literacy learners. Building, or scaffolding, upon what students are able to do and guiding them to new understandings are the keys to creating a comprehensive literacy.

Reciprocal Relationship between the Whole Child and Text

As educators identify the developmental stage of a reader, they are charged with the task of providing appropriate text for the student to read in order to maintain their current level of reading ability as well as propel their reading capacity forward. In order to be successful outside of the classroom, "…students must be able to read and comprehend independently and proficiently the kinds of complex texts commonly found in college and careers" (CCSS 2010). So the goal of supporting all students to be strategic readers who are capable of meeting the reading demands outside the school setting is worthwhile and demands attention. The common practice of matching a reader to a "just right" text has merit, especially when it is accompanied with the additional effort of propelling a student to read text that is slightly outside their comfort zone, as well. Frustration is not the goal here, stretching to reach the next level of reading capacity is key. As educators, we must ensure that students are provided the opportunity to read a wide variety of texts in the sense of genre, complexity, access to background knowledge, and enjoyment of reading. Instead of binding a student to a specific band of text, we must identify the characteristics of text that will provide varying levels of access for the reader and provide him or her with opportunities to engage with these varying levels of text.

Three measures of text characteristics have been identified as important in evaluating a text for students: *qualitative, quantitative,* and *reader* and *task considerations* (CCSS 2010). By carefully considering these three aspects of text, educators will have the tools necessary to match a reader with a text or a text with a reader, which in turn will support and stretch the reader's developmental growth. To consider the *qualitative measures*, one must look at components of the text that are measured by the reader, such as levels of meaning or purpose, structure, language conventionality, clarity, and knowledge demand. These aspects can be difficult to measure; however, research to determine best practices for defining qualitative measures is underway (CCSS 2010). To consider *quantitative measures*, one must look at components of the text that are measured by word length, sentence length, and text cohesion. These measures are typically measured by computer software because of the number-based nature of this text measure. For *reader and task considerations*, one must think about the motivation, knowledge, and experiences of a reader as well as the complexity of the task at hand. This piece of the triad is where the educator's professional judgment, experience, and knowledge of their students come into play, which leads to the necessity of ongoing professional development to build teacher expertise in the area of reading development, as well as in the selection of texts that are appropriate for a reader at a given time. Figure 1.5 demonstrates the three equally important parts for measuring text complexity.

Figure 1.5 The Standards' Model of Text Complexity

(CCSS 2010)

Assessing Through Conversational Coaching: Teacher Talk

To bring students to a metacognitive level with their reading strategies, you will need to be highly aware of the questions, statements, and prompts you are using to support learning. You can use this type of Teacher Talk as a tool embedded into your conversations as you coach your students to process and think strategically. Conversational Coaching is a form of Teacher Talk in the classroom. Asking students to stay in the realm of "why" they are learning a specific content is necessary in having them process the information at a deeper level of understanding. "In our brains, processing turns data into stored knowledge, meaning, experiences, or feelings" (Jensen and Nickelsen 2008, 105). Teacher Talk should ask questions (e.g., "What words or phrases did the author use to help you create an image in your mind?"), make statements (e.g., "Try to picture in your mind someone who reminds you of a character in the story"), or provide prompts (e.g., "I can imagine what it is like to...") that bring readers to process the information. Students who are exposed to higher-order thinking and questioning comprehend more than students who are passively asked lower-order questions (Amer 2006; Anderson and Krathwohl 2001; Bloom and Krathwohl 1956; Conklin 2012; Eber 2007; Kunen, Cohen, and Solman 1981; Redfield and Rousseau 1981; Taylor 2008). Teacher Talk is the link to scaffolding instruction to help students be aware of their use of strategies and to think about the processes that are occurring to apply a particular strategy. This metacognitive awareness is imperative for students to possess in order to develop into strategic readers. Chapters 2–5 incorporate a variety of Teacher Talk to support deeper learning. The Teacher Talk is aligned to Bloom's (1956; Anderson and Krathwohl 2001) Taxonomy and the hierarchy of Webb's Depth of Knowledge (DOK) (2002), which relies more on complexity than difficulty. Merging these ideas extends the context in which the verbs are applied and the depth of thinking required. Danger lurks for those who stay at just the knowledge level. According to Confucius, a famous Chinese philosopher, "He who learns but does not think is lost. He who thinks but does not learn is in great danger." Let's use our most valuable weapon, which is our voice through conversational coaching, to move our students out of the "danger zone" and into more accountable talk.

I = Instruction

Instruction is the final aspect of a CAI comprehensive-literacy classroom. Instruction is an "act" that supports active learning. The instructor "can have a profound influence on student learning" (Marzano, Pickering, and Pollock 2001, 3). The initial instruction needs to be clear, concise, and meaningful to engage the learners. An instructional framework begins with establishing a physical environment and a classroom community that is conducive to learning. The teacher should have knowledge of the whole reader as he or she scaffolds instruction systematically. Using the scaffolding model, teachers gradually release instruction through literacy phases. As teachers align instruction with the needs of students, they may need to respond to intervention through differentiating their techniques. Effective instruction considers the conditions for optimal learning and then actively strives to combine the art and science of teaching to create strategic readers.

Conditions for Optimal Learning

In order for a comprehensive-literacy classroom to be successful, expectations, procedures, and an environment conducive to learning all need to be determined and in place. Cambourne's (1995) conditions for learning is one model that continues to help teachers implement the conditions that should be in place for optimal learning. In all their literacy endeavors, teachers should examine these nine conditions and the literacy approaches that align with them, all the while remembering that their ultimate goal is superlative learning. Figure 1.6 defines each condition and shows the alignment of the condition with a comprehensive literacy classroom.

Figure 1.6 Conditions for Optimal Learning

Condition	Description	Comprehensive Literacy Classroom	Centers/Literacy Stations
Immersion	To be exposed to an environment rich in authentic spoken and written language	Provides multiple opportunities for reading, writing, listening, speaking, and language, using a wide variety of materials and resources Provides opportunity for community building	Provides a print-rich environment with words and labels around stations Immerses students in books and book talk Encourages students to talk to one another as they develop skills and strategies
Demonstration	To observe models of proficient, strategic reading and writing	Models what students need to know and be able to do, is explicit and deliberate during modeled instruction Read-alouds and modeled writing	Models for students before any activity is placed in a station Explains the what, why, and how of each task Models process as well as product Revisits demonstrations as needed

Condition	Description	Comprehensive Literacy Classroom	Centers/Literacy Stations
Expectation	To believe that literacy strategies and skills can and will be acquired	Identifies and posts reasonable expectations and procedures with students and establishes goals Ongoing informal and formal assessments	Teaches and models expectations for station use Sets up stations in a supportive yet challenging manner
Engagement	To want to try authentic reading and writing strategies and techniques To be confident about support	Interacts in experiences of successful readers and writers Focuses on relevant tasks responsive to literacy Participates in shared, interactive literacy Provides cooperative learning experiences	Connects mini-lessons to the station experiences in the classroom Gives students many opportunities to practice and apply skills and strategies Shares the purpose of each activity with purpose cards at stations
Use	To apply authentic reading and writing throughout daily life	Integrates with other content areas in real time for acquisition Is relevant to life application, long-term retention, and critical thinking Participates in guided/small groups and independent literacy	Gives students many opportunities to practice and apply skills and strategies at stations
Approximations	To inquire and be free to explore and make attempts at what proficient, strategic readers and writers can do	Promotes risk taking and supports instruction at the learner's need level Builds trust and positive social skills Participates in guided literacy and critical literacy	Provides many opportunities in stations without expecting mastery 100 percent of the time Values the process, not just the finished product Places examples in stations to support student learning
Response	To receive feedback on attempts to read and write strategically	Gives specific, timely, and relevant feedback Gives voice to students Includes conferences, small groups, and journal responses	Invites students to positively respond to the work of peers Encourages and informs students about their progress Responds supportively and constructively
Responsibility	To be able to make choices and decisions To be engaged rather than an observer	Provides opportunities to make choices Allows for student ownership and self-regulation Participates in independent literacy	Sets up stations so the learner can make meaningful decisions about reading and writing Allows for choice within stations

(Adapted from Cambourne 1995; Nations and Alonso 2014)

Rigorous Instruction

Questions all educators should ponder about their instructional practices:

- What are ways you will assess the student to demonstrate how much content has been attained and to what level of achievement?

- How have you applied Bloom's Taxonomy and/or Webb's DOK within the lesson for students to form their own answers and demonstrate inquiry-based learning?

- What ways have you incorporated for students to connect the content and bring meaning to what is being studied?

- What ways have you combined the content to demonstrate conceptual relationships among cross-curricular instruction?

- Have you applied the gradual release of responsibility throughout the learning experience?

- Have you designed the lesson to consider the multiple intelligences of your students?

- What ways have you allowed for self-regulated learning to occur?

The term *rigorous instruction* has motivated educators to closely evaluate their instruction, the environment within their classroom, and the conversations with students in an effort to attain the level of instruction expected to create college- and career-ready students. The term *rigor* is defined as "the quality of being extremely thorough, exhaustive, or accurate." Rigorous instruction is not what you teach but how you teach and how students demonstrate their wide mental grasp of the content presented. The instructional process and the student product must be thorough, exhaustive, and accurate. Content acquisition is apparent through student conversations, project-based learning, and critical thinking. As a by-product of being thorough, exhaustive, and accurate, long-term retention is evident when students are able to display their understanding over time and apply concepts in various relevant contexts. Instruction is integrated and overlapping with the boundary lines of content areas becoming blurred, as critical thinking is required to connect concepts across all content areas. The learner carries a great deal of responsibility within the safe confines of a classroom environment where failing safely is the norm and soaking in a concept over time offers the opportunities to develop ownership of knowledge. Effective rigorous instruction does not mean *more* of what we have already been doing or *more* workload for our students. If there is more of anything, it is the reflective practice educators must engage in to effectively reach learners, knowing when to adjust instruction and revisit a concept, when to move on from a concept, and how to unite future instruction with current understandings. This is the art and science of teaching. The techniques within this book have been scrutinized to employ the features of rigorous instruction, demonstrating what effective instruction looks like in the classroom.

Gradual Release Through Scaffolding = I → We → With You → By You

Scaffolding instruction is a concept that focuses on how individuals learn (Collins, Brown, and Newman 1989; Vygotsky 1978) and provides support in the development of their learning. The support is given "to students within their zone of proximal development enabling them to develop understandings that they would have not been capable of understanding independently" (Many et al. 2007, 19). Pearson and Gallagher (1983) further developed the scaffolding research with their concept about the Gradual Release of Responsibility (GRR). GRR calls for support to be given by the teacher while students are learning a new concept, skill, or strategy; that support then slowly diminishes as students gain responsibility for their own learning. The GRR framework gradually moves from the teacher modeling ("I do it") through collaboration, by sharing ("We do it") and guiding ("Done With You"), to a state of self-sufficiency ("Done By You"). The techniques found in this book have the GRR model embedded within so educators have a consistent picture of how this looks within the classroom. Each technique has four phases. Although written in more of a step-by-step format, the intention here is not to teach in a linear fashion. Each phase will need to be revisited over time to ensure that true learning has occurred and mastery of concepts is achieved.

"I" Learning Phase: In reading, modeling by the teacher occurs with new learning experiences and is imperative before the student can be expected to attempt the unknown. Initially, the teacher models what he or she wants students to be able to do (e.g., a strategy within one of the five components of reading). Teachers should continue to utilize GRR throughout their instruction of the curriculum.

"We" Learning Phase: After teacher modeling of each strategy, students need time to interact with the teacher to gain further understanding. This phase incorporates shared learning mainly as a whole group, allowing a risk-free environment to occur with support from the teacher.

"With You" Learning Phase: When students begin to try the strategy on their own, the teacher or other support (partners, group members, volunteers) should be there to guide them. However, the responsibility of learning is mainly on the individual student to apply their newfound knowledge collaboratively in a guided environment.

"By You" Learning Phase: The final phase of this scaffolding process is for the student to apply the strategy independently. The goal is for students to become independent, self-directed learners. What is important to note here is the idea that GRR is not a linear process that can be accomplished in one lesson in one day. While some students may be able to walk through these learning phases and acquire new behaviors very quickly, it is much more common for students to need to return to modeling and collaborating again and again before mastering new learning. Students who are struggling with a concept need repeated guided practice with scaffolding to guarantee success in the long term. This repeated practice can come in the form of whole-group, small-group, or one-on-one instruction, which means the flexibility of the instructional design within the classroom must be responsive to learner needs (Fisher and Frey 2010). This will empower students to be self-regulated learners who return to a source of knowledge as they travel the course that leads to mastery. According to Routman (2003), "when teachers understand and internalize this model, teaching and learning become more effective, efficient, and enjoyable" (43). Comprehensive-literacy classrooms are conducive to this maturation of learning because students have the opportunity to become sophisticated, strategic readers and writers in a supportive, risk-free environment.

Instructing the Whole Child = Creating a Strategic Reader

In order for students to become responsible for their learning, educators need to empower them to be intrinsically motivated, strategic, and able to direct their own learning. This form of self-regulation is the ultimate design of a strategic reader (Hilden and Pressley 2007; Horner and O'Connor 2007; Paris, Wasik, and Turner 1991; Parsons 2008; Perry, Hutchinson, and Thauberger 2007; Zimmerman and Schunk 2013). When designing instruction, teachers reflect on and utilize the data gained through assessing the whole child (e.g., interests, motivation, levels, styles). Instructing the whole child involves tapping into the interests and motivations of the learner. Igniting this aspect of the whole learner will inspire effort and bring forth engagement on the part of the student, ultimately increasing student achievement (Brophy 1983; Dewey 1913; Fink and Samuels 2008; Harackiewicz et al. 2008; Jang 2008; Jensen 2005; Kohn 1993; Lavoie 2007; Skinner and Belmont 1993). Figure 1.7 highlights the concepts of interest, motivation, and engagement. The techniques in this book incorporate these concepts through the process of creating strategic readers.

Figure 1.7 Interest, Motivation, and Engagement

Interest	Motivation	Engagement
The awareness in which the student is aroused, demonstrates curiosity about, and shows drive and passion toward the task.	The factors that stimulate and give incentive (intrinsic and extrinsic); reason, action, and desire that causes a certain behavior.	The degree to which the student is actively and passionately connected to the learning experience.
What are the student's passions? What is the student doing after school or in his or her free time? What does the student talk about/express most? What are the characteristics of his or her appearance (i.e., clothes, hair)?	Why did he or she do what was done? Does the student initiate action when given the opportunity? Is the student exerting intense effort in the learning tasks? Is the student demonstrating enthusiasm and curiosity toward the given learning experience?	Is the student willingly participating? Does the student genuinely care about the learning experience? Is the student actively involved in the outcome of the experience? Does the student share in the responsibility of his or her learning?

The process of planning this type of instruction begins with the end in mind (Covey 1989, 2006; Tomlinson and McTighe 2006; Wiggins and McTighe 2005). Educators need to think in a way similar to architectural designers and ask questions like *What would be an interesting and engaging technique to design in order to uncover the main purpose of the lesson?* Instructing the whole child requires teachers to be knowledgeable of the strategies (curriculum), the learner (assessment), and the techniques (instruction). Techniques are the specific structures and rigorous instruction designed to teach a strategy. Chapters 2–5 incorporate a variety of techniques; teachers can select the ones that best support the strategy they are teaching and align with the needs of their students. Each technique begins with stating the purpose (why) and is constructed to gradually release the responsibility of learning to the self-regulated student. It is essential that students have the opportunity to observe the teacher modeling the initial engaging instruction and then to interact as they emulate the strategy the technique is designed to support. Teachers should begin with high-quality, effective instruction to reach the whole child. However, if a student becomes weakened in an area and demonstrates a need for additional support, it is critical for the teacher to respond with immediate rigorous instruction as a form of intervention. This response accelerates the mending and repairing needed to get back to the "whole" of the fragmented child.

A fragmented learner is one who needs the educator to respond to their intervention needs. Response to Intervention (RTI) is what effective teachers have been implementing for years with struggling readers. It is the act of providing high-quality instruction to meet the struggling readers' needs. The Individuals with Disabilities Act of 2004 (IDEA) combined with the NCLB Act form the foundation for the "official" trademark of RTI. RTI is an instructional practice based on scientific research that analyzes the learning rate over time to make important educational decisions about students with learning disabilities (Allington and Walmsley 2007; Batsche et al., 2005; Reutebuch 2008). It recommends a multitiered-intervention approach based on monitoring the progress of the instructional practice in general, and special favoring for small-group and individualized tutoring (Allington 2008; Fuchs and Fuchs 2008; Vaughn, Linan-Thompson, and Hickman 2003). "What is essential is the idea that we address the needs of most learners by providing high-quality and culturally responsive instruction in the least intrusive environment" (Ellery and Rosenboom 2010, 18–19).

The Challenge

The CAI cycle continues throughout the learning process. All three components need to be present in a comprehensive, systematic, and explicit approach to meet the multiple needs and diverse learning styles within today's classrooms. Figure 1.8 shows the student as the core of a comprehensive-literacy classroom. It is imperative to keep the student at the center of all decisions on curriculum, assessment, and instruction; the Venn diagram depicts how CAI intersects and allows flexibility for the teacher. Curriculum, assessment, and instruction are the infrastructure that, when aligned, create a powerful comprehensive-literacy classroom.

Figure 1.8 The CAI Cycle

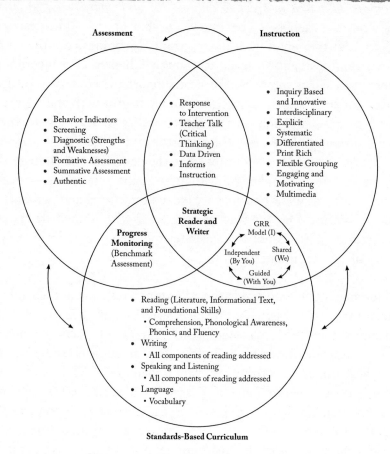

We challenge you, the educator, to identify the characteristics of your readers; know your readers. Know what motivates them and how to engage them in their learning process. You will be empowered when you know your students' developmental stages (emergent, early, transitional, or fluent) and learning levels. Once you identify these reading stages through appropriate assessments, it is then necessary to align strategies and techniques in all of the components of reading instruction at a suitable level for students as needed. It is our hope that you will be encouraged to have a repertoire of strategies, techniques, and Teacher Talk to meet the individual needs of the diverse learners within your classroom. You may apply the strategies, techniques, and Teacher Talk presented in this book in any order according to the needs of your students.

The final challenge is for you to consider reading as an art and a science. See yourself as an architectural artist and a savvy scientist. Imagine your students' minds as canvases, just waiting for you to give color and meaning with a deeper level to their learning, so you can create the ultimate masterpiece—strategic readers!

Phonological Awareness and Phonics

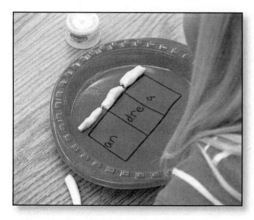

Blending and Segmenting Sounds with Silly Segmenting Technique

Analyzing Sounds with Roll Read Record Technique

Word study is the art of examining closely how words are designed phonemically (sounds), phonetically (alphabetic principle), morphologically (structure of words), and orthographically (spelling). This inquiry process of working words is foundational for the literacy strand of reading. According to the reading strand within the Common Core State Standards for English Language Arts, the reading foundational skills consist of print concepts, phonological awareness, phonics and word recognition, and fluency (CCSS 2010). Word-Study areas should be taught with a cross-curricular approach and in conjunction with all literacy strands (i.e., reading, writing, language, listening and speaking) in an authentic, yet systematic approach. In this chapter, we will focus on phonological awareness and phonics to include within these areas an emphasis on structural analysis and spelling. The Word Power chapter (Chapter 3) focuses on vocabulary and will go into more depth within the study of morphology (i.e., roots, affixes, inflectional endings).

Phonological Awareness

Phonological awareness is a vital cornerstone to the success of every reader having a solid foundation in the area of word study. To support students in becoming proficient readers, it is important to understand what phonological awareness is, why it is essential, what strategies and techniques to implement, and how to conversationally coach (Teacher Talk) students so they will think strategically. Phonological awareness is the general consciousness of language at the spoken level. Phonemic awareness is the understanding that speech is composed of a sequence of sounds combined to form words, and it is the main component of phonological awareness.

According to the International Reading Association (IRA 1998), phonological awareness encompasses larger units of sound, whereas phonemic awareness stems from this concept but refers to smaller units of sound. These small units of speech correspond to letters of an alphabetic-writing system; these sounds are called phonemes and can make a difference in a word's meaning. For example, the word *met* has three phonemes, /m/ /e/ /t/. By changing the first phoneme to /j/, we can produce a new word, *jet*, with a completely different meaning.

A student's awareness of phonemes has been shown through extensive research to hold predictive power toward their reading development (Cunningham and Stanovich 1998; Juel 1988; Melby-Lervag, Lyster, and Hulme 2012, Menzies, Mahdavi, and Lewis 2008; Moats and Tolman 2009; Snow, Burns, and Griffin 1998; Spencer et al. 2011). Phonological awareness can demonstrate various levels of learning and can develop in a continuum that consists of listening to sounds, word awareness, rhyming, syllable awareness, and phonemic awareness (being able to isolate, identify, categorize, blend, segment, delete, add, and substitute phonemes). These levels can be intermittently applied depending on the purpose and students' ability to gain achievement. It is important to note that phonemic awareness, phonological awareness, and phonics are not interchangeable nor are they the "end to themselves rather they are necessary components of an effective comprehensive reading program designed to develop proficient readers with the capacity to comprehend texts across a range of types and disciplines" (CCSS 2010, 15). The goal is for students to become familiar with the sounds (phonemes) that letters (graphemes) represent and to become familiar with hearing those sounds within words to determine meaning.

Phonics

Phonics refers to the relationship between phonemes and graphemes. Being able to read, pronounce, and write words by associating letters with sounds represents the basis for the alphabetic principle. Coupling this foundational reading component with the brain's capacity to make connections allows phonics to be a support in the reading process and makes phonics one of the means to a very important end—that is, meaningful reading.

Phonics is part of the graphophonic-cueing system that demonstrates the relationship between sounds in speech and letters in print. Proficient strategic readers use the graphophonic-cueing system to demonstrate their awareness of graphemes (the visual representations of phonemes), sound-symbol associations, and the structural analysis of a word. This ability to decode unknown words while simultaneously using a semantic-cueing system (reading for meaning), and a syntactic-cueing system (using grammatical structure and word order), supports reading fluently with comprehension and aids in becoming a strategic reader.

Research by neuroscientists and cognitive scientists suggests that the most effective phonics instruction is planned, sequential, explicit, systematic, multisensory, and, most important, meaningful (Archer and Hughes 2011; Campbell, Helf, and Cooke 2008; Herron 2008; NICHD 2000; Shaywitz and Shaywitz 2007; Stahl, Duffy-Hester, and Stahl 1998). Explicit instruction in the classroom is "a series of supports or scaffolds, whereby students are guided through the learning process with clear statements about the purpose and rationale for learning the new skill, clear explanations and demonstrations of the instructional target, and supported practice with feedback until independent mastery has been achieved" (Archer and Hughes 2011, 1). Therefore, teaching phonics in a comprehensive literacy program allows for specific focused instruction within the confines of purposeful teaching.

The word-study strategies presented in this chapter are aligned to the various instructional approaches to include synthetic phonics, analytic phonics, embedded phonics, analogy phonics, onset-rime phonics, and spelling. Teachers need to identify the effective strategies within these approaches and "make a conscious effort to examine and reflect upon the strategies they use for teaching phonics in order to select the best type of experiences for the children they teach" (Morrow and Tracey 1997, 651). Implementing an ongoing Word Study Journal, (e.g., spiral notebook, composition book), will provide the opportunity for learners to apply the strategies and techniques presented in this chapter and document their word-study journey. This Word Study Journal is included throughout the procedures and can be used as an observational tool for assessing progress with the word-study strategies. Systematic word-study instruction should be integrated with the other components of reading instruction (language-vocabulary, foundational skills-fluency, and reading literature and informational-text comprehension) to create a comprehensive literacy classroom. All components are leading toward bringing meaning to reading; therefore, the goal on this literacy journey should be that all roads lead to comprehension. It is important that there is an integration of the components and not on judging reading competence on phonological or phonic strategies alone. Too often, educators interchange phonological awareness, phonemic awareness, and phonics. Figures 2.1 and 2.2 help illustrate the relations among phonological awareness, phonemic awareness, and phonics using a nature metaphor.

Figure 2.1 Descriptions of Phonological Awareness, Phonemic Awareness, and Phonics

Terminology	Definition	Metaphor Description
Phonology	The study of the unconscious rules governing speech and sound production; the linguistic component of language	Sky Governing the big picture
Phonological Awareness	The awareness of sound structure; the ability to notice, think about, or manipulate the larger unit of sound auditorily and orally	Clouds Look up and become aware of the cloud(s) in the sky
Word Awareness	The ability to recognize that spoken language is made up of words and that words form sentences	Raindrop Comes out of the cloud (a component of phonological awareness)
Rhyming Awareness	The ability to recognize, isolate, and generate corresponding sounds, especially ending sounds	Raindrop Comes out of the cloud (a component of phonological awareness, e.g., hair/care)
Syllable Awareness	The ability to identify syllables (i.e., the smallest unit of speech with a vowel sound), distinguish between one and two syllables, and count, blend, and segment syllables in words and sentences	Raindrop Comes out of the cloud (a component of phonological awareness; /wa/ /ter/)
Phonemic Awareness	The awareness that spoken language consists of a sequence of phonemes (i.e., the smallest unit of sound)	Hail Also comes out of cloud but contains a combination of particles (onset and rimes, blending, segmenting,
Phonics	The system by which symbols represent sounds in an alphabetic writing system; the relationship between spelling patterns and sound patterns	Ground Foundation; rain hits the ground intermittently, helping to make the ground fertile (products of phonological awareness)
Metalinguistic	The ability to think about and reflect upon one's language	Seed Planting a seed after making the connection between water and the ground
Orthography	The method of representing the spoken language with written symbols	Roots Branching off from seed (punctuation, stages of spelling)
Graphemes	The written symbol used to represent a phoneme	Stems The parts you see (letters)
Morphemes	The structure of meaningful language units.	Leaves Parts of a plant (prefixes, suffixes)
Decode and Write Words	The ability to derive a pronunciation for a printed sequence of letters based on knowledge of spelling and sound correspondence.	Flower The product of rain and good soil (reading and writing)

Figure 2.2 Illustration of Relationship Among Phonological Awareness, Phonemic Awareness, and Phonics

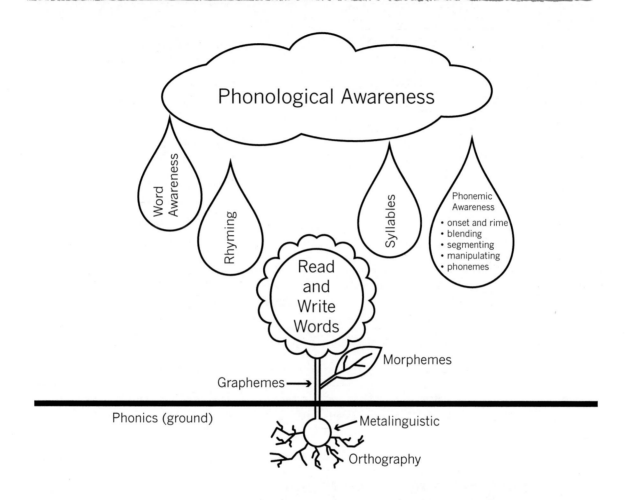

To be effective, when using the strategies and techniques presented in this chapter, teachers should allow ample time for teacher modeling and student application long before independent application is expected. Teachers should select and model reading and thinking aloud from appropriate text to apply the techniques in a meaningful manner, which supports authentic learning for strategic reading. By using this process, students are able to see first the whole text (i.e., appropriate text), then see the parts systematically (i.e., strategies and techniques), and finally, apply the parts back to the whole (i.e., become metacognitively aware of strategies while reading text). Using quality literature and informational text and promoting language development throughout the techniques will help to enhance students' development of the Word Study strategies. The Word Study strategies and their corresponding techniques detailed in this chapter are listed in Figure 2.3.

Figure 2.3 Word Study Strategies and Techniques in Chapter 2

Strategy	Corresponding Techniques in This Chapter	
Rhyming	Musical Rhyme (page 39) Rappin' Rhymes (page 40)	Rhyming Jar (page 42) Draw a Rhyme (page 43)
Isolating and Identifying Sounds	Mirror/Mirror (page 47) Alliteration Activation Creation (page 48)	Hot Seat (page 50) Think Sounds Abound (page 52)
Blending and Segmenting Sounds	Chime With Rimes (page 57) Body Blending (page 58)	Egg-Cited About Sounds (page 60) Silly Sound Segmenting (page 61)
Synthesizing Sounds	Stir It Up (page 65) Stretch It (page 66)	Bingo/Bongo (page 68) Syllable Juncture Structure (page 69)
Analyzing Sounds	Roll-Read-Record (3Rs) (page 74) DISSECT (page 76)	Word Ladders (page 77) Rappin' with Roots (page 79)
Embedding	Blinders (page 82) Predict/Preview/Polish/Produce (4 Ps) (page 83)	Word Detectives (page 84) Clued on Clues (page 86)
Spelling	Interactive Word Walls (page 92) Working With Words (WWW) (page 93)	Brain Tricks (page 95) Look/Say/Cover/Write/Check (page 96)
Recognizing	Letter Recognition (page 100) High-Frequency Words (page 101)	Irregular and Sight Words (page 102)

Word Study Strategy: Rhyming

Rhyming provides students with an opportunity to begin developing an awareness of sounds, and it is one of the early phases of phonological awareness. Rhyming allows for students to explore the rhythm of language and even enhances students' ability to express with some animation in their voice instead of just saying a statement in a monotone voice. Readers need many opportunities to hear and identify rhymes (end parts that sound alike but do not necessarily look alike) and to repeat the ending sounds by producing words with similar sound groups, which increases students' ability to grasp phonemic awareness strategies more effectively (Papadopoulos, Kendeou, and Spanoudis 2012; Reynolds, Callihan and Browning 2003; Runge and Watkins 2006). Providing students with opportunities to explore the similarities and differences in the sounds of words helps them to have an insight that language has not only meaning and message but also physical form (Adams 1990; 2011).

To support Rhyming while reading, a set of skills is required to effectively implement this reading strategy. The synchronized application of several reading strategies results in making meaning while reading a text. The skills, additional integrated reading strategies, and their reading components found in corresponding chapters are listed below.

Focus Skill(s):

- Concepts of words
- Rhythm of language

Integrated Strategies:

- Isolating and Identifying Sounds (Chapter 2)
- Associating (Chapter 3)
- Determining Importance (Chapter 5)

Accountable Teacher Talk for Rhyming

Following is a list of suggested Teacher Talk that encourages readers to think strategically as they employ the Rhyming strategy. To effectively increase levels of thinking, these suggestions incorporate Bloom's Taxonomy's higher-order questioning (Anderson and Krathwohl 2001) and Webb's Depth of Knowledge (2002).

Remembering and Understanding (Recall)

- What is a rhyming word?
- Of these three words_____, _____, _____which two words rhyme (e.g., cat, bat, fish)? Why did you pick the two words you did?

Applying (Skill/Concept)

- Draw what rhymes with _____. How did you know what to draw?

Analyzing (Strategic Thinking)

- Explain how these two words are alike. What part of the word makes the rhyme? What facts can you gather that explain the difference between rhyme and rime? Generate another word that would rhyme with these words.

Evaluating and Creating (Extended Thinking)

- Listen to the text read aloud. Select the words that rhyme within the text. What criteria did you use to determine if the words rhyme? Produce a list of words that have the same rhyme as the one presented.

- Create a sentence that includes a key vocabulary word used as a rhyming word. Explain how you used the rhyming word to rhyme with another word that supported meaning. What added support was given to bring meaning to the vocabulary word?

Behavior Indicators for Rhyming

As you assess students' ability to rhyme, use the following behaviors as a guide. Do students exhibit these behaviors never, rarely, often, or always?

- ❑ Hear and recognize rhymes
- ❑ Repeat ending sounds and produce new words with similar sounds
- ❑ Apply rhyme in context for meaning

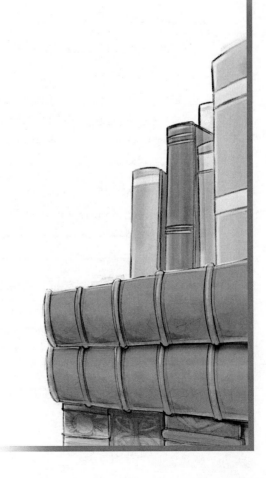

Techniques for Rhyming

 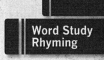
Musical Rhyme

Purpose:	ELL Technique:
To recognize and produce rhyming words	Yes

Materials:

- text with rhymes
- *Musical Rhyme Pictures* (see musicalrhyme.pdf)

- music that has a fun beat, preferably without words
- stuffed animals such as teddy bears

Learning Phases

I

Select pictures that correspond with rhyming words you are studying (multiple rhymes are permissible), or use the *Musical Rhyme Pictures*. Think about students' names and generate authentic or nonsense words that rhyme with their names.

Read aloud a section from the selected text that highlights rhyming. Using your voice to emphasize the words that rhyme, identify orally the parts within the words that sound alike. After reading and identifying the rhyming words in the text, model how we can use our names to produce words that rhyme. Give a few examples of people's names and create a word that rhymes.

We

Have students listen to the word you call out. If they think their names have the same ending sound, have them stand up. Students listen to the rhyming word and determine if they are the match. If they hear their rhyming match, have them identify themselves by stating their name and creating more words that rhyme with their names.

Create a class list of the ones you demonstrate. Continue to add to the list regularly. **Suggested Teacher Talk:** *Explain how these two words are alike. What part of the word makes the rhyme? Generate another word that would rhyme with these words.*

With You

Make a large circle on the floor with the *Musical Rhyme Pictures*, and have each child stand behind one of the cards. Use music to start and stop along the way, as done in musical chairs. Start the music, and have students begin walking around the picture circle. Intermittently pause the music, and have students stop in front of a card. Call out a word, and have students check to see if the picture they are standing in front of rhymes with the stated word.

Invite the student with the rhyming picture to jump into the middle of the circle, say aloud their rhyming word, and add another word that rhymes. Students standing around the outside of the circle can have a chance to "unload" any rhyme thoughts and contribute by jumping inside the circle and saying their rhymes and then jumping back out.

By You

Place the *Musical Rhyme Pictures* in an area where students can revisit the technique again and produce rhyming words and record in their Word Study Journals. Post poetry such as traditional rhymes, nursery rhymes, or contemporary poetry for students to read aloud and recognize the rhyme within the text.

Differentiation

Use various rhyming words (e.g., cat-hat; weather-feather; persist-exist) depending on the instructional levels of students.

Extensions

- Read a poem from a content area or a theme, or use clapping games such as "Miss Mary Mack." Choose a body signal (e.g., hands up or down; sway to right or left) to identify the initial rhyming word and demonstrate the rhythm of the poem using that signal.

- Split the class into heterogeneous small groups of four or five students and give each group a stuffed animal or an object. Play music while the stuffed animal or object is passed around like a "hot potato." When the music stops, whoever is holding the stuffed animal produces a rhyming word that corresponds with a given word. Circulate among the teams to support them as they implement the technique.

Rappin' Rhymes

Purpose:	ELL Technique:
To recognize and produce rhyming words to rhythm	Yes

Materials:
• poems, songs, or raps that correlate to content being studied   • Internet access to websites

Learning Phases

I

Share a selected text (poem, song, or rap) that correlates with the content being studied. Search a variety of websites for modeled-rhyming support and modeled poetry, songs, and raps (e.g., Educationalrap.com; Flocabulary.com; Rhymer.com; Rhymerzone.com; Smartsongs.com).

Demonstrate the rhythm within the text and highlight the featured words that rhyme by dramatizing the poem as you create movements/body signals that feature attention to the rhyming words and possibly change their prosodic functions (i.e., stress, pitch, tone) for the rhyming words highlighted.

We

As a class, select a poem, song, or rap, and dramatize it with specific movements/body signals that feature attention to the rhyming words, using their voices to emphasis the rhyming words. **Suggested Teacher Talk:** *Listen to the text read aloud, and select the words that rhyme within the text. What criteria did you use to determine if the words rhyme? Produce a list of words that have the same rhyme as the one presented.*

With You

Divide students into teams. Have each team select text to dramatize on its own, using the same process as modeled previously. If desired, allow students to use forms of beat boxing and freestyle rapping to enhance musical elements and rhyming. Invite students to rap about things they see and encourage them to incorporate objects, people, situations, and even sounds into their raps.

Circulate among the teams to support them as they work. Then, have teams present their dramatized-selected text to other groups. Students watching the presentation should analyze movements and determine the pattern of the body signal and the rhyming pattern within the context of the poem, and then turn and talk with partners to discuss how they think the musical rhythm corresponds with the content.

By You

Give each student two vocabulary words that correlate with the content being studied. Have them reflect on the group's dramatized presentations. Have students use the vocabulary words to create their own two rhyming couplets in which the last words in lines one and two rhyme with each other, and the last words in lines three and four rhyme with each other.

Extension

Create a talking photograph using a website such as Fotobabble (http://www.fotobabble.com/). Students upload a photograph and then record themselves saying words that rhyme with the objects in their photographs to create a "talking image."

Rhyming Jar

Purpose:	ELL Technique:
To generate rhyming words that associate and focus on what is essential to determine meaning in a chosen content area	No

Materials:

- *Rhyming Jar Sentences* (see rhyming jar.pdf)
- jar
- strips of paper

- display options (chart paper, dry-erase boards, interactive whiteboard)
- Internet access to websites

Learning Phases

I

Label a jar as the Rhyming Jar. Write or copy *Rhyming Jar Sentences* on strips of paper that correspond with a concept of particular content you are studying (e.g., habitats, immigration). For additional sample sentences see the *Rhyming Jar Sentences*, omitting the final rhyming word (e.g., color words: I want a new bed, and I will paint it _____ [red]). Then, place the strips into the Rhyming Jar.

Select a strip from the Rhyming Jar and read it aloud, emphasizing the first rhyming word (e.g., whisper the word *bed* in the first sentence above). Leave out the rhyming word at the end of the sentence, and model how you have to think about the word you emphasized because the omitted word will have the same ending sound (rhyme) as that particular emphasized word.

We

Generate with students other words that would rhyme with the selected words. Read text that has words that rhyme with the identified word. Display this list for all students to see the rhyme identified (e.g., bed/red). Have students stand every time they hear a word that rhymes with the identified word in context.

Return to the Rhyming Jar, pull another sentence from the jar, and invite students to work in pairs to select the word that completes the sentence. If additional support is needed, give the initial sound for the omitted rhyming word. Add that rhyming pair to the chart, and have students share other words that rhyme to add to the list.

With You

Distribute strips from the Rhyming Jar to students, and have them work with partners to create the ending part to the rhyming sentences. Students analyze the vocabulary words, the rhyming ability, and the correlation to the content meaning in order to know whether the word(s) they've selected make sense. **Suggested Teacher Talk:** *Does your rhyming word at the end of the sentence make sense? Why or why not?*

As a class, add the rhyming pairs to the list. Partners can go on a detective hunt to search for words that rhyme with their selected rhyming words from their sentence strips. Add the discovered rhyming words found on their rhyming detective hunts to a posted class-generated list.

By You

Have students be "rhyme detectives," looking for other oral and written words that rhyme with the word pairs on the list. If desired, students can listen to chants, poetry, or rap from various sources. Challenge them to create individual sentences that support meaning for the vocabulary words that will be within the rhyming sentences. **Suggested Teacher Talk:** *Explain how you used the rhyming vocabulary word within the sentence to rhyme. What added support was given within the statement to bring meaning to the vocabulary word?*

Differentiation

For visual learning support or English language learners, use picture cards as the initial rhyme instead of words in the sentence.

Draw a Rhyme

Purpose:	ELL Technique:
To determine a rhyming word that makes sense in a story in order to complete a sentence and to create a visual representation of the rhyme	Yes

Materials:	
• *Draw a Rhyme Poem* (see drawrhymepoem.pdf)	• scissors
• display options (chart paper, dry-erase boards, interactive whiteboard)	• felt
	• foam board
	• drawing paper or dry-erase boards
• rhyming poems	• Internet access to websites

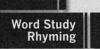

Learning Phases

I

Model the *Draw a Rhyme Poem* and read the first few lines aloud, omitting the ending rhyming words. Demonstrate and display an image that would correlate with the meaning of what you read.

Model how you can create a poem for concept of study in any content area (a body system in science, a multiplication equation in math, etc.). The words at the end of every two lines should rhyme. For example, the first two lines might read *In digestion everything begins here, In an opening that is between your ears*. Omit saying the word *ears* when reading the sentence aloud and draw a picture of a mouth.

We

Read the next two lines, and ask a student to continue creating the concept image that correlates with the meaning of the text. For example, the next two lines might read *When you chew and chew your food, it must go through this long, long tube*. The student would draw an esophagus attached to the mouth as anatomically correct as possible. **Suggested Teacher Talk:** *Draw the concept the rhyme refers to (e.g., concept: esophagus, rhyme: food and tube). How do the rhyming words in the poem support your understanding of_____ (e.g., digestive system)?*

With You

Have partners take turns reading a different poem from *Draw a Rhyme* (Fitzpatrick 1997) to each other. One will read while the other one listens and draws the rhyme. Partners revisit the poem and compare the one that illustrated the rhyme with the actual poem for accuracy. They can also create their own Draw a Rhyme poem to share.

By You

Record some poems for use with this technique and place them at the listening center. Have students listen to the poems on their own and draw the rhyming words or have precut shapes from felt or foam board that represent the desired rhymes. Have students put together the felt or foam pieces to "build a rhyme."

Extension

Introduce students to a variety of rebus stories. For example, read *I Love You: A Rebus Poem* (Marzollo 2000). As a class, compare the Draw a Rhyme technique to a rebus story. Create a group rebus story to correspond with a current content subject or piece of text. (Nursery rhymes make great rebus examples and can be found on the Internet (e.g., Enchantedlearning.com.) Reread the text, noting rhymes in the text by whispering them when you encounter them as you are reading.

Word Study Strategy: Isolating and Identifying Sounds

Isolating sounds is a strategy that allows students to recognize individual sound(s) in a word. Attending to these phonemes increases students' phonemic awareness that words are made up of individual sounds that connect to form a word. The Foundational Skills strand within the Common Core State Standards (CCSS 2010) emphasizes isolating and identifying as the essence of the foundation for phonological awareness, phonics, and word recognition. When students apply this strategy, they are demonstrating their ability to think about and separate individual sounds from one another within a word (e.g., the first sound in dog is /d/, the medial sound in wet is /e/, and the final sound in like is /k/). Students need to explore the articulation of these alphabetical sounds with techniques that support the correct positioning of their mouths. "This type of explicit attention to vocal gestures can be helpful at the beginning of phonemic awareness instruction" (Manyak 2008, 659). Positioning of the lips, tongue, and jaw is vital to speech, motor coordination, and articulating sounds correctly and has a positive effect on students' word reading (Castiglioni-Spalten and Ehri 2003; Anthony et al. 2011).

Students who are applying this strategy are able to think about separate distinct sounds, and notice that two or more words may have the same initial sound (e.g., *ball*, *bat*, and *balloon*), medial sound (e.g., *met*, *Greg*, and *tell*), or final sound (e.g., *call*, *pool*, and *doll*). Identifying these sounds is important, as students lay a solid foundation in the area of phonological awareness as they move through the developmental stages of reading, and it provides students with a tool for reading as well as writing.

To support Isolating and Identifying Sounds while reading, a set of skills is required to effectively implement this reading strategy. The synchronized application of several reading strategies results in making meaning while reading a text. The skills, additional integrated reading strategies, and their reading components found in corresponding chapters are as follows.

Focus Skill(s):

- Concepts of words
- Awareness of sounds
- Formation of mouth position

Integrated Strategies:

- Analyzing Sounds (Chapter 2)
- Analyzing Words (Chapter 3)

Accountable Teacher Talk for Isolating and Identifying Sounds

Following is a list of suggested Teacher Talk that encourages readers to think strategically as they employ the Isolating and Identify Sounds strategy. To effectively increase levels of thinking, these suggestions incorporate Bloom's Taxonomy's higher-order questioning (Anderson and Krathwohl 2001) and Webb's Depth of Knowledge (2002).

Remembering and Understanding (Recall)

- What is the difference between the sound and the letter? What sound does the letter _____ make?

- What other words start the same as the word _____?

Applying (Skill/Concept)

- Think of the words that begin with the same sound as _____ and compose your own form of alliteration. What do you notice about your tongue/lips/jaw when you say the sound _____?

Analyzing (Strategic Thinking)

- Distinguish where you hear the sound /_____/ in the word _____. Is the sound closer to the beginning or ending of the word? Explain your choice.

Evaluating and Creating (Extended Thinking)

- Explain why you positioned your mouth that way to make the word _____. Think of other words that would have that same mouth shape and make the same sounds.

- Create a list of words that start the same as _____ and forms an alliteration with the same beginning sounds. Compose these words into several sentences that denote appropriate meaning.

Behavior Indicators for Isolating and Identifying Sounds

As you assess students' ability to isolate and identify phonemes, use the following behaviors as a guide. Do students exhibit these behaviors never, rarely, often, or always?

- ❑ Isolate and identify individual sounds by positioning the mouth, lips, jaw, and tongue to correspond with appropriate sound

- ❑ Isolate and pronounce initial sounds (e.g., cup, car, ball), medial vowel sounds (e.g., cup, cap, cop), and final sounds (e.g., pan, pal, pad) in spoken-syllable words

- ❑ Distinguish long- from short-vowel sounds in spoken single-syllable words when reading regularly spelled one-syllable words

Techniques for Isolating and Identifying Sounds

Mirror/Mirror

Purpose:	ELL Technique:
To identify and demonstrate positioning of the mouth, lips, jaw and tongue with isolated sounds in a spoken word	Yes

Materials:

- a piece of familiar text
- hand held mirrors (or visit http://www.ValerieEllery.com for Mouth It Mirrors)
- basket
- Word Study Journals
- digital camera
- chart paper

Learning Phases

I

Select a word with three sounds from a familiar text and say it aloud, isolating the beginning sound. Look into a handheld mirror and notice the position of your mouth (lips, tongue, jaw). Being specific, tell students what you see in the mirror. For example, "When I produce the /d/ sound in the word *dog*, I see my lips are open, and I feel my tongue touching the roof of my mouth."

We

Have students practice positioning their mouths to say the sound you isolated. Select several volunteers to describe the formation of their mouths on a particular sound given. Have students place their hand on their throats as they vocalize a sound, a syllable, or a word and notice the rhythmic feature of the highlighted sound(s).

With You

Have students work with a partner and select a word from a familiar text. One student will produce sounds from the word, study their mouth in a mirror, and describe to their partner what they notice for their mouth position. Partners will then switch roles, so each one is able to observe the position of their mouth and verbalize their observation. Select another word with three sounds from a familiar text and ask partners to isolate the medial or final sound in the word. Partners will again observe their mouth and describe what they see to their partner. **Suggested Teacher Talk:** *What do you notice about your tongue/lips/jaw when you say the sound _____ ?*

By You

Provide mirrors during independent writing time for students to utilize while encoding words. They may check the position of their mouth for specific sounds (e.g., initial sounds, vowel sounds, syllables, affixes, or roots of a word). Students can record (illustrations or narrative) in their Word Study Journals what they observed as they positioned their mouth for the specific sounds.

Differentiation

Substitute sounds for a multisyllabic word from a familiar text or content area, and say it aloud, isolating the syllables (e.g., reflecting or equation). **Suggested Teacher Talk:** *When I produce the /r/ sound in the first syllable (re-), I see my lips are the shape of a circle, and I feel my tongue lifted and then moving down toward my chin.*

Extensions

- Create a chart with four or five letters as the categories. Collect items that correlate with the letter sounds in a basket. Have students select an item, check the position of their mouth in the mirror, and then place an object under a corresponding picture to complete the chart. **Suggested Teacher Talk:** *How do you position your mouth when you start the word _____ for the final sound in the root _____?*

- Create a digital portfolio of sounds by having students use a webcam, voice recording software, or an app. Students produce a sound while taking a picture of their mouth formation and recording the sound they pronounce.

- Using a digital camera, have student groups take pictures of their mouths as they form letter sounds. The pictures can be used to create digital books by importing them into a PowerPoint™ slideshow. If desired, have students record and insert the sounds that are demonstrated in each picture.

Alliteration Activation Creation

Purpose:	ELL Technique:
To identify initial sounds and create additional words that begin with the same sounds to supply rhythm, repetition, and meaning in a story, poem, or song to demonstrate a form of figurative language	Yes

Materials:

- text with alliteration (poetry, jingles, song lyrics)
- small objects (e.g., ball, pencil, marker)
- bucket or bag
- Word Study Journals
- chart paper
- clip art or pictures of common recognizable items (e.g., dog, car, child)
- drawing paper

Learning Phases

I

Select a piece of text (poem, story, or a song) and small objects that highlight alliteration. Read aloud the selected text. Emphasize with your voice the various words that highlight the repetition of initial sounds.

Discuss how this literary style creates a unique rhythm in the text, where the initial sounds are repeated in close succession. Select and place a few chosen objects in a bucket or a bag to use during the "We" section.

We

Ask students to listen and determine words that have repeated sounds that form a rhythm from selected text with alliteration. Brainstorm words that begin with the same beginning sound for alliteration. Have students take turns choosing a small object from the bucket or bag, saying the name of the object, and then thinking of an adjective or word beginning with the same sound as the object. For example, a student could take a pencil out of the bag and say "peculiar pencil."

Continue to pass the bucket or bag around the room and have students generate alliterations for the objects. List students' responses on chart paper. **Suggested Teacher Talk:** *Think of words that begin with the same sound as _____.*

With You

Divide students into groups of three or four. Distribute a picture or clip art from a chosen content of study to each group. Have them think of vocabulary words to align with the picture and create a list of words that demonstrate alliteration and also denote appropriate meaning. Then, have the students create a sentence using the vocabulary word, using as much alliteration as possible.

Example:

Content: Anne Frank

Vocabulary Word: rucksack

Illustration: picture of a rucksack; two-word alliteration: rugged rucksack

Sentence Sample: After *resting*, Anne *ran rapidly* to see the *rationed* books in the *rugged rucksack*. (italicized words are other vocabulary words in text)

By You

Continue to have students search for alliteration in text (books, poems, songs) and record examples in their Word Study Journals. **Suggested Teacher Talk:** *Create a list of words that start the same as _____ and form alliterations because of their beginning sounds. Compose these words into several sentences that denote appropriate meaning.*

Extensions

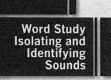

- Use a student's name followed by a verb after his or her name that has the same beginning sound (e.g., Derek dreams, Jacey jumps, Brooke bounces) to produce alliteration. Have students create tongue twisters with their names (e.g., Bailey bakes biscuits before breakfast).

- Have students create their own poetry prose, using alliteration with illustrations and sentences that incorporate as many vocabulary words from a specific content-area text. **Suggested Teacher Talk:** *What kind of figurative language did you hear in the text that was read aloud? Think of the words that begin with the same sound as _____ and compose your own alliteration creation.*

Hot Seat

Purpose:	ELL Technique:
To recognize and dramatize positioning of isolated sounds	Yes

Materials:	

- three cups, one set per pair of students
- chairs
- small items to use as markers (e.g., marbles, counters, buttons)
- Word Study Journals
- three index cards
- text
- Hula-Hoops™ *(variation)*
- chart (optional)
- markers

Learning Phases

I

Mark the index cards each with one letter—*B* (beginning sound), *M* (middle sound), and *E* (ending sound). Mark each set of cups with the same letters. Line up three chairs in the front of the room. Attach one (*B*, *M*, or *E*) card to each chair and explain that these are the "hot seats." Select a word from a familiar text or content area of study.

Isolate one sound from the word by saying it aloud, and then sit in the chair that correlates with the position of the sound in the word. For example, if the word chosen is *pig*, say the /p/ sound, and sit in the first seat. Continue to move to each chair, saying aloud the sound within the word that correlates with the chair (sit in the middle chair and say the /i/ sound in *pig*; sit in the last chair and say the sound /g/ in *pig*).

We

Select students to line up and take turns sitting in the hot seats. Ask a student to sit in the correct chair that correlates with another sound in the original word. Have the student explain his or her reasoning for selecting the chosen chair. Select another word from a familiar text with more sounds than the number of chairs. **Suggested Teacher Talk:** *Where do you hear the /____/ sound in ____?*

Once the student is sitting in the selected hot seat, continue having him or her lean toward the chair that represents the answer. **Suggested Teacher Talk:** *Is the /____/ sound closer to the beginning of the word or closer to the end of the word?* Verify answers by breaking the word into phonemes and counting how many sounds are before and after the highlighted sound.

With You

Distribute a set of cups and a marker to each pair of students, explaining that the cups now represent the chairs from the previous phase. Demonstrate how to use the cups and a small item as a sound marker.

Instruct students to line up cups in order, and choose words from a familiar text to have them demonstrate positioning of the sounds by placing a marble in the correct cup that represents the isolated sound and then defend their decision. **Suggested Teacher Talk:** *Move your cup in the direction that represents the closest proximity to the highlighted sound. Verify your response.*

By You

Students analyze words during independent reading or words directly from their independent writing to determine the number of sounds or syllables. They can record their exploration in Word Study Journals. Variation: Use Hula-Hoops™ to substitute chairs by placing the hoops on the floor and letting students stand inside the circles, or place at a center.

Differentiation

Select and isolate a multisyllabic word from a familiar text or content area of study, highlighting features such as affixes. For example, if the word is *equation* and the syllable /tion/ is isolated, the student would sit in the last seat because it is the final syllable. The number of chairs/cups can increase depending on how many syllables are being studied.

Extensions

Create a class graph labeled *prefix*, *root*, *suffix*, listing isolated syllables in the appropriate categories when possible. If an isolated syllable correlates with one of the headings, it can be added to the graph. For example, in the word *equation*, the syllable /tion/ could be written under the label *suffix*. Post in the classroom as a visual reminder of roots and affixes.

Think Sounds Abound

Purpose:	ELL Technique:
To isolate, identify, and match beginning and ending sounds in words	Yes

Materials:

- *Think Sounds Pictures* (see thinksoundspics.pdf)
- paper or recording device
- Word Study Journals
- basket
- masking tape
- six to eight objects to complete a Think Sounds Train

Learning Phases

I

Select a word from a content area of study or from a text that is familiar to students. Say the word aloud, isolating the ending sound. Then, produce another word in which the beginning sound is identical to the ending sound in the starter word (e.g., starter word is *cloud*, which ends with the /d/ sound, so the second word could be *dense*) *Think Sounds* (Zgonc 1999). Continue producing other content words that connect by the ending sound of one word becoming the beginning sound of the following word (e.g., *cloud, drizzle, latitude, dense, snow, ozone*). If a literary text is read, the words could be related to elements from the story (e.g., characters, emotions, and settings) to create a train of related words.

We

Create a class Think Sounds Train from a content area you are studying or a piece of literature you are reading by asking a student to produce a starter word. Students then think of a word that begins with the final sound in the word. Have the next student say a word that begins with the ending sound of the last word. Invite students to give word choices that would keep the class "train" in production mode, moving forward with words that have the initial sound as the former word's ending sound.

Discuss how some words end with a letter that's different from the sound (e.g., /s/ is the final sound in dense, not the letter or sound for the e which is silent). If a word is given and the group is unable to add a word to the class train, then "stop the train" and start over on a "new track" with a new word to create a new train of words.

With You

Divide students into teams of five to six. Provide teams with different words to use for their Think Sounds Trains. Have each group designate a Recorder to capture the words on paper or by an electronic recording device (e.g., tablet, smartphone) for review. Select a student to start each team train. Remind students to pay attention to the final sound, not the final letter, when creating a new word. **Suggested Teacher Talk:** *Think about the word* density *from our science unit on matter. What sound do you hear at the end of the word? Take the final sound, and think of a word that begins with that sound and correlates with our content of study.*

Instruct teams to continue adding to their Think Sounds Trains as long as possible. Allow teams to present their trains to the class. Have students share meaning behind each word as they present it and how the words may be connected to one another.

By You

After reading an informational text independently, ask students to create their own Think Sounds Train with pictures or words related to the main concept in the text. If a literary text is read, students may come up with characters, setting, emotions, and so forth from the story to create their train. Ask students to share their Think Sounds Train with a partner or the class and justify their choice of words in relation to the chosen concept.

Differentiation

- For visual-learning support or English language learners, use *Think Sounds Pictures* to represent the words in the Think Sound Train instead of words.

- While orally creating the Think Sounds Train, clap a rhythmic beat to keep the train moving at a steady pace. For example, ask the group to clap two times, and then tap their knees once in rhythm. When knees are tapped, the next word in the Think Sounds Train should be produced. This process supports kinesthetic learners and students who respond well to music and movement.

Extension

Select six to eight objects that could complete a Think Sounds Train. Label the beginning object with a numeral 1, using masking tape and the ending object with the final number. Place the objects in a basket for students to try to order into a Think Sound Train during a center or workstation.

Word Study Strategy: Blending and Segmenting Sounds

Blending and Segmenting Sounds is a strategy that involves listening to a sequence of spoken sounds or syllables and then combining the sounds to form a meaningful whole (blending), and hearing a word, and then breaking it into its separate parts (segmenting). The blending strategy allows students to move from knowing sounds individually or isolating sounds in a choppy-pause sound, to a smoother sound while having a continuous flow of connecting the sounds. Segmenting allows for students to examine the parts of the words. Parts can be the beginning letter(s) that precedes the vowel (onset) and the rhyming pattern that follows the onset (rime). "Sets of words with matching rimes, such as *bell*, *tell*, *sell* are nothing more or less than phonograms or word families" (Adams 1990, 139). Nearly 500 words can be derived purely from using 37 rimes (Wylie and Durell 1970). Readers can decode and encode these words by dividing them between the onset and rime and then blending these two parts together (e.g., /b/-/ike/ blended together is bike).

As students get a solid understanding of Blending and Segmenting Sounds, they are able to use this strategy to manipulate phonemes. Manipulating phonemes involves blending and segmenting by adding, deleting, and substituting phonemes in words. This combination of connecting and separating phonemes and graphemes (letters) helps students associate phonemic awareness with application to reading and writing (Allor, Gansle, and Denny 2006; Ball and Blachman 1991; Edelen-Smith 1997; Lundberg, Frost, and Petersen 1988; Melby-Lervag et al. 2012). Tangible objects (e.g., buttons, paper clips, or other counters) representing letter sounds serve as visual support for students, and these objects can then be replaced by their respective letters when segmentation is done in written form such as phonics (Newbury 2007). Figures 2.4 and 2.5 identify a variety of ways to demonstrate blending and segmenting competencies.

Figure 2.4 Blending Samples

syllable	/gar/den/ = *garden*
onset and rime	/b/ (onset) /ike/ (rime) = *bike*
individual phonemes	/c/-/a/-/t/ = *cat*

Figure 2.5 Segmenting Samples

sentences to words	*The dog barks* becomes /The/ /dog/ /barks/
words to syllables	*garden* becomes /gar/den
words to onset and rime	*bike* becomes /b-/ike/
words to individual phonemes	*cat* becomes /c-/a/-/t/

To support Blending and Segmenting Sounds while reading, a set of skills is required to effectively implement this reading strategy. The synchronized application of several reading strategies results in making meaning while reading a text. The skills, additional integrated reading strategies, and their reading components found in corresponding chapters are listed below.

Focus Skill(s):

- Concepts of words

- Awareness of sounds; onset and rimes

- Connecting

- Separating

Integrated Strategies:

- Isolating and Identifying Sounds; Analyzing Sounds (Chapter 2)

Accountable Teacher Talk for Blending and Segmenting Sounds

Following is a list of suggested Teacher Talk that encourages readers to think strategically as they employ the Blending and Segmenting Sounds strategy. To effectively increase levels of thinking, these suggestions incorporate Bloom's Taxonomy's higher-order questioning (Anderson and Krathwohl 2001) and Webb's Depth of Knowledge (2002).

Remembering and Understanding (Recall)

- How many words do you hear in the sentence?

- How does hearing the onset and then the rime help you to form the word?

Applying (Skill/Concept)

- Demonstrate the number of syllables (or sounds) you hear in the word by pushing your counters together.

Analyzing (Strategic Thinking)

- Try to say the word slowly to hear the individual sounds in the word _____ and determine other words that are close to the same number of sounds. How does slowly hearing each individual sound and blending the sounds as you go help you when forming a word?

Evaluating and Creating (Extended Thinking)

- Isolate the second syllable in the word _____. How many letters are represented within the highlighted syllable? What is the vowel that is in the highlighted syllable? Explain how thinking about syllables supports your ability to decode/sound out a word.

- Investigate words by their syllables. What information can you gather to support your understanding of syllables? Explain the steps you used to determine where the syllable breaks are in the word.

Behavior Indicators for Blending and Segmenting Sounds

As you assess students' ability to blend phonemes, use the following behaviors as a guide. Do students exhibit these behaviors never, rarely, often, or always?

- ❏ Blend and segment onsets and rimes of single-syllable spoken words

- ❏ Orally produce single-syllable words by blending sounds (phonemes), including consonant blends

- ❏ Segment spoken single-syllable words into their complete sequence of individual sounds (phonemes)

- ❏ Identify and separate a sentence to individual words, individual words to syllables, words to onset and rime, individual units of sound in a word, and structural analysis of a word

Techniques for Blending and Segmenting Sounds

Chime with Rimes

Purpose:	ELL Technique:
To hear and analyze two segments of a word, such as the onset and rime and blend them together to form the word	Yes

Materials:

- text
- word list from text with onsets and rimes
- puppet
- magazines
- dry-erase boards and markers
- online clip art programs
- *Rimes Poster* (see rimesposter.pdf)
- Word Study Journals
- chart paper
- markers

Word Study
Blending and
Segmenting
Sounds

Learning Phases

I

After reading a sentence from a selected text, present students with a word from the text. Read the word to students, noting the particular rime sound you are studying (e.g., *ight*). Use a puppet to introduce blending onset and rimes by chanting a jingle as follows: Use two different voices. Your voice: "It starts with /n/." Puppet voice: "and it ends with /ight/." Your voice: "put it together, and it says *night*."

We

Select a student to listen to the puppet say the onset and have the student create a rime that would make the new word. Rimes can be selected from the *Rimes Poster* to create a word to chant the jingle and have the student fill in the word at the end of the sentence. For example, "I know a word that begins with /c/ and ends with /ake/. Now put it together and it says _____[cake]."

Continue to use the puppet and have students listen to the onset and rime (e.g., /r/-/ake/) and blend the two together in their minds to create a visual representation of the chosen onset and rime word. **Suggested Teacher Talk:** *Explain how these words are similar.*

With You

Ask groups to cut pictures out of a magazine or use electronic illustrations that represent a word with an onset and rime. Students can collect the pictures in a Word Study Journals, identify the segmentation in the word, and blend the word beside the picture in written form.

By You

While independently reading, have students search for onset and rime words to analyze and demonstrate segmentation in their Word Study Journals. They can place a / to demonstrate the segmentation(s) in the word (e.g., r/ake, p/eek).

Differentiation

To support visual learners and English language learners, use two different-color markers (one color for the onset *n* and the other color for the rime *ight*) to highlight the word for all students to see; record the word on a chart, using markers with these same colors.

Word Study Blending and Segmenting Sounds

Extensions

- Have students segment the word either by syllables (pen/cil) or phonemes (/d/-/e/-/s/-/k/).

- Challenge teams to think about or search in their text for words that have a particular rime, such as *-ight*, as a part of the words (e.g., *frightened, mighty, delightful*).

Body Blending

Purpose:		ELL Technique:
To hear the individual units of sound in a word and act out the blending of the phonemes to form the word		Yes

Materials:	
• Hula-Hoops™	• index cards
	• Word Study Journals

Learning Phases

I

Place one Hula-Hoop™ on the ground for each phoneme represented in a chosen word (e.g., *met* has three phonemes (/m/-/e/-/t/) = three hoops). Say each sound individually as you step into one hoop at a time. Move from left to right to represent the order of sounds in a word.

After saying the last sound, step out of the final hoop and blend all the sounds represented and say the word aloud. **Suggested Teacher Talk:** *How does slowly hearing each individual sound and blending the sounds as you go help you when forming a word?*

We

On individual cards, segment words into sounds or syllables. Choose volunteers to represent the proper number of sounds for students to "be a phoneme or syllable" in a predetermined word (e.g., log). Ask each student to stand behind a hoop. Invite the first student to step into the hoop and begin by saying the first sound (e.g., /l/). The next student steps inside his or her hoop and says the second sound (e.g., /o/) while linking onto the first student and orally combines the first sound with the second sound (e.g., /lo/).

Continue until all students standing in the hoops have said their sounds and linked arms to form a word. Have all the linked students take one step forward out of their hoops and pronounce the entire word in unison (log).

Word Study Blending and Segmenting Sounds

With You

With small groups at a center/station, students can practice Body Blending using phonemes, or they can select one onset card and one rime card from the stacks and hop into the first Hula-Hoop™ and pronounce the onset. Then, hop into the next Hula-Hoop™ and say the rime. Finally, hop out of the Hula-Hoop™ and pronounce the blended word. **Suggested Teacher Talk:** *When you hop out of the final hoop, what are you doing to the word?*

By You

Have students select words from their independent reading or writing to segment and blend sounds. After segmenting the sounds in a chosen word, have students draw circles (representing the hoops) from left to right for each sound in the word.

Instruct students to then write the grapheme(s) that correlate with each sound in the appropriate circle and the blended word below the circles. Students can use index cards to create segmentation cards by writing each sound segment on a card to share with others to scramble and blend.

Differentiation

Blend and segment the given words by syllables, affixes, and root words (e.g., if the word is multiplication, and you are working with syllables, the first student will say /mul/, and the second student will say /ti/ and then blend /mul/ and /ti/ together by saying /mul/ti/. The third student will say /pli/, followed by /mul/ti/pli/). Continue this process until students form the entire word.

Extension

Using key academic vocabulary words, write the letters on a note card that represents a unit of sound. Mix up the letter cards representing the word and pass them out to teams of students. Teams work to unscramble the letters and then perform their word, not by showing their letter cards but by saying the sounds and forming the word using the process described in the technique. If several letter cards could blend together to be an affix, have those students stay inside a Hula-Hoop™ together or stand shoulder-to-shoulder as they present their sounds. The rest of the class listens to the sounds and tries to discover the word. Instruct students to record the newly blended words in their Word Study Journals.

Egg-Cited About Sounds

Purpose:	ELL Technique:
To hear individual units of sound in words, and segment spoken syllable words into their complete sequence of individual sounds (phonemes)	Yes

Materials:

- text
- plastic eggs or a close and open container
- objects for counters (e.g., colored candies, paper clips)
- Word Study Journals

Word Study Blending and Segmenting Sounds

Learning Phases

I

Select words from a text you are reading in class. Pronounce one word and orally segment the phonemes in the word while dropping a counter into the egg or container. Close the container. Orally produce each phoneme again, shaking the egg/container with each phoneme.

We

Distribute one plastic egg (or a container that can be opened and closed) and four to six counters to students, and orally share a word from the text. Have students decide how many sounds are in the word and place a counter in the egg to represent each sound. **Suggested Teacher Talk:** *Determine how many sounds you hear in the word, and place a counter to represent each sound. How many counters did you place inside your egg? Why?* Have students close the eggs and pronounce the word slowly by isolating each sound as they shake the egg to the rhythm of the sounds.

With You

Divide students into pairs. Designate one student as Partner A and the other Partner B. Have Partner A search through the selected text and choose a word to have Partner B segment according to the desired outcome (sounds, syllables) using the process described in the previous section. Then, Partner A checks the accuracy of Partner B's ability to segment and they reverse roles with alternative words.

By You

Ask students to select a word from their independent reading or writing and write the word in their Word Study Journals. Specify the type of segments (sounds, syllables), and have students search in the text and highlight the chosen segment. Have students place the appropriate number of counters in the egg and shake out the word independently.

As the student pulls each counter out, instruct him or her to draw circles or boxes for the sounds represented in the word and then blend them all together by writing the word under the circles or boxes and revisiting the word in context.

Differentiation

Analyze a variety of segments (syllables, root and inflectional endings, affixes and roots in the word) while dropping a counter into the egg to represent each form of segmentation.

Suggested Teacher Talk: *Isolate the second syllable in the word _____. How many letters are represented within the highlighted syllable?* For example, if the word is *hibernation*, then students would place three counters in the container for the letters in /ber/. Then, students can analyze the highlighted syllable segment to determine from the number of letters how many sound units are within the syllable. For example, in the /ber/ syllable from the word *hibernation*, there are only two sounds: /b/ and the r-controlled vowel /er/.

Silly Sound Segmenting

Purpose:	ELL Technique:
To separate individual units of sounds in a word and demonstrate sounds through a tangible representation	Yes

Materials:

- text
- clay
- Word Study Journals
- sticky notes
- picture card

Learning Phases

I   Select a word from a familiar text, or show a picture card that represents the word. Roll a ball of clay into a long "silly snake" to represent the selected word. Orally segment each phoneme in the word, breaking off a chunk of clay as you say each phoneme, making sure to use the entire strip of clay since it represents the whole word.

Pick up the first piece of clay and say the phoneme it represents. Repeat this process with each piece of clay, presenting each phoneme within the word. Demonstrate blending the segments by picking up the first piece of clay again and say the phoneme it represents.

Next, pick up the second piece of clay and say the phoneme it represents while connecting the first and second pieces of clay. Orally produce the sound segment the first two phonemes represent. For example, if the *chosen* word is *fish*, the sound segment that represents the first two phonemes is /f/ + /i/ = /fi/. Continue this process until each phoneme is blended back together to form the original word.

We

Display sticky notes instead of clay for the whole group to see. Each sticky note denotes a syllable in the example word. Use a pointer or your finger to glide under each sticky note as you repeat the word. Share a word with the class, and ask volunteers to come up and count out how many sticky notes will be needed to represent the determined segments. Have the volunteers say the designated sounds and stick the note card on display, gliding to demonstrate blending the sounds. **Suggested Teacher Talk:** *Demonstrate how many sounds you hear in the word _____.* Repeat the process with a new word from the text you are reading.

**Word Study
Blending and
Segmenting
Sounds**

With You

Divide students into small groups. Provide each group with several small balls of clay, and ask them to shape their clay into a log roll like a snake. Pronounce a word directly from a chosen text and have students separate their "snakes" into a corresponding number of sound units, reminding them that each segment represents a phoneme. Have students demonstrate a one-to-one correspondence with each section of their snakes as they say the phonemes separately. Then have them pick up each individual segment while pronouncing the corresponding phoneme, pinching the individual segments together as they fuse the phonemes to re-form the word by blending. **Suggested Teacher Talk:** *What sounds do you hear in the word? Separate the sounds and represent each segment with a separate piece of clay. Which visual representation shows the _____ (e.g., the second) syllable in the word _____? (e.g., word = bicycle, second syllable = cy)*

By You

Ask students to select words from a familiar literary or informational text the class has read or the student has read independently. Invite them to segment and blend phonemes in the selected words, creating a visual representation of each phoneme with clay, using the process previously described.

Differentiation

Have students blend the word in a variety of ways (e.g., syllables, prefix, or suffix, root word) and analyze the vowel sounds within each segment of the word while physically and orally reforming the word.

Extensions

- Break each syllable into individual phonemes by putting a tally mark on a syllable sticky note or break each piece of clay apart again to denote the number of phonemes in each syllable. Stack the sticky notes on top of each other as you say each syllable. Say the first syllable and pick up the first visual note. Continue to connect sticky notes, creating a visual representation of each syllable blending with the previous syllable to reform the word.

- Select a mystery word. Write clues for other students to demonstrate a word that would best represent the mystery word. For example, "I am thinking of a four syllable word—the first syllable vowel is /i/, it is a book of words with their definitions" (dic-/tion/-/ar/-/y). In a Word Study Journal, students may record the word and the number representing how many segments are in the word (e.g., phonemes, syllables, affixes) and any mystery clues they create.

Word Study Strategy: Synthesizing Sounds

Students apply the word-study strategy of Synthesizing Sounds by converting letters (graphemes) into sounds (phonemes) and then combining those sounds to create a meaningful word. *Synthesizing* means to combine parts or elements to form a whole. This strategy mirrors the synthetic-phonics approach which demonstrates integration between visual and phonological representations (Johnston, McGeown, and Watson 2011). Some educators use the term *synthetic* with the term *explicit* when referring to phonics to detail the precise way letters and sounds are associated and then blended together through decoding. Adams (1990) defines *explicit phonics* as "the provision of systematic instruction or the relation of letter-sounds to words" (49). This provision is necessary for students who have little prerequisite knowledge about alphabetic principle and phonemic awareness.

"The more students pay attention to what their mouths do when they make a speech sound, the more likely they are to remember the association of sound to letter" (Herron 2008, 80). Implementing the synthesizing strategy systematically enhances the identification and blending of phonemes by providing opportunities to merge sounds incorporating instructional techniques that support these associations enables students to become independent strategic readers.

To support Synthesizing Sounds while reading, a set of skills is required to effectively implement this reading strategy. The synchronized application of several reading strategies results in making meaning while reading a text. The skills, additional integrated reading strategies, and their reading components found in corresponding chapters, are listed below.

Focus Skill(s):

- Concepts of words
- Manipulating sounds
- Connecting sounds

Integrated Strategies:

- Isolating and Identifying; Sounds Blending and Segmenting Sounds (Chapter 2)
- Associating; Analyzing Words; Word Awareness (Chapter 3)

Accountable Teacher Talk for Synthesizing Sounds

Following is a list of suggested Teacher Talk that encourages readers to think strategically as they employ the Synthesizing Sounds strategy. To effectively increase levels of thinking, these suggestions incorporate Bloom's Taxonomy's higher-order questioning (Anderson and Krathwohl 2001) and Webb's Depth of Knowledge (2002).

Remembering and Understanding (Recall)

- Look at the letters and think about the sounds that they make to blend the word.

- How many sounds do you hear in the word _____?

Applying (Skill/Concept)

- Describe the actions you would take to determine how many syllables are in the word.

Analyzing (Strategic Thinking)

- What was the original word? What is the new word? How are they different?

Evaluating and Creating (Extended Thinking)

- Based on what you know about syllables, how would you determine the number of syllables in a word? Explain your thinking.

- What criteria would you use to determine how many phonemes are in the word? How would you verify your response?

Behavior Indicators for Synthesizing Sounds

As you assess students' ability to synthesize, use the following behaviors as a guide. Do students exhibit these behaviors never, rarely, often, or always?

❏ Recognize that sounds can be associated with letters

❏ Combine parts (sounds, affixes, inflectional endings, syllables) to form a whole word by decoding

❏ Demonstrate basic knowledge of one-to-one letter-sound correspondences by producing the primary sound or many of the most frequent sounds for each consonant

Techniques for Synthesizing Sounds

Stir It Up

Purpose:	ELL Technique:
To listen and identify sounds and letters in words and produce additional words that have the same identified letter-sound or syllable correlations	Yes

Materials:

- text
- ABC card set (*optional: can be created on index cards; one letter for each card*)
- cookie sheet
- magnetic letters
- display options (chart paper, dry-erase boards, interactive whiteboard)
- chef hat
- bowl
- magazines with food pictures

Word Study
Synthesizing
Sounds

Learning Phases

I

Hold up an ABC card and state the letter name and sound associated with the grapheme. Name a food that begins with the sound on the ABC card. Repeat with two or three more ABC cards. Place ABC cards in a circle or oval shape on the floor, and put a chef hat in the middle.

We

Have students stand on the outside of the circle so they can walk around the cards. Turn on music, and have students begin to march around the cards like a game of musical chairs until you turn it off. When the music stops, have students look down at the card closest to them.

Call out a letter or a letter sound, and have students determine if they are standing by a matching ABC card (the same letter you called). The student standing by the selected letter jumps into the circle and can hold the chef hat. The student "chef" adds to the pretend class soup a food object that begins with the sound or letter called. Create a class word list for all to see, and discuss the meaning of the words generated throughout the technique:

- If the added ingredient begins with the same sound that was called, the other students say, "Stir it up, stir it up," while they are making a stirring motion. If the ingredient does not match, the "chef" student says, "Take it out, take it out" while making a motion that pretends to be pulling it out and throwing it over his or her head.

- Have additional cooks (i.e., students with ingredients they think should be added for the selected letter/sound) jump into the pot and share their "ingredient" for the soup. Then, start the music again and repeat.

Have teams or partners review the generated list and study each word. Students should discuss the application of the word to the content of study, how they have used the word, and retell a story using the words.

Invite students to use the words from the created class word list to sort them by various word characteristics (e.g., number of phonemes or graphemes, beginning sounds, positioning of vowels).

Extensions

**Word Study
Synthesizing
Sounds**

- Say a food item or a purposeful word from a content-related text (instead of a letter) and think aloud the number of syllables in the word. Demonstrate standing by that word, jumping into the pot of soup, and saying another food- or content-related vocabulary word with the same number of syllables incorporating the analyzing strategy. Discuss how the chosen word adds value to the content.

- Place a magnetic letter on each of the ABC cards and have the student who adds an ingredient to the soup place his or her magnetic letter in a large bowl in the middle of the circle. After several students have added to the soup bowl, use a large spoon to "stir it up." Pour the letters out on to a magnetic cookie sheet, and have students use the letters to try to make words that relate to the unit of study.

- Ask students to find pictures in cooking magazines that correlate with a specific letter sound. Collect the pictures in a large class cooking pot and display as a springboard to future learning.

Stretch It

Purpose:	ELL Technique:
To recognize and demonstrate combined knowledge of all letter-sound correspondences	Yes

Materials:	
- text - rubber bands	- *Stretch-It Strips* (see stretchstrips.pdf) - visit http://www.ValerieEllery.com for hands-on Stretch-It Strips (*optional*)

Learning Phases

I

Hold a rubber band while stretching the words. Select a regularly spelled, single-syllable word from a familiar literary or informational text. While saying each phoneme, stretch the word apart. After the final phoneme, snap the word back together and say the initial word.

Orally segment the phonemes in the word one at a time. Use the *Stretch-It Strips* or the hands-on Stretch-It Strips to represent each sound. Write the grapheme(s) that represent each sound inside a box on the *Stretch-It Strip*.

Figure 2.6 Sample Stretch-It Strip

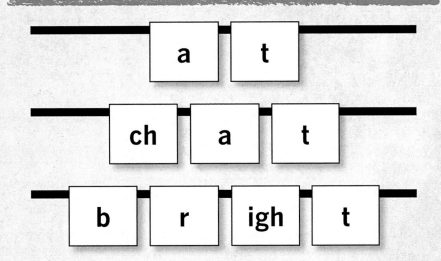

We

Have students pretend to hold a rubber band while stretching the words in the air and singing along. Select another word from a familiar text and segment the phonemes as a whole group, stretching the word in the air. Examine the number of sounds in the selected word and draw a box for each sound. **Suggested Teacher Talk:** *How many sounds do you hear in the word _____?*

Elicit letter(s) that represent each box and record them within the boxes. Then put the word in a sentence that makes sense or reread the text where the word was found in order for students to hear it in context.

With You

Distribute copies of the *Stretch-It Strips*, which can be laminated, or use the hands-on *Stretch-It Strips*. Have students write the letter(s) that correspond with each sound on each square. If using the hands-on *Stretch-It Strips*, have students stretch the elastic word and then slowly bring the word back together while merging the sounds. **Suggested Teacher Talk:** *When you stretch the word, what is happening?* If using the *Stretch-It Strips*, have students wave their hands over the boxes from left to right as they say the sounds in the word, carefully blending all the sounds together.

Word Study Synthesizing Sounds

Have students select words from their independent reading or writing and record them on the *Stretch-It Strips*, identifying the segments within the word. Have students write the word in a sentence that makes sense or reread the text, using the word(s) students stretched to hear and possibly see them in context.

Differentiation

For an analytical approach, provide a variety of Stretch-It Strips (two, three, and four boxes) and ask students to decide which strip to use based on the number of sounds in a provided word (two, three, or four).

Bingo/Bongo

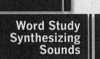
Purpose:	ELL Technique:
To listen to and identify manipulated letters and sounds	Yes

Materials:

- text
- display options (chart paper, dry-erase boards, interactive whiteboard)
- colored markers (e.g., counters, chips, or small manipulatives)
- *Bongo Letters and Word Cards* (see bongocards.pdf)
- bowls or baskets

- *Bingo/Bongo Three-Column Chart* (see bingobongothree.pdf)
- *Bingo/Bongo Blank Board* (see bingobongoblank.pdf)
- *Bingo/Bongo Directions* (see bingodirections.pdf)
- *Bongo Initial, Ending, and Vowel Boards* (see bongoinitial.pdf)

Learning Phases

I

Create five letter cards with the individual letters B, O, N, G, and O on individual cards or print the *Bingo/Bongo Letter Cards*. Place these cards in a container such as a bowl or basket. Copy and cut the *Bingo/Bongo Word Cards*. Place these word cards in a separate container.

Say to students a single-syllable word (e.g., *bed*), and think aloud how you can change one sound in the word (beginning, middle, end) to form a new word (e.g., red, bid, bet). Demonstrate this with several different words.

We

Work with the class to create other words that can be changed by changing a beginning, middle, and/or ending sound. Generate a class chart of words, using a different-color marker to note the letter/sound changes in the words.

With You

Distribute a *Bongo Initial, Ending, or Vowel Board* and eight markers to each student, or one card and eight markers to each student pair. Pull a *Bingo/Bongo Letter Card* out of the bowl or basket, and pull a *Bingo/Bongo Word Card* out of the other bowl or basket. Call out the selected *Bingo/Bongo Letter* and the selected *Bingo/Bongo Word*. Remind players which sound they are changing in the Bingo word (initial, ending, or vowel). For example, if the letter is *B* and the Bingo word is *dog*, and the focus is initial sounds, you may say, "B—dog. Look under the B heading on your *Bongo Initial Card* and try to find a word (or picture) where the initial sound is changed from /d/ to another sound but the /og/ still remains."

Students place a marker on the bongo word or picture that is the same as the presented word, but with the selected sound changed. **Suggested Teacher Talk:** *Place a marker on the bongo word that is the same as dog with the initial sound changed to /l/. Explain how you found your word or picture.* Continue calling out Bingo words until you have a Bongo winner.

By You

Ask students to select a word from their independent reading text, and record it under the Chosen Word section of their *Bingo/Bongo Three Column Chart*. Have them select a sound to change, and record the Bongo word under the New Bongo Word on the *Bingo/Bongo Three Column Chart*.

Differentiation

- For visual support, especially for English language learners, select the picture boards from the Bingo/Bongo Boards (e.g., initial, ending, vowel).

- Select words that contain affixes or inflectional endings but have the same root word (e.g., for the root word complete, you could use the words *incomplete*, *completely*, *completing*, *completion*, or *semi complete*). Use several root words and be specific about which part of the word to change (affix or inflectional ending).

Syllable Juncture Structure

Purpose:		ELL Technique:
To combine knowledge of all letter/sound correspondences and recognize syllabication patterns to decode and read accurately unfamiliar words in context and out of context		Yes

Materials:	
• text	• mirrors
• index cards	• basket
• *Syllable Rummy Directions* (see syllablerummy.pdf) (*optional*)	• *Syllable Structure and Jingle Examples* (see syllablejingle.pdf)

Learning Phases

I

Select several words that have two syllables (e.g., using students' names, like *Derek*). Write each syllable segment on an index card and place all the syllable segment cards in a basket. Introduce a jingle that represents the syllable pattern being highlighted if applicable. Sample jingles are provided in Figure 2.7. Pull two cards out and pronounce the syllable representation on each card. Try to combine the two syllables to see if they can form one of the selected words.

Continue until two syllable structures are combined to form a word (e.g., /pen/ /cil/). Say the new word aloud and keep your hand just below your jaw so you can demonstrate how your jaw drops down and touches your hand for each syllable in the word.

We

Have students practice saying specific words from a content area unit you are studying. Have them place their hands under their jaw to feel the number of times their jaw touches their hands. Ask partners to watch one another's mouths and notice the structure formation of the jaw, as the various words are spoken. Allow students to sing/rap the applied jingle if applicable.

With You

Have teams select multisyllabic words from a text or a unit of study and write each syllable representation within the selected words on index cards. Collect all team cards, and distribute one card to each student. Ask students to move about the room and find partner(s) to form a complete word and determine the type of syllable structure. See Figure 2.7 for examples of syllable structures.

Figure 2.7 Syllable Structure and Jingle Examples

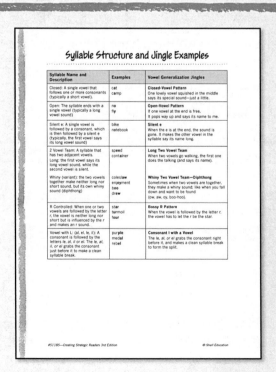

Word Study
Synthesizing
Sounds

By You

Have students study words from a text and notice the dropping of their jaws as they read the words. They can even use the mirrors from the Mirror/Mirror technique earlier in this chapter. **Suggested Teacher Talk:** *Think about how each word is broken into syllables. Explain the steps you used to determine your process for each of the segmentations.*

Extension

Divide the class into teams of four to six students per team. Distribute predetermined syllable cards and the Syllable Rummy Directions to each team. Have the teams play Syllable Rummy (Johnston et al. 2009) as they focus on combining syllables to form words. Students use the Analyzing Word Study Strategy to create their own multisyllabic rummy cards by segmenting the words into syllables on index cards.

Word Study
Synthesizing
Sounds

Word Study Strategy: Analyzing Sounds

Analyzing a word requires students to take an identified word and examine its sound parts. This strategy encourages students to explore the letter-sound relationship while analyzing the word structure. Students use the Analyzing Sounds strategy to read a whole word and then "take it apart" to investigate how the word works. Research has proven that our brain is constantly searching for patterns as a new stimulus is introduced, and we should give it every opportunity to investigate and organize these patterns and help our students become pattern detectors (Cunningham 2000). Working with patterns can reinforce letter-sound combinations and students' ability to merge these combinations together to read words accurately.

Applying the Analyzing Sounds strategy into word study instruction aligns the concepts of the analytic and analogy phonics approaches to examine the word parts. Word parts can be the beginning letter(s) that precede the vowel (onset) and the rhyming pattern that follows the onset (rime) or the analysis of morphemes (affixes, roots), known as the *morphological knowledge* (Bowers, Kirby, and Deacon 2010) within words.

"Once words are broken into parts, students can use their knowledge of word parts to attempt to deduce their meaning—if they understand how word parts function" (Graves 2006, 103). Students discover implicitly the intricacies of word parts when they utilize analyzing as a word study strategy and apply it to their ability to read words while determining meaning.

To support Analyzing Sounds while reading, a set of skills is required to effectively implement this reading strategy. The synchronized application of several reading strategies results in making meaning while reading a text. The skills, additional integrated reading strategies, and their reading components found in corresponding chapters are listed below.

Focus Skill(s):

- Concepts of words
- Manipulating sounds
- Separating

Integrated Strategies:

- Isolating and Identifying Sounds; Blending and Segmenting Sounds (Chapter 2)
- Categorizing; Analyzing Words (Chapter 3)

Accountable Teacher Talk for Analyzing Sounds

Following is a list of suggested Teacher Talk that encourages readers to think strategically as they employ the Analyzing Sounds strategy. To effectively increase levels of thinking, these suggestions incorporate Bloom's Taxonomy's higher-order questioning (Anderson and Krathwohl 2001) and Webb's Depth of Knowledge (2002).

Remembering and Understanding (Recall)

- What is a word part?
- What features of the words are alike?

Applying (Skill/Concept)

- Classify these words. What do you notice about the words?

Analyzing (Strategic Thinking)

- What sound occurs in all of these words? Explain the rule or generalization you see in these words.

Evaluating and Creating (Extended Thinking)

- What alternative word would you suggest that has that same "pattern chunk" in it? How does this word fit the pattern in the other words? What criteria would you use to assess these words?
- What information can you gather to support your idea about the parts of the words you are studying? Test your hypothesis on several words, and draw a conclusion about the parts you are analyzing.

Behavior Indicators for Analyzing Sounds

As you assess students' ability to analyze, use the following behaviors as a guide. Do students exhibit these behaviors never, rarely, often, or always?

- ❑ Focus on the whole word, and then identify specific aspects within the word
- ❑ Identify and explain parts and patterns within words
- ❑ Decode and sort words according to common syllabication patterns and morphology (roots and affixes) to accurately read unfamiliar-multisyllabic words in and out of context

Techniques for Analyzing Sounds

Roll-Read-Record (3 Rs)

Purpose:	ELL Technique:
To focus on a word and analyze it for the specific parts within the word	Yes

Materials:

- text
- *Roll-Read-Record (3Rs) Chart* (see rollreadrecord.pdf)
- display options (chart paper, dry-erase boards, interactive whiteboard)
- large and small number cubes
- chart paper
- Word Study Journals

Word Study Analyzing Sounds

Learning Phases

I

After reading a familiar literary or informational text, roll a number cube and search for a word within the text that has the same number of phonemes or syllables as shown on the cube. Orally analyze the word for the correct number of phonemes or syllables and record the word on a class column chart labeled one through six. **Suggested Teacher Talk:** *Look at your word and think about how the word is designed. Compare and contrast the individual sounds within the words. Explain why each word is categorized.*

We

Together complete the process of the 3 Rs.

- **Roll:** Ask a volunteer to roll a number cube and search for a word within the text that has the same number of phonemes or syllables on the cube.

- **Read:** Students read the selected word slowly, reflecting on the parts within the word.

- **Record:** Have students record selected words or objects on the *Roll-Read-Record (3Rs) Chart* or a class chart.

With You

In small groups, review the generated chart from the class *Roll-Read-Record (3Rs) Chart*. Have students review their knowledge about the words and reflect on the words by giving the same number of features about the words that was depicted on the number cube. For example, if the number cube landed on number 5, the word analyzed from the weather unit might be *clouds* (phonemes /c/ /l/ /ou/ /d/ /s/) or *precipitation* (syllables /pre/ /cip/ /i/ /ta/ /tion/), and then students could share five things they learned about clouds or the concept of precipitation.

By You

Give each student a number cube. Ask students to select words from their independent texts based on the number rolled. Specify whether students are searching for the number of phonemes or syllables. Students can record their findings on the *Roll-Read-Record (3 Rs) Chart* or in a Word Study Journal.

Differentiation

- For visual and kinesthetic support, have students roll the number cube and then use the palm of their hands as a "mat" to push out with their finger the number of sounds in the analyzed parts to support them as they determine how many sounds are in the word by the one-to-one correspondence (finger to sound).

- For visual support, and to assist English language learners, use pictures or objects as a substitution for the words in this technique.

- Modify the criteria for each number on the cube, and have students search their selected text for words that meet those requirements. For example:

  1. a word with a prefix
  2. a word with a suffix
  3. a word with an inflectional ending
  4. a word with a prefix and a suffix
  5. a word with a prefix and an inflectional ending
  6. free choice

Word Study Analyzing Sounds

DISSECT

Purpose:	ELL Technique:
To examine a word by decoding its parts, use other resources to read the word successfully, and describe this problem-solving process	Yes

Materials:

- text
- small toy
- Word Study Journals
- dictionary

- lab coat and science goggles (*optional*)
- *DISSECT Chart* (see dissectchart. pdf)
- *Deeper DISSECTing Chart* (see deeperdissect.pdf) (*optional*)

Learning Phases

Word Study Analyzing Sounds

I — Use a small toy to "dissect" and describe how each of the parts creates the whole (e.g., a plastic toy frog with dissectible parts; a toy that can easily be disassembled). You can choose to wear a lab coat and/or goggles to help create an authentic environment.

We — Select several words from a text or content area to model DISSECTing (examining) the words using the DISSECT acronym to guide you through your "lab" work.

- **D**iscover a word in text
- **I**solate the sounds
- **S**eparate the syllables
- **S**ay the word slowly
- **E**xamine the parts of the word
- **C**heck for understanding
- **T**ake it back to the text

With You — Divide students into groups called *Investigative Lab Teams*. Distribute copies of the *DISSECT Chart* and instruct the teams to work together as they dissect words from a piece of text or a previously generated list, using the chart as their guide. Have them record their dissecting progress on their *DISSECT Chart*.

By You — Have students apply the DISSECT technique in their independent reading and writing to examine challenged words. Students may record the process in a Word Study Journal.

Differentiation

Select words that contain roots or affixes. Have students dissect the root words or words with affixes, using the Deeper DISSECTing Chart acronym as they investigate their words. This can also be used as an extension idea for other students as they become more familiar with this technique.

Deeper DISSECTing Acronym (adapted from Deshler and Schumaker 1988, Lenz and Hughes 1990)**:**

- Discover the context by examining syntactic and semantic cues.

- Isolate the prefix by dividing it from the base or root word.

- Separate the suffix from the base or root word.

- Say the stem by reading what is left of the word.

- Examine the stem by applying phonetic-knowledge generalization guidelines.*

- Check with someone.

- Try a reference resource (such as a dictionary).

*Examples of phonetic generalizations:

- **Generalization 1:** If the stem or part of the stem begins with a vowel, separate the first two letters. If it begins with a consonant, separate the first three letters and pronounce the rest. Follow through with Generalization 1 until the stem is reached.

- **Generalization 2:** If the student cannot make sense of the stem after using Generalization 1, take off the first letter of the stem and use the rule again.

- **Generalization 3:** The student can check the hints for pronunciation when two different vowels are together.

Word Study Analyzing Sounds

Word Ladders

Purpose:		ELL Technique:
To use word-analysis skills (examine sound-symbol relationships) and context as a clue to the meaning of a word		Yes
Materials:		

- text

- *Word Ladder* (see blankwordladder. pdf)

- display options (chart paper, dry-erase boards, interactive whiteboard)

Learning Phases

I

Select words from a familiar text or from the class Working Word Wall and create several Word Ladders, or use premade Word Ladders (e.g., *Daily Word Ladders* by Tim Rasinski 2008). Model the beginning of a class Word Ladder, thinking aloud the steps along the way as you work your way up a few rungs on the ladder. Demonstrate what happens if the guess is not correct (e.g., have to go back to the word from the previous rung and think about the clue given and determine what other words might make sense to "move" you up the ladder). Explain to students that when we read, we must make sure our words look right, sound right, and are meaningful.

We

Continue working from the class ladder, demonstrating with the class how to complete the ladder going from the bottom to the top. Ask students to use the meaning clue and structure clue you give to slowly change words on the class ladder to form new words that visually look right and are meaningful.

With You

Distribute a *Blank Word Ladder* to each of the students. Have students work together in small groups or in pairs to select words (e.g., content area unit, text, premade Word Ladder). Have them create clues or use clues previously determined by you or other resources to complete another ladder. **Suggested Teacher Talk:** *How do you know your answer is correct? Why couldn't it be____?* Review the ladder together, having students justify their answers.

By You

Challenge them to create their own Word Ladders to submit to the class. These can be placed in centers/workstation areas, as well.

Word Study
Analyzing
Sounds

Differentiation

Change words for the ladders based on content (general-academic and domain-specific words—math, science, or social studies) or structure (prefixes, suffixes), depending on the needs of students.

Rappin' With Roots

Purpose:	ELL Technique:
To recognize and use known root words and affixes to derive conceptual knowledge of a word through rhythm	Yes

Materials:

- rapping online website and apps
- informational text
- Word Study Journal
- display options (chart paper, dry-erase boards, interactive whiteboard)
- note cards or sticky notes

Learning Phases

I
Rap a few examples of ways to incorporate rhythm into learning. Examples are available on various online websites (e.g., http://www.educationalrap.com).

We
Provide a list of key-vocabulary terms from the text or unit of study for students, or brainstorm the list together and display it. Create a class rap using several of the academic key-vocabulary words from the list. Consider using an app or a website to enhance the rap and engage your students in the word-study learning process in a rhythmic format. (e.g., AutoRap App: maps the syllables of speech to any beat; creating a unique rap).

With You
Divide students into small groups. Distribute Latin and Greek roots and affixes note cards or sticky notes to students to create a group lyrical rap to describe the meanings and purposes, using the assigned roots and affixes. Have students compare and contrast their root-word choices and determine if it will add meaning to their rap. **Suggested Teacher Talk:** *What information can you gather to support your idea about the parts of the words you are studying? Test your hypothesis on several words, and draw a conclusion about the parts you are analyzing.*

By You
Give each student a root word and have them all individually add a verse to their group rap that specifically has to do with the unit of study. Students can maintain their raps in a Word Study Journal.

Word Study Analyzing Sounds

Differentiation

Depending on student need and interest, focus on various phonics elements within rap (e.g., phonograms, vowel patterns, suffixes).

Word Study Strategy: Embedding

In Embedding, students use letter-sound correspondences and integrate this association with context clues to form a word. Context clues are hints within the text that help students decode unknown words. Embedding is a strategy that helps students assume responsibility for applying several cueing systems as they investigate words they encounter in their reading. "High-quality texts expose children to all possible sound-letter relationships and therefore have potential for children to make discoveries" (Hornsby and Wilson 2011, 10). Acquiring this strategy empowers students with another way to identify unfamiliar words they encounter as they engage in ongoing authentic reading and writing. When phonics instruction is embedded in the context being used, it promotes the usefulness of decoding skills. "If, as reading detectives, children are clued up on clues, they can achieve success with unknown words and gradually internalize strategies to help them in the future" (Farrington 2007, 9).

Students use whole, meaningful text (semantic cues); an awareness of letter-sound association (graphophonic cues); and their understanding and probability of the language (syntactic and collocation cues) to support contextual reading. The teacher may employ the whole-part-whole approach of teaching "with, through, and about whole written texts," breaking a section of the text into a specific part and then embedding the part "within the context of meaningful reading and writing" (Strickland 1998, 43). This phonics embedded approach (Adams 1990; Krashen 2002; Manning and Kamii 2000; NICHD 2000) allows students an opportunity to apply the embedding strategy to solve unknown words encountered in text.

To support Embedding while reading, a set of skills is required to effectively implement this reading strategy. The synchronized application of several reading strategies results in making meaning while reading a text. The skills, additional integrated reading strategies, and their reading components found in corresponding chapters are listed below.

Focus Skill(s):

- Letter/Sound correspondence

- Discovering context clues

- Decoding

Integrated Strategies:

- Synthesizing (Chapter 2)

- Contextualizing; Analyzing (Chapter 3)

Accountable Teacher Talk for Embedding

Following is a list of suggested Teacher Talk that encourages readers to think strategically as they employ the Embedding strategy. To effectively increase levels of thinking, these suggestions incorporate Bloom's Taxonomy's higher-order questioning (Anderson and Krathwohl 2001) and Webb's Depth of Knowledge (2002).

Remembering and Understanding (Recall)

- What questions can you ask yourself to help you to figure out the unknown word?

- How do the words around the unknown word help you?

Applying (Skill/Concept)

- What words were easy for you to predict? Why? Explain how you make predictions for unfamiliar words.

Analyzing (Strategic Thinking)

- After seeing the onset, what word would make sense and visually match the part shown? Verify your reason.

Evaluating and Creating (Extended Thinking)

- I know_____ is happening from the clues in the text, so I predict this word must be _____ because _____ (e.g., it looks right with the letter-sound connection).

- Investigate and draw conclusions about how the clues embedded in the text give a reader hints to decode unfamiliar words. Design a plan that supports readers to figure out unknown words.

Behavior Indicators for Embedding

As you assess students' ability to embed, use the following behaviors as a guide. Do students exhibit these behaviors never, rarely, often, or always?

- ❑ Recognize and describe the use of "peripheral vision"

- ❑ Decode or clarify an unknown word based on context clues to determine meaning

- ❑ Apply the structural cues of the unknown word based on the meaning of the surrounding words

Techniques for Embedding

Blinders

Purpose:	ELL Technique:
To recognize and use "peripheral vision" when attempting to read unknown words	Yes

Materials:

- Word Study Journals
- books
- text
- index cards
- pictures of horses wearing blinders on their eyes

Learning Phases

I

Show pictures of horses wearing blinders (leather flaps attached to a horse's bridle) on their eyes and discuss how the blinders are meant to obscure clear perception and prevent the horse from looking around. Compare how some people are like horses when they try to read as if they have blinders on their eyes. They do not "look around" by using context clues to help decode an unknown word.

Explain how when readers take in all the surrounding words (use their "peripheral vision"), they are able to use the words to support the strategy of contextualizing. **Suggested Teacher Talk:** *How does using your peripheral vision help you?*

We

Have students hold books or their hands on each side of their faces to block their peripheral vision, and have them attempt to walk around the room without bumping into one another. Ask students to remove the books or their hands, walk around the room again, and note the differences.

Discuss with the class how this analogy is similar to reading—that is, students only look at one word at a time to figure out unknown words. Point out that they have "blinders" on when they are only attending to a particular word. **Suggested Teacher Talk:** *What happens when you read with blinders?*

With You

Distribute index cards and have partners place one card in front of a word in the selected text and the other card behind the word. Have the partners take turns sliding the cards along where only a word at a time is showing in the sentence. Invite the partner that is not moving the cards to try to read the words aloud one at a time. Reverse roles, and discuss the process.

#51185—Creating Strategic Readers 3rd Edition

Have students read independently, being conscious of their peripheral vision and how the awareness of the surrounding words in text can support them. Have them record their blinders experience in their Word Study Journals.

Extension

Record several sentences from a text you are reading, underlining a phrase in the middle of the sentence. Ask students to focus their eyes on the underlined phrase and use their peripheral vision to read the words before and after the underlined section. For example: "There is a house, a napping house, where everyone is sleeping" (excerpt from *The Napping House* 1984).

Predict/Preview/Polish/Produce (4 Ps)

Purpose:	ELL Technique:
To predict words that would make sense in the text by using the surrounding words	Yes

Materials:

- text
- sticky notes or highlighting tape
- marker
- laminated construction paper
- dry-erase boards
- display options (chart paper, dry-erase boards, interactive whiteboard)

Word Study Embedding

Learning Phases

I   Display and read a section from a text and omit one word by covering it with a sticky note, saying the word *blank* or silently touching your lips for the omitted word. Model thinking about the context of the text and this particular section. **Suggested Teacher Talk:** *I know _____ is happening from the clues in the text, so I predict this word must be _____ because it looks right with the letter/sound connection.*

Uncover the word and reiterate how your thinking supported you in solving the unknown word with context clues, using the cueing systems to cross-check (semantic, syntactic, and graphophonic).

We

In the same text, cover another word a few pages after the first word. When you get to this page, have several volunteers practice applying the 4 Ps to process the unknown word.

Predict what they think is the omitted word. Have students record their predictions on dry-erase boards or paper, or chart some students' predictions for display. Then, have students discuss why they chose their predicted words.

Preview the first letter of the omitted word while pulling back the sticky note or tape to expose only the first letter (or instead of the first letter, cover the ending letters or vowels). **Suggested Teacher Talk:** *What would make sense here and match the beginning letter of this covered word?*

Polish predictions by checking their previous predictions for the omitted word with the preview provided. **Suggested Teacher Talk:** *After seeing the onset, what word would best make sense and visually match the part shown? Verify your reason.*

Produce the omitted word by revealing the entire word and reread the sentence.

With You

Write and display four to five sentences for students to view as a team, and cover one word in each sentence. Have the sentences follow a similar word pattern (e.g., covering the final word, covering the digraph words, or covering the words with blends). Students *"Guess the covered word"* (Cunningham 2000), record the words, and write about how they discovered the covered word.

By You

Distribute a piece of laminated construction paper that is about the same size of the print in a text that students are reading independently. Write four Ps on it with a permanent marker. Remind students when they come to an unknown word, they can place the paper over the word as a visual reminder to use the context of the text and apply the four Ps.

Word Study Embedding

Differentiation

Implement this technique using content area domain-specific vocabulary words.

Word Detectives

Purpose:	ELL Technique:
To use context clues to figure out unknown words	Yes

Materials:	

- text
- highlighter tape
- *Word Detectives Badge Poster* (see worddetectives.pdf)

Learning Phases

I

While reading a selected text, demonstrate how to use highlighting tape to mark words that are unknown. Introduce the "detective work" for solving an unknown word, using the supports found on the *Word Detectives Badge Poster*.

Word Detective Supports

- Look at words around the highlighted word. What do you notice?

- Do the words around the highlighted word remind you of something you already know?

- Look at the first letter of the highlighted word. How does it give you support?

- Make a guess at what words you think would start with those letters. I predict the word will be _____.

- Do the words you guessed make sense with the rest of the sentence? What would make sense here?

We

After reading, ask students to return to the highlighted words and become "Word Detectives." Display the *Word Detectives Badge Poster* and have students use the badge to support their strategic word solving. Each point of the star on the badge has one instruction. **Suggested Teacher Talk:** *What questions did you ask yourself that helped you to solve the case of the unknown word? How do the words around the unknown word help you?*

Word Study Embedding

With You

To report their findings, have students meet with a "sheriff" (a designated word-solving helper). The sheriff can give students feedback and support, as needed.

By You

Students use the feedback from meeting with a class "sheriff" and apply the supports to solve other unknown words in a text they are reading or writing independently.

Extension

Each time students apply these supports in their reading and writing, they can record on their *Word Detective Badge Poster* or put their initials on a class *Word Detective Badge Poster* to earn their way to becoming a "Certified Deputy Sheriff Word Detective."

Clued on Clues

Purpose:		ELL Technique:
To decode unknown words using context clues from the text		Yes

Materials:

- text
- word list
- highlighter tape
- sticky notes
- sentence strips
- index cards
- Word Study Journals

Learning Phases

Word Study Embedding

I

Select a particular graphophonic part of a word to study (short vowels, digraphs, rime). For example, using a phonogram or rime (e.g., -ab), list several words on index cards that are formed using this phonogram (e.g., *lab, grab, cabin, crab*). Present a sentence (orally or displayed) that uses one of the created words, omitting the selected word from the sentence as you read it to the class (e.g., *We went to _____ this weekend*).

Demonstrate how you reread the sentence and placed each word in the blank on the sentence to determine which words would best make sense in the sentence. Emphasize how you were "clued on the clues" in order to solve the mystery word.

We

Display a different word list (e.g., content-area words) and other predetermined sentences with omitted words. Have a student read one of the sentences aloud and review the word list to determine which word would complete each sentence based on the clues within the text. Have students explain their reasoning and review acceptable alternatives.

With You

Divide students into partners and have them compare responses and discuss how changing the letters/sounds can completely change the meaning of a word. Give each partner a word and a sentence strip to create a sentence, focusing on embedding clues. Remind students to leave a blank where their specific word would be.

Have partners exchange their sentence with another partner to try to clue in on the clues in the sentences to determine the unknown word. **Suggested Teacher Talk:** *How do the words around the unknown word help you determine what word completes the sentence?*

By You

Have students read independently and place a sticky note on words that have the particular phonics element they are studying. Have them select several of the sentences that they marked with a sticky note and use that sentence to create their own "Clued on Clues" sentences to share with others. In their Word Study Journals, have them record how activating this embedding strategy allows them to be clued on the clues to decode and bring meaning to what they are reading.

Differentiation

Use this same technique to select a syntactic-morpheme part of a word (e.g., prefix, suffix) to use instead of a graphophonic-word part.

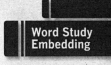

Word Study Embedding

Word Study Strategy: Spelling

Spelling as a strategy helps readers transform sounds into letters and letters into written-word form. Proficient strategic readers use their memory functions of phonological and phonics knowledge to enable them to decode (read) and encode (write) words (Cunningham and Allington 2007; Gentry 2006; Kast, Baschera, Gross, Jäncke, and Meyer 2011; Roberts and Meiring 2006). Reading and spelling are interdependent; students need many opportunities to explore sound and letter relationships in real text, manipulate letters to form words, search for patterns within words, and sometimes decode words sequentially. It is through reading that students visually store shapes of words so that when writing, they can recall how the words looked when they were read. "When students decide that a word doesn't look right, they rewrite the word several different ways using their knowledge of spellings patterns" (Tompkins 2001, 114). Guiding students through using their visual memory of the word is one technique teachers use rather than always asking students to sound out words when they are trying to spell a word (Conrad 2008; Moustafa 1997).

When students view spelling strategically, they are able to evolve through the developmental stages and "attack" with the thinking process that occurs as they gain word power. Explicit spelling instruction does allow students to transfer word knowledge over time into independent composing (Amtmann, Abbott, and Berninger 2008; Liow and Lau 2006). Gaining word power requires students to process spelling through word studies that enable them to explore, inspect, visualize, chunk, sound out, approximate, and use memory devices, patterns, and their multiple senses (e.g., hearing, seeing, and feeling). Strategic readers and writers think of spelling as a strategic tool on their quest to gain word power. Keeping the formal procedures and routines of word study as simple and predictable as possible allows students to become inventors, choreographers, and word explorers (Calkins 2001).

Many studies have noted the various spelling stages and their characteristics (Bear et al. 2011; Freeman 1995; Gentry 1989; Gentry and Gillet 1992; Graves 1982; Pinnell and Fountas 1998; Sharp, Sinatra, and Reynolds 2008; Tompkins 2000; Vacca, Vacca, and Gove 1995). Following are the stages and some suggested approaches to support the growth of the speller within each stage. Note that researchers and practitioners use multiple names when referring to the similar spelling stages.

Prephonetic/Precommunicative/Emergent Stage

Students in this initial stage are not yet connecting letters with the words they are writing to convey a message; they are using scribbles and letter-like forms to represent a message. Their messages may be randomly arranged on the pages (e.g., right to left, top to bottom, left to right, or all over) or may be in a nonsense form and often cannot be read by others. Approaches to support students who are trying to develop at this stage of spelling include listening to pattern books, identifying words within the text, matching initial and final consonants with sounds, playing with the sounds in words, drawing pictures and then writing about their drawings, dictating stories, and exploring directionality.

Semiphonetic/Early-Phonetic/Early-Letter-Name/Alphabetic Stage

Students demonstrate the early signs of connecting letters and sounds in writing and reading. Their spelling includes single letters to represent words, sounds, and syllables. Students at this stage omit vowels most of the time. Approaches for this stage are using word walls for names, high-frequency words, and easy word patterns; language experiences (e.g., writing personal experiences with teacher support to connect written form with oral language); sorting words according to the initial or final consonant sounds; and changing the onsets of words to form a new word.

Phonetic/Early/Within-Word Pattern Stage

Students in this stage spell words the way they hear them and, at times, by patterns they see from other words. Vowels, consonants, and some blends and digraphs may appear in their writing of words, but they may be inconsistent. This stage is important because it represents the beginning use of word segmentation in students' writing. Approaches that support phonetic spellers include using word walls; reading texts with reasonable picture support, appropriate level high-frequency words, and patterned words that can be decoded with ease; exploring long and short vowel sound relationships; using rhyming words; and incorporating phonemic-awareness activities.

Structural/Syllables and Affixes/Transitional Stage

Students at this stage demonstrate the use of structural elements (e.g., syllables, inflectional endings, affixes) in their writing. They are consistent in using a vowel in every syllable and are beginning to use the morphemic relationships of words (e.g., *happy, happier, happiest, unhappily, happiness, happily*). Their spelling is moving from a dependence on phonology (sound) to relying more on visual representations and structures of words. Approaches for this stage are using word studies on more-complex spelling patterns and structural elements, using a word wall, reading more-complex text with less picture support, practicing solving multisyllabic and irregular technical words, and proofreading.

Conventional/Meaning/Derivational/Advanced/Correct/Fluent Stage

In this last stage, students are spelling the majority of the words correctly in their writing. Students are aware of and use a variety of rules and generalizations of the orthographic (written) system and know how to use historical roots to derive meaning. Approaches that support this advanced speller are using word studies on root words and their meanings, examining vowel alterations in derivationally related pairs, and reading complex text with specialized-content vocabulary and many multisyllabic words.

To support Spelling, a set of skills is required to effectively implement this reading strategy. The synchronized application of several reading strategies results in making meaning while reading a text. The skills, additional integrated-reading strategies, and their reading components found in corresponding chapters are listed below.

Focus Skill(s):

- Letter/Sound correspondence
- Decoding
- Encoding

Integrated Strategies:

- Synthesizing; Analyzing Sounds; Recognizing (Chapter 2)
- Analyzing Words (Chapter 3)

Accountable Teacher Talk for Spelling

Following is a list of suggested Teacher Talk that encourages readers to think strategically as they employ the Spelling strategy. To effectively increase levels of thinking, these suggestions incorporate Bloom's Taxonomy's higher-order questioning (Anderson and Krathwohl 2001) and Webb's Depth of Knowledge (2002).

Remembering and Understanding (Recall)

- How does knowing how to spell _____ help you spell _____?
- Look at the word you wrote. Does it look right? Why or why not?

Applying (Skill/Concept)

- If this word spells _____, how might you spell this word _____? Explain your reasoning.

Analyzing (Strategic Thinking)

- Think about other "chunks" that are within the word to help you spell the word. What is the secret word that uses all of these letters?

Evaluating and Creating (Extended Thinking)

- Evaluate other words according to how they relate to this word (look, sound, meaning) and explain the similarities and differences. What categories would you sort your words into, based on the patterns you see within the words?

- Investigate the spelling pattern of a set of words. What information can you gather to support your understanding of the pattern? Explain the steps you used to determine the pattern and how it supports how you spell the words.

Behavior Indicators for Spelling

As you assess students' ability to spell, use the following behaviors as a guide. Do students exhibit these behaviors never, rarely, often, or always?

❑ Create associations to remember how to spell words

❑ Connect words by spelling patterns and generalizations (word families, position-based spellings, syllable patterns, ending rules, meaningful word parts) in writing words (encoding)

❑ Spell untaught words phonetically and phonemically (manipulating letters to discover letter-sound relationship)

Techniques for Spelling

Interactive Word Walls

Purpose:	ELL Technique:
To interact with displayed words and use spelling patterns and generalizations when reading and writing words	Yes

Materials:	

- words for wall
- space on wall or board
- different colors of paper
- scissors

- spiral notebooks or file folders (*optional*)
- digital portfolio (*optional*)
- Word Study Journals (*optional*)

Learning Phases

I

Each week, select high-utility words to display on an active *word wall* (Cunningham 2000, 2012; Hoyt and Therriault 2008). Choose how to display each word visually (see Extension section for ideas). Present words used in the context students will encounter in their reading and writing. Share why you will be placing words on a class Interactive Word Wall to showcase intentional words.

Place the words on the wall in a chosen category that illustrates a principle or complements the class unit of word study. **Note:** Avoid overcrowding the Interactive Word Wall. Remember to interact with the word wall throughout various instructional opportunities and to change up words, remove words, maintain some key vocabulary, or revisit concepts as a unit progresses.

We

Allow students time to interact and use the wall as a resource for word study (e.g., clapping, chanting, and writing the words; playing word games; discovering words by clues given; writing the word in sentences; and doing word sorts). **Suggested Teacher Talk:** *How does the word wall help you? Try to check the word wall to see how _____ is spelled.*

With You

In small groups, have students interact with words from the class Interactive Word Wall by selecting and removing a word to create factual statements about the chosen word, or compose a summary about a topic using several words from the wall.

#51185—*Creating Strategic Readers 3rd Edition*

By You

Have students make individual portable word walls in their Word Study Journals, spiral notebooks, file folders, or by digitally creating a word wall, using various websites as a tool to create an eWord wall (e.g., http://padlet.com; http://www.thinglink.com). As students are independently writing and focusing on spelling certain words, they can reflect and even go physically to the class Interactive Word Wall to check for clarification.

Differentiation

Use a variety of high-utility words to display on the word wall (e.g., patterns, content, irregular words, diphthong vowel patterns) according to students' needs and interests.

Extensions

- Use a variety of ways to display words (e.g., on cards, on colored paper, cut around or outline configuration) or organize words (e.g., linear rows, group clusters, webs).

- Use a variety of types of walls (e.g., alphabetical, literature-based story elements, tier-level words, seasonal, parts of speech, phonetic, writing tools).

Working with Words (WWW)

Purpose:	ELL Technique:
To explore, inspect, visualize, chunk, sound out, approximate, and use memory devices, patterns, and multiple senses (i.e., hearing, seeing, and feeling)	Yes

Materials:	
• *Working with Words (WWW)* (see workingwords.pdf)	• clear counters
	• dry-erase markers
• display options (chart paper, dry-erase boards, interactive whiteboard)	• index cards
	• bins

Word Study Spelling

Learning Phases

I

Model for students how to "work a word" (adapted from Gaskins et al. 1996).

- Present a word to students and have them say it aloud. (*The word is _____.*)

- Encourage students to stretch the word like a rubber band or use *Stretch-It Strips* (see Synthesizing Strategy, this chapter). Compare the word to other words that are about the same length in sound. (*Say the word slowly.*)

- Have students use their hand as a flat mat and the other hand to "push out" the number of sounds in the word with their fingers as they say the sounds. (*I hear _____ sounds.*)

- Display the word for students to look at, and then have them record the word. (*Write the word down.*)

- Have students tap out the letters in the word on their hands or desk. (*The word has _____ letters, and because it has _____ sounds, there will/will not be one sound for each letter.*)

- Investigate the word for any spelling patterns and highlight them. (*The spelling pattern is _____.*)

- Report the investigation findings about the words. (*This is what I know about the vowels in the word _____.*)

We

Display *Working with Words (WWW)* for all to see and follow along with the steps presented on *Working with Words (WWW)*.

With You

Give each team a bin with a laminated *Working with Words (WWW)*, clear counters, dry-erase markers, and index cards with the chosen developmental words. Select a team captain to pick a card, read the word to the group without showing the card, and have the team begin to work the word on their mats (collaborating together and explaining the *why* behind each step).

By You

Students can also practice working with words during their independent reading and writing time to compare and contrast the word with other words on the word wall. (*Another word on the word wall with the same vowel sound is _____. The spelling patterns are the same or different because _____.*)

Word Study
Spelling

Differentiation

Each week give teams a list of developmental spelling words to "work," using a laminated *Working with Words (WWW)*. Assign students to groups according to their spelling development. (See stages listed in this chapter on spelling.) (**Note:** You can use a spelling-inventory assessment to assign teams by their developmental spelling stages/levels.)

Brain Tricks

Purpose:	ELL Technique:
To create associations to remember how to spell words	Yes

Materials:

- text
- *Brain Trick Connection Puzzles* (see braintrick.pdf)
- real-picture frames (*optional*)
- Word Study Journals

Learning Phases

I

Select a word to work from a familiar text or content area you are studying. Display a *Brain Trick Connections Puzzle* for all students to view. Write the word at the top of the form in the puzzle pieces and model the connections you can make about the word (e.g., rhymes with, starts like, goes with, it means). Reread the word and discuss how making connections about the word assists you when spelling.

We

Display a large picture frame as the visual. Have students pretend that they are taking a picture of a word. Ask students to close their eyes and try to see the word, putting a frame around the pictures they took. Students can hold up their hands and "click" the word as if they are using a camera to take a picture of the word presented. When students open their eyes, have them share how to spell the word as you or a volunteer write it inside the puzzle pieces for all to view and begin to generate connections to the framed word.

With You

Distribute a copy of the *Brain Tricks Connection Puzzle* to each student. Divide students into small groups, and have them write the words they are studying in the middle of the puzzle piece. Ask students to take each word and record connections which they can make about the word (e.g., rhymes with, starts like, goes with). Have students continue this for all of the chosen words, sharing and discussing the connections. **Suggested Teacher Talk:** *Try to visualize the word in your mind and "take a picture" of it.*

By You

Have students search for words from their independent reading or writing to use the *Brain Tricks Connections*, or record the thinking process in their Word Study Journals.

Word Study Spelling

Differentiation

Assign students to groups according to their spelling development. (See stages listed in this chapter on spelling.) (**Note:** You can use a spelling-inventory assessment to assign teams by their developmental spelling stages/levels.)

Extension

Have students create mnemonics to remember spellings of certain words. For example, to remember how to spell the word *friend*, say, "I'll see my friend at the end of the week on Friday." **Suggested Teacher Talk:** *What are some ways you try to think out how to spell a word?*

Look/Say/Cover/Write/Check

Purpose:	ELL Technique:
To visualize and spell words	Yes

Materials:

- *Look/Say/Cover/Write/Check Bookmark* (see looksaybookmark.pdf)
- *LSCWC Icons* (see lscwcicons.pdf)
- *If I Can Spell Form* (see ificanspell. pdf)
- text
- kinesthetic materials (e.g., salt, sand, molding dough, and bread dough)

- words
- notebook paper
- display options (chart paper, dry-erase boards, interactive whiteboard)
- index cards, folder, or chart
- Word Study Journals

Learning Phases

Display the words Look, Say, Cover, Write, Check or use the *LSCWC Icons* and model (LSCWC) concept (adapted from Pinnell and Fountas 1998), using the steps below:

 Look: Select a word from a text, and look at the word to visualize the overall letter patterns within the word and to see the shape of the word. Model closing your eyes, imagine the word in your mind, and describe how you are visualizing the word (e.g., letter shapes, configuration, spelling pattern).

 Say: Say the word. Point out to students that this is their time to "talk" the word. You can say or chant to a rhythm each of the letters, sounds, syllables, or noticeable patterns. You can use the *Stretch It* technique from this chapter to stretch the word to hear the sounds and look for patterns.

Cover: Place something over the word to cover the word. Close eyes again and model how you revisit the image of the word from the first time you looked at the word.

Write and Check: Take a moment to think about how the word is spelled, recalling the pattern, configuration, and even the rhythm of how the word sounds. Then, write the word. Uncover the word to check in the text to see if spelling is correct.

We

Choose some spelling words and display them for all students to see. Ask several students to demonstrate the LSCWC steps, focusing on one word at a time for the class. Encourage the other students to follow along and share various ways in which they visualized the word, or give ideas how to "say" the word (e.g., rap, sing, whisper pattern).

With You

Have students create a file folder by cutting the top to the centerfold to make three even flaps. Have students use the folders in pairs. Partner A calls out a word, and Partner B begins the LSCWC steps. Together, the partners check the work of Partner B and determine if any changes are needed. Then, have students reverse roles.

By You

Have students practice spelling words using the LSCWC file folders and bookmark to help them remember the process. **Suggested Teacher Talk:** *Look at the word you wrote; does it look right?*

Differentiation

- Assign students to groups according to their spelling development. (See stages listed in this chapter on spelling.) (**Note:** You can use a spelling-inventory assessment to assign teams by their developmental spelling stages/levels.)

- For kinesthetic support, place salt, sand, or flour on a tray and have students trace the words. Or have students use string, play dough, or bread dough to form the words.

Extension

Have students use words from their spelling lists to identify words that have same spelling pattern. In their Word Study Journals, have them share words that follow the same pattern, and complete the *If I Can Spell Form* and verify why they are grouped together.

Word Study Spelling

Word Study Strategy: Recognizing

Students who apply the Recognizing strategy are able to identify words quickly and automatically. Word recognition is foundational in proficient readers. The cognitive process allows for instant recognition of words in written form. Using text that is predictable and easy to memorize supports beginning readers in gaining word-recognition abilities (Bear et al. 2011). The speed and accuracy with which a student is able to use this strategy determines the student's fluency and comprehension. "When students recognize words immediately, they find it easier to focus on the meaning of what is being read" (Bishop and Bishop 1996, 53). The techniques in this section focus on supporting students in recognizing letters, sight words, high-frequency words, and irregular words. See Figure 2.8 for a distinction among the various word types.

Figure 2.8 Various Word Recognition Types

Type of Word	Description of Type of Word	Examples of Type of Word
Sight Words	Words recognized and pronounced immediately also can include high-frequency words and irregular words	*was, the, with, want, this*
High-Frequency Words	Some of the most commonly used words in printed language; can be decodable or undecodable	*was, that, with, which, know*
Irregular Words	Sounds that are unique to the word or only a few words with uncommon phoneme-grapheme relationships and are not decodable	*was, give, come, would, who*

To support Recognizing, a set of skills is required to effectively implement this reading strategy. The synchronized application of several reading strategies results in making meaning while reading a text. The skills, additional integrated reading strategies, and their reading components found in corresponding chapters are listed below.

Focus Skill(s):

- Irregular spelling patterns
- Sight words
- Decoding and encoding

Integrated Strategies:

- Isolating and Identifying Sounds; Synthesizing and Sounds; and Analyzing Sounds (Chapter 2)
- Visual Imaging and Analyzing Words (Chapter 3)

Accountable Teacher Talk for Recognizing

Following is a list of suggested Teacher Talk that encourages readers to think strategically as they employ the Recognizing strategy. To effectively increase levels of thinking, these suggestions incorporate Bloom's Taxonomy's higher-order questioning (Anderson and Krathwohl 2001) and Webb's Depth of Knowledge (2002).

Remembering and Understanding (Recall)

- How does recognizing the words by sight help you when you are reading?
- Why do we want to be able to recognize words?

Applying (Skill/Concept)

- Explain how you would sort these letters. What pictures would you select to represent this letter? Why?

Analyzing (Strategic Thinking)

- Examine the word _____ to see if it has a smaller word inside it to help you remember it.

Evaluating and Creating (Extended Thinking)

- Using the five senses, examine the word _____ and describe how each of the senses influenced how to recognize the word in text.
- What changes would you make to the letter _____ to form the new letter _____?

Behavior Indicators for Recognizing

As you assess students' ability to recognize, use the following behaviors as a guide. Do students exhibit these behaviors never, rarely, often, or always?

❑ Recognize words instantly

❑ Identify high-frequency words

❑ Examine words using the multiple senses

Techniques for Recognizing

Letter Recognition

Purpose:	ELL Technique:
To recognize letters by matching, sorting, and creating them	Yes

Materials:

- uppercase and lowercase letters (foam, wood, magnetic)
- small bag (e.g., paper or cloth bag)
- Word Study Journals
- art materials (optional)

Learning Phases

I — Select several letters to place in a bag. Place your hand in the bag and begin to describe aloud the letter you are feeling. **Suggested Teacher Talk:** *This letter has several curves. I think it could be an "s."*

We — Have volunteers reach in the bag and begin to describe a letter prior to pulling it out. Have the class think of the way the volunteer is describing the letter, and begin to predict which letters have those features and could possibly be the letter in the bag.

With You — Divide students into small groups, and have them begin to dialogue and list the features of each letter and create a reference chart. *Optional:* Display a diagram of how to properly write the letter and note the specific features (e.g., sticks, curves, circles, tails, tunnels).

By You — Have students practice writing letters in their Word Study Journals and note the key features that support their letter recognition.

Word Study Recognizing

Extensions

Use a variety of other interactive ways to have students practice letter recognition:

- **Letter Matching and Sorting**: Have students match uppercase letters with corresponding lowercase letters or classify letters according to various attributes.

- **Letter Art:** Have students make a design with a specific letter, using a variety of materials including physical formations with their bodies.

High-Frequency Words

Purpose:	ELL Technique:
To recognize high-frequency words in text	Yes

Materials:

- text
- index cards
- highlighters, highlighting tape, or chenille sticks
- chart paper
- online resources for practice and word-search templates
- magnetic letters
- Bingo Bongo Cards

Learning Phases

I

Share with students how some words are called *high-frequency words* (sight words) because they appear often in many texts. Explain how if you can learn to recognize these words instantly, it will help you read smoothly and clearly without stopping and also help you to know what the text means. Give a few words as examples. **Note:** Often these words do not follow common phonics generalizations and cannot be sounded out.

We

Create a class list of high-frequency words students are encountering. As you record new words on the chart, point out the features of the words and why each word might be confusing.

With You

In small groups, have teams select various games to create and play using the class list of words. Examples include:

Concentration—Write high-frequency words on index cards, shuffle the cards and lay them facedown. Have students take turns turning over two cards at a time to see if they have a match. If the cards do not match, the other student takes a turn. Both are trying to recall where the words are located. After all words have been collected by the readers, have students read them aloud and then search for them in context.

Wordo (Bingo)—Place words on the grid card instead of numbers.

Go Fish—Write each word on two cards. Shuffle, deal, and play the match card game.

By You

Give students as many opportunities as possible to use these words in their writing and to recognize them in their reading. This will be valuable in students learning instant recognition of the words. **Suggested Teacher Talk:** *How many times have you used your high-frequency words in your writing this week? How does recognizing the words by sight help you when you are reading?*

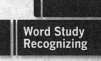

Word Study
Recognizing

Extensions

- Use online resources to provide practice with high-frequency words, or create word searches, using online resources for templates.

- Have students use highlighters, highlighting tape, chenille sticks, or any other tool to set the high-frequency word apart from other words in the text they are reading.

Irregular and Sight Words

Purpose:	ELL Technique:
To recognize words instantly, using the five senses	Yes

Materials:

- text
- display options (chart paper, dry-erase boards, interactive whiteboard)
- fly swatter
- scissors

- index cards
- Word Study Journals or word bank (*optional*)
- dough and oven (*optional*)
- audio recorder (*optional*)

Learning Phases

I

Select appropriate irregular words and/or sight words (i.e., words that are not easily decoded) from a text currently being read in class. Introduce the words by displaying them in teacher-created sentences or directly from a text. Create a word mask by cutting a section out of the middle of a fly swatter. Place the word mask over the word to make it stand out from the other words in the sentence.

We

Have students use their senses to process the word into memory. See Figure 2.9 for words to begin instruction on how to read and write the basic 30 irregular words using their senses.

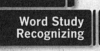

Figure 2.9 Basic 30 Irregular Words

Thirty Irregular Words				
the	would	were	too	as
you	are	do	should	mother
said	people	what	your	is
his	some	could	of	one
know	to	who	there	put
was	they	two	because	whose

(*Adapted from Moats and Tolman 2009*)

Examples:

Sight: Have students visualize each word by pretending to "take a picture" of the word. Then, students "develop" this picture by writing it into their Word Study Journals or word bank. An actual object or a picture that corresponds to the word can be shown to the student. **Suggested Teacher Talk:** *How does your sense of sight help you to recognize words?*

Hear: Listen to the words. Students may also record the new word to replay it in the future.

Touch, Smell, and Taste: Roll out dough and use it to form the letters for the word. Bake the words (dough), and then have students eat the letters as they spell out each word.

Write the word on an index card and cut the letters apart to allow small groups to remake the word.

Have students read books and other texts that contain the focus words. **Suggested Teacher Talk:** *Why do we want to be able to recognize words?*

Differentiation

Divide students into groups for this technique and provide them with varying words and types of words (i.e., sight, high-frequency, irregular) depending on student needs.

Extension

Explicitly point out the irregular aspect of the unexpected spelling of the words. Write an irregular word on an index card, and outline the configuration. Gradually add words to a class Word Wall where students can practice and study the displayed words. Place students in teams, and have them go on word searches to find words and arrange them in a grid. In addition, students can create their own word search using graph paper.

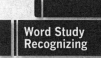

Word Study
Recognizing

Word Study Wrap-Up

Word Study instruction gives students a foundation to apply their knowledge of phonological awareness and phonics as an integral part of reading. "Teachers should recognize that acquiring phonemic awareness is a means rather than an end. Phonemic awareness is not acquired for its own sake, but rather for its value in helping learners understand the alphabetic system to read and write" (NICHD 2000, 2–6). The strategies, techniques, and Teacher Talk presented in this chapter support teachers in maximizing their students' potential in becoming strategic readers and creating a comprehensive-literacy classroom. In the craft of teaching reading, teachers use these strategies, techniques, and Teacher Talk as artistic tools to add dimension to the strategic readers they are helping to create.

Vocabulary

Contextualizing with Context Complex Clues Techniques

Associating with Reflection Connection Technique

Vocabulary instruction should be an integral component in a comprehensive literacy classroom. Research shows that the size of a reader's vocabulary influences their phonological awareness (Nagy 2005; Rosenthal and Ehri 2008), comprehension, and fluency (Beck, McKeown, and Kucan 2002, 2008; Blachowicz and Fisher 2010, 2006; Flood et al. 1991; NICHD 2000; Robb 1997). Spiraling vocabulary instruction beginning in the early years is critical to reading success. Emphasis on vocabulary in the primary grades is a significant predictor of reading comprehension in the middle and secondary grades (Cunningham 2005; Cunningham and Stanovich 1997; Chall and Dale 1995; Denton et al. 2011). Students need many opportunities for developing a rich vocabulary through listening, speaking, reading, and writing in an integrated manner. Integrating vocabulary instruction provides students with numerous opportunities to manipulate and learn new vocabulary words. Incorporating vocabulary instruction throughout the content areas will encourage students to make connections to new and already-known information, discuss meanings of new words, and demonstrate and appropriately apply the new words, providing multiple re-exposures to the words. Encouraging students to think strategically when learning new words is essential. Vocabulary knowledge is cumulative and takes multiple exposures in a variety of meaningful contexts for words to be applicable and committed to long-term memory (Akhavan 2007; Ellery and Rosenboom 2010; Marzano and Simms 2013; Misulis 1999; Stahl and Nagy 2006). Vocabulary word power travels on a developmental trajectory towards success.

Isabel L. Beck, Margaret G. McKeown, and Linda Kucan (2002, 2008) have outlined a useful model for conceptualizing categories of words readers encounter in texts, and for understanding the instructional and learning challenges that words in each category present. They describe three levels, or tiers, of words in terms of the words' commonality (more- to less-frequently occurring) and applicability (broader to narrower) (see Figure 3.1).

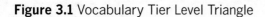

Figure 3.1 Vocabulary Tier Level Triangle

Tier 3— Domain-specific words; close tie to content knowledge; more common in informational text

Tier 2—General academic words; mainly appear in written texts (informational, literary, and technical) rather than in speech; they are highly generalizable and used across instructional areas

Tier 1—Everyday speech words; mainly learned through conversation

(Adapted from Common Core State Standards [NGA and CCSSO 2010 Appendix A, 33]; Beck et al. 2008)

This chapter offers vocabulary strategies and techniques that enhance students' understanding of new words and concepts within the tier leveling. These strategies include giving both definitional and contextual information about new words, performing cognitive operations when introducing words, and talking about new words constantly (McEwan 2002). If students do not understand the meaning of the words they read, the reading process merely becomes meaningless decoding (Pinnell and Fountas 1998). These strategies will help provide students with powerful, in-depth learning as they strive to become successful readers.

The strategies and techniques detailed in this chapter are as shown in Figure 3.2.

Figure 3.2 Vocabulary Strategies and Techniques in Chapter 3

Strategy	Corresponding Techniques in This Chapter	
Associating	Move to the Meaning (page 110) Compare 'n Share (page 111)	Reflection Connection (page 113) Semantic Feature Analysis (page 114)
Contextualizing	Cloze Passages with Semantic Gradients (page 118) Contextual Redefinition (page 119)	Collaborate and Elaborate (page 121) Context Complex Clues (CCC) (page 123) Go Figure (page 124)
Categorizing	Academic Word Walls (page 129) Picture and Word Sorts (page 131)	Alphaboxes (page 132) List/Group/Label/Reflect (page 134)
Visual Imaging	Museum Walk (page 139) Four Corners (page 140)	Eye Spy With My Eye (page 142) Comic Connections (page 143)
Analyzing Words	Playing With Plurals (page 147) Vocabulary Tree Notebook (page 148)	Flip-a-Chip (page 150) Rootin' Root Words (page 153)
Personalizing	Word Jars (page 157) Journal Circles (page 158)	Knowledge Rating (page 159) Quick-Writes (page 160)
Wide Reading	Accountable-Talk Read-Alouds (page 164) Author Study (page 165)	Book Talks and Trailers (page 166) Genre Study (page 167)
Referencing	Resource Buddies (page 172) Defining Moment (page 173)	Glossary and Thesaurus Use (page 174) Start Your Engines (page 176)

To be effective, the strategies and techniques presented in this chapter should allow ample time for teacher modeling and student application long before independent application is expected. Teachers should select and model reading aloud appropriate literature to apply the techniques in a meaningful manner, which supports authentic learning for strategic reading. By using this process, students are able to see first the whole text (i.e., appropriate literature), then see the parts systematically (i.e., strategies and techniques), and finally apply the parts back to the whole (i.e., become metacognitively aware of strategies while reading appropriate literature). Using quality and complex text and promoting language development throughout the techniques will help to enhance students' development of the strategies. In addition, teachers can use the motivation and engagement feature within many techniques as an additional means (e.g., multiple intelligences) of motivating the whole child and creating 21st-century learners. (See Chapter 1 for a description and illustration of the whole child.) This allows for differentiation within the technique as needed to educate the whole child.

Vocabulary Strategy: Associating

The ability to associate words enables students to make a connection between words. Proficient readers develop flexibility in using and manipulating words as they apply various techniques to acquire word associations. Understanding how words connect enables the proficient reader to analyze and synthesize information, determining the ways in which words relate to one another to enhance retrieval of conceptual information by assessing semantic networks (Baldwin, Ford, and Readence 1981; Johnson and Pearson 1984; Pittelmann et al. 1991). To associate words, a reader processes in "linguistic form that includes print and meaning and nonlinguistic form that includes visual and sensory images" (Bromley 2007, 531).

Word associating allows readers to use alternative words to construct meaning from the text. To link prior experiences with new information, one may construct many kinds of word relationships. "The students who can associate the words with each other can expand their vocabulary and choose the right word for the right context" (Isticifi 2010, 364). When readers use analogies, they draw inferences, and an opportunity for critical thinking occurs. This process of attaching a new concept to an existing one allows the reader to connect and bring meaning to the text.

To support Associating while reading, a set of skills is required to effectively implement this reading strategy. The synchronized application of several reading strategies results in making meaning while reading a text. The skills, additional integrated reading strategies, and their reading components found in corresponding chapters, are listed below.

Focus Skill(s):

- Make connections
- Make comparisons and determine similarities

Integrated Strategies:

- Contextualizing, Categorizing; Visual Imaging; Analyzing Words (Chapter 3)
- Synthesizing (Chapter 5)

Accountable Teacher Talk for Associating

Following is a list of suggested Teacher Talk that encourages readers to think strategically as they employ the Associating strategy. To effectively increase levels of thinking, these suggestions incorporate Bloom's Taxonomy's higher-order questioning (Anderson and Krathwohl 2001) and Webb's Depth of Knowledge (2002).

Remembering and Understanding (Recall)

- What made you think of that association?
- What features do these words have in common?

Applying (Skill/Concept)

- What are examples/nonexamples of the word (i.e., synonyms and antonyms)?

Analyzing (Strategic Thinking)

- How are these words similar and different?

Evaluating and Creating (Extended Thinking)

- Examine your words to determine if they are similar in meaning and how they relate or do not relate. What criteria did you use to make your determination?
- Develop a plan that involves movement or a visual image to connect to a word or phrase to demonstrate meaning. Justify your choice.

Behavior Indicators for Associating

As you assess students' ability to associate words, use the following behaviors as a guide. Do students exhibit these behaviors never, rarely, often, or always?

- ❏ Make connections among words
- ❏ Determine how words relate to form deeper meaning
- ❏ Generate analogies to extend content knowledge

Techniques for Associating

Move to the Meaning

Purpose:	ELL Technique:
To use movement or visual images to connect words with their meaning	No

Materials:

- text
- hip-hop music
- musical instruments

Learning Phases

I

Select words from a text in which movement can be created to associate with the meaning of the word (e.g., emotion words such as *excited* and *scared*, or weather words such as *thunder* and *rain*). Read the section from the text, highlighting the chosen words. Record the words for students to see.

Use a musical instrument to model your interpretation of movement to the meaning of the chosen words. Reread the section, inserting the musical association as you read aloud and move to the meaning.

We

Have students think of words from a familiar text that could have movement and music illustrations to enhance meaning. Create a class list, and discuss how associating words to movement or visual images can have an impact on their ability to connect to and with words.

Distribute musical instruments. As you read aloud the familiar text, have students create movement to associate the selected words. Stop on the selected word, and allow students to artistically bring meaning to the word.

With You

Assign a selection of text for partners or teams to read and select several words to highlight. Have students determine the way they will interpret a word through a specific action and possibly add music to enhance meaning. **Suggested Teacher Talk:** *Develop a plan that involves movement or a form of visual image to connect to a word or a phrase to demonstrate meaning. Justify your choice.*

Ask teams to share their movement and musical creation of their words and describe why they chose the instruments, tune, and rhythm for their words.

Invite students to review their independent writing and think about their word choices. Have them include words and phrases that signal precise actions and emotions to strengthen their writing. Have students share how they use their word choices to inform about or convey thoroughly an experience.

Extension

Use a hip-hop song such as "The Chipmunk Rap" found on the Flocabulary website (http://www.flocabulary.com) and other hip-hop songs to help students make connections to words from well-known children's literature. Create your own hip-hop or rap songs using selected vocabulary words.

Compare 'n Share

Purpose:	ELL Technique:
To make connections among words demonstrating shades of meaning	Yes

Materials:	
• text	• colored index cards
• plain index cards	• music

Learning Phases

I

Select a word within a text and think aloud other words that you could use to convey similar meaning of the selected word (e.g., *cold* and *frigid*). Reread the sentence inserting different words that relate (e.g., It was a *cold* December night. It was a *frigid* December night.).

Compare and share if the new associated word changed the meaning of the sentence. Discuss the concept in which words may appear similar in meaning but really are just different enough to change the meaning. This is known as a word having "shades of meaning."

 We

Select five words from the text that are academically appropriate for your students' level and record them on plain index cards. These words can be general academic words or content-related words.

With the class, produce other words that would connect in meaning to each of the original words. For example, if you selected *sleep* as one of your five words, then you might record the words *rest*, *nap*, and *slumber* as three other words to record on cards. Discuss the various connections that can be made among the words. Have students think about and search for examples of how these words are used in the text you are reading.

With You

Distribute an index card to each student with a predetermined vocabulary word written on it (e.g., *affordable*). Have students hold their cards and stand up around the room. Begin to play music, and have the students exchange cards with various partners until the music stops. Then, have them partner with the closest student to them and turn back to back.

Have each student read the word on his or her card, think about the meaning of the word, and then turn around to face the back-to-back partner. Then, partners "compare 'n share" their words (e.g., *cheap* and *low-priced*). **Suggested Teacher Talk:** *Examine your words and determine if they are similar in meaning and how they do or do not relate. What criteria did you use to make your determination?*

Encourage students to record on their index cards several synonyms that mean almost the same thing as their pair words but have a slight difference in meaning (e.g., *economical, thrifty, on sale*).

By You

Give each student a blank colored-index card. Have them read from their independent reading text and select three to five words to create their own set of word cards. On each card, have them record several examples of something that fits the description given by each word card.

Collect all these example cards to use in whole-group discussions to further the Compare 'n Share technique and enhance students' ability to associate words.

Extensions

- Distribute a stack of the word cards (15–20 cards) and example cards to teams of players (three to four students). Each student selects five example cards and then places the word cards in a stack in the center of the group. Each student then takes a turn revealing the word card. Students who did not reveal the word card try to find an example card in their hand that best fits the revealed word card. If they have one that relates, they discard it and justify why they feel their example is associated with the center word. The first player to discard all of their cards is the winner.

- Have students use the online graphical dictionary Visuwords™ (http://www.visuwords.com) as a visualization tool to look up words to find their meanings and associations with other words and concepts in a web format.

Reflection Connection

Purpose:	ELL Technique:
To connect words that relate to one another and determine relationships among the words	Yes

Materials:

- text
- *Puzzle Pieces* (see puzzlepiece.pdf)
- Vocabulary Journal
- digital camera *(optional)*

- *Reflection Connection Chart* (see reflectionchart.pdf)
- index cards
- chart paper

Learning Phases

I

Select two related words from a familiar text. Cut the *Puzzle Pieces* apart. Write one word on each side of the puzzle. Think aloud about how the words relate, referring to the text for evidence that validates the connection.

Discuss the type of analogy represented (e.g., synonym, antonym, whole-to-part). (See the *Reflection Connection Chart* for types of analogies.) **Suggested Teacher Talk:** *What connects these examples?*

We

Choose five sets of words from the selected text that are related (e.g., *sleep/night*, *dirty/torn*). Use a range of grade-appropriate, general-academic and domain-specific words, focusing on one or several types of relationships/analogies. List five of the words on chart paper or on one side of five puzzle-piece sets so that students can review the meaning of each word.

As you read the text, ask students to listen for a word that relates to one of the five words in the teacher-generated list. Ask students to justify the related words with text evidence. While reading together, have students identify a related word for each word on the chart.

With You

Divide students into two groups, and give each student a word or a phrase card from the puzzle-piece sets. Have students read their word cards and work together to determine which words or phrases connect and, if so, how the words connect.

Students revisit the text they are reading and identify the text evidence that supports their reasoning for connecting the words. **Suggested Teacher Talk:** *What is the relationship between these two words? Explain your thinking.* Figure 3.3 shows an example of the process using the book *Owen* by Kevin Henkes.

Figure 3.3 Reflection Connection Sample

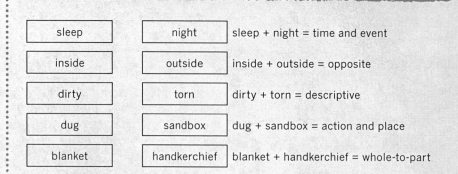

sleep	night	sleep + night = time and event
inside	outside	inside + outside = opposite
dirty	torn	dirty + torn = descriptive
dug	sandbox	dug + sandbox = action and place
blanket	handkerchief	blanket + handkerchief = whole-to-part

 By You

Have students identify related words from their independent reading, and examine the connection among the words. These words can be collected in their Vocabulary Journal or written on puzzle pieces to share with a reading partner or the whole class.

Extensions

• Have students use four words from a familiar text to complete the following sentence: _____ *is to* _____ *as* _____ *is to* _____ *because* _____. Have students determine how the words connect and record their results on the *Reflection Connection Chart*. Then, have students record the words used to fill in the blanks above on their pieces and share in small groups. Students can revisit the text to examine the relationship of words in context.

• Use illustrations for one side of the puzzle piece instead of a word. You may draw the illustrations and write the matching word or phrase for students to put together, or provide students with a word for one side of the puzzle and ask them to illustrate the meaning of the word on the other side. Students could search for pictures in magazines that illustrate a designated vocabulary word or go on a word hunt around the school, using a digital camera to capture examples of key vocabulary.

Semantic Feature Analysis

Purpose:	ELL Technique:
To explore how sets of key vocabulary words relate to one another and extend content knowledge	Yes

Materials:

• text

• *Semantic Feature Analysis Matrix* (see semanticfeature.pdf)

• Vocabulary Journals or chart

Learning Phases

I

Consider key concepts or topics that represent larger ideas students will encounter as they read a text. Use a range of grade-appropriate, general academic and domain-specific words, and move toward more-abstract ideas over time. Discuss how readers can arrange these key concepts on a graphic organizer to visually see how words relate to one another.

Display the *Semantic Feature Analysis Matrix* and share how it is designed to enhance retrieval of conceptual information by assessing semantic networks. Model how this type of grid serves as a thinking tool to associate vocabulary words and concepts.

We

On the left column of the *Semantic Feature Analysis Matrix*, write 5 to 10 key words or phrases that relate to the chosen topic. The topics or key concepts you choose to work with from the reading may start out concrete (e.g., sea animals, baseball) and gradually become more abstract (e.g., environmental issues, government).

Have students discuss the properties, features, or characteristics of the topic and list their suggestions horizontally across the top row of the matrix. **Suggested Teacher Talk:** *What features do these words have in common?*

With You

Before you read the text, have students collaborate with partners, work in small groups, or work independently to record on a matrix their predictions about the relationships. For each vocabulary word down the left side of the matrix, have students work their way horizontally across the matrix and ask themselves whether the vocabulary word possesses each of the features or properties written across the top.

Ask partners to write a plus (+) or minus (–) symbol in each box to indicate the presence or absence of a particular feature. Encourage students to explain their findings and to identify terms or features that they still are questioning.

By You

After reading the text selection, have students modify any portion of their matrix to reflect what they have learned from the reading. Students may add across the top of the matrix any additional features they discover that assist in the understanding of the concept. They might also record a summary of their findings in Vocabulary Journals to use to create a "group findings" chart or discuss them with partners. **Suggested Teacher Talk:** *How are these words alike or different?*

Extension

Select words from the *Semantic Feature Analysis Matrix* and create a Venn diagram to show the distinguishing relationship among words.

Vocabulary Strategy: Contextualizing

One of the most effective strategies to increase vocabulary comprehension is to use the context that surrounds an unknown or challenging word to discover its meaning. This discovery process transpires through clues contained in the context. The reader can use various cueing systems such as structure (syntax), meaning (semantic), or visual (graphophonic) when dissecting the context to help convey meaning. Context clues can be embedded in different formats. For example, the meaning of a word occasionally can be explained within the same sentence.

At times, synonyms of the unknown word can clarify words within the sentence. Sometimes, the reader may need to make an inference or continue reading to figure out the relationship between the unknown word and the clues around the unknown word. Strategy instruction is necessary to support the reader in explicitly using context within the text to comprehend even a shade (degree) of meaning.

Students need to "realize that it is okay to take a stab at unfamiliar words and figure out an approximate meaning from the context" (Calkins 2001, 168). After students identify the unknown word, they may predict its possible meaning from the context. The context enables students to take an inquisitive stance toward word meaning and to monitor and verify predictions (Blachowicz and Fisher 2010; Greenwood and Flanigan 2007; Nelson 2008; Tierney and Readence 2005). The text structures (e.g., descriptive, sequence, cause and effect, problem and resolution, compare and contrast) can also support the reader to contextualize by attending to the structure of how the information in the text is organized. Using a variety of contextual analysis techniques allows the student to be active rather than passive in the discovery of new words.

To support Contextualizing while reading, a set of skills is required to effectively implement this reading strategy. The synchronized application of several reading strategies results in making meaning while reading a text. The skills, additional integrated reading strategies, and their reading components found in corresponding chapters are listed below.

Focus Skill(s):

- Using context clues
- Text structures

Integrated Strategies:

- Associating; Categorizing; Analyzing Words (Chapter 3)
- Predicting; Inferring and Drawing Conclusions (Chapter 5)

Accountable Teacher Talk for Contextualizing

Following is a list of suggested Teacher Talk that encourages readers to think strategically as they employ the Contextualizing strategy. To effectively increase levels of thinking, these suggestions incorporate Bloom's Taxonomy's higher-order questioning (Anderson and Krathwohl 2001) and Webb's Depth of Knowledge (2002).

Remembering and Understanding (Recall)

- When you come to a word you don't know, how do you use context clues to determine the meaning of the unknown word?

- What do you know about the word _____ from this sentence?

Applying (Skill/Concept)

- Describe how you used the word in context (definition, cause and effect, opposite).

Analyzing (Strategic Thinking)

- What clues are in the sentence that helped you figure out the word?

Evaluating and Creating (Extended Thinking)

- Think about the possible shades of meaning that would make sense in the given context. Determine which word out of the choices is the best for bringing strong correlation to the text. Verify your choice.

- Think of how you can use this word as a noun or as a verb (or other parts of speech, as applicable). Produce sentences using the word as a noun and as a verb. How can you verify which meaning to use?

Behavior Indicators for Contextualizing

As you assess students' ability to contextualize, use the following behaviors as a guide. Do students exhibit these behaviors never, rarely, often, or always?

❑ Predict and verify omitted words using surrounding context clues

❑ Cross-check the meaning of unknown words, using cueing systems

❑ Analyze how specific word choices shape meaning

Techniques for Contextualizing

Vocabulary Contextualizing

Cloze Passages with Semantic Gradients

Purpose:	ELL Technique:
To determine a gradient (shades of meaning of words) and predict an omitted word using surrounding context, cross-checking with several cueing systems	No

Materials:

- text
- correction tape or large sticky notes
- learning logs or Vocabulary Journals
- hue paint strips (found for free at local hardware stores)

Learning Phases

I   Select a pair of words that are opposite (e.g., *cold* and *hot*), and display the words left and right of each other. Read aloud the words, and lean your body left to right as you read the words. Create several words that correspond with each of the selected pair words.

cold  hot

Word Bank: warm, cool, tepid, chilly

Explain the concept of shades of meaning by creating a different-color "paint strip" for each word pair (e.g., blue hue strip for the cold words and orange hue strips for the hot words). Use the visual color strip boxes to record the words that have a gradient of meaning for each of the word pairs on a different colored strip. Discuss how you have painted an array of related words on a continuum of meaning.

scorching	arctic
boiling	freezing
hot	cold
warm	chilly
tepid	cool

We — Select a short passage from a text, and display it visually for all students to see. Choose several words to omit, and place correction tape or a large sticky note over the words. Guide students in figuring out the missing words by using the "sense" of the surrounding words or other sentences. Have students generate ideas for words that would best complete each of the sentences, thinking about various shades of meaning for words.

With You — Visit the 4 Ps in the Word Study Chapter to practice predicting, previewing, polishing, and producing the omitted words through the contextualizing strategy. Using the list of words students generated to complete the passage, have them work collaboratively to determine where the words could be placed on a continuum (see the example with the paint strips in the above example).

Have students justify their placements. **Suggested Teacher Talk:** *Think about the possible shades of meaning that would make sense. What word do you think has the strongest meaning to complete this sentence? Why?*

By You — Instruct students to record their process in figuring out the unknown word in their Vocabulary Journals. Have them analyze word choices from their independent writing and select a few words to consider replacing to enhance an array of words within their writing piece.

Extension

At a center or literacy station, have students create their own semantic gradient on a paint strip either by using a partially completed gradient with the words to choose from and place on the gradient or by generating words from the two extreme ends of the continuum.

Contextual Redefinition

Purpose:	ELL Technique:
To predict and use deductive reasoning to examine the meaning of multiple-meaning words and to verify the correct meaning of a word through the context	No

Materials:

- text
- index cards
- dictionary (print or online)
- scissors (optional)
- paper
- Vocabulary Journals
- *What Do You Mean? List* (see whatdoyoumean.pdf)
- display options (chart paper, dry-erase boards, interactive whiteboard)

Learning Phases

Vocabulary Contextualizing

I

Select multiple-meaning words from a text and display the words in isolation for all students to see. Think aloud about a word, such as *order* and record on an index card your definition for the word based on what you might know about the word or the word parts.

Share the word in a sentence, "I need to place my *order*." Display two other example sentences using the word *order* as a noun and a verb (e.g., I need to get my room in *order*; I would like to *order* a hamburger).

Model the process of deduction by looking at the two example sentences and figuring out the meaning of the word *order* in the original sentence based on the context. Share how you are paying close attention to the word order, syntax, and parallel concepts to verify or refute your original prediction of the meaning.

Use two additional cards and record two other representations (e.g., an illustration, a written definition, or the word used in a sentence) of the meaning of the word. Explain how *contextual redefinition* (Readence, Bean, and Baldwin 2007) provides an opportunity to redefine a word as needed based on how it is used in context.

We

Create additional multiple-meaning word cards as a class, and pass them out to volunteers. Read sentences from the text, using the word in context, and have the volunteer that is holding the correct "meaning example" stand up or step forward.

Discuss their reasoning as you check for understanding. Read aloud from the text, or write and present each word in its appropriate context. Develop new sentences that provide contexts for each word. **Suggested Teacher Talk:** *How does the context help you understand the meaning of the words?*

With You

Ask students to share with partners their original prediction and allow them a chance to ask questions to either change or confirm their predictions. Discuss how hearing or seeing the context helped them understand the actual meanings of the words.

Students can verify the word meanings by using resources such as a dictionary, and discuss how the two steps of contextual redefinition—seeing the words in isolation and seeing them placed in context—were different. **Suggested Teacher Talk:** *What words within the sentence help support the meaning of (word)?*

By You

When reading independently, invite students to be aware of making predictions of unfamiliar words they encounter. Have them cross-check their predictions and decide what type of clues they used as they tried to figure out the unknown word. They can record their thinking process in their Vocabulary Journal and title the section "Using Context to Define Words."

Differentiation

Select words that contain meaningful morphemes for analysis (e.g., prefixes and roots) for aligning to students' instructional and independent levels.

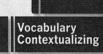

Extensions

- Create a two-tab 3-D graphic organizer by folding a piece of paper in half horizontally and then folding in half again vertically. Unfold the paper just once so that the fold is in the middle, and cut the top flap up to the fold. Write the word on the outside of one of the tabs, and under the tab demonstrate through illustration or in descriptive words one way to use the word in context. Continue on the opposite tab to model a different way the word can be used in context.

- Have students create a cartoon character to share their interpretation of the word. Invite them to use a speech bubble to write the two different ways they used the multiple-meaning word. Students can also illustrate the scene around the character to correspond with the appropriate meaning of the word.

- Invite students to choose words from the *What Do You Mean?* List to use in two different sentences. Have one partner create a sentence using the word as one part of speech (e.g., a noun) while the other partner uses the word as a different part of speech (e.g., a verb) in a different sentence. Invite students to explain their thinking, demonstrating the multiple meanings of the word.

Collaborate and Elaborate

Purpose:	ELL Technique:
To explore, discuss, and formulate a definition that students perceive from clues within the sentence or related sentences and integrate newly-formed words into a working vocabulary	Yes

Materials:	
• text	• dictionaries or glossaries
• chart paper	• Vocabulary Journals

Learning Phases

I

Select three to four content-area words from a text being read in class. Share the value of working with others or using online tools to collaborate on the meaning of selected words, using the context hints within the text to determine the appropriate use of the selected words.

Initiate a class list of ways readers can figure out unknown words. Record an example (e.g., text structure) and elaborate how it supports your ability to determine meaning based on the organization and clue words in the text.

We

Engage in a class discussion of the meaning of one of the specific content-area words. Enlist students' elements of support when trying to find meaning of a word (e.g., examples and non-examples of the word's meaning, ways students have seen the word in context before, application of the word in everyday conversations, visual images that enhance meaning).

Record and display students' responses on a class list. Read the word in context, and refer back to the class chart to examine the meaning of the word, based on each of the elements given.

With You

Arrange students in groups to explore, discuss, and formulate a definition of the words or phrases previously discussed that they perceive from clues within the sentence or related sentences.

Have teams select a recorder to capture their examples and non-examples of the word from personal experiences and background knowledge, which helps to illustrate what the word is or is not, depending on the related words in context.

Have the group agree upon a definition that best describes the meaning of the word or phrases according to the related words, and compare it with resources (e.g., dictionary, teacher, glossary).

By You

Arrange students in groups to explore, discuss, and formulate a definition of the words or phrases. Invite students to write unknown words or phrases they encounter in their Vocabulary Journal. Students continue to add new vocabulary words as they encounter them in their reading and then apply them in proper context to strengthen their independent word knowledge and their writing.

Ask them to be prepared to elaborate on the various ways to implement the use of and demonstrate meaning of their words **Suggested Teacher Talk:** *How have you used your new word in your written or oral presentation?*

Differentiation

Use a range of grade-appropriate general academic and domain-specific words based on students' instructional or independent level.

Extension

Visit online vocabulary software tools to help create interactive flashcards for increased memory of newly formed words. Examples of online resources include Anki (http://ankisrs. net), Flashcard Machine (http://www.flashcardmachine.com), and Brainflips (http://www. brainflips.com).

Context Complex Clues (CCC)

Purpose:	ELL Technique:
To use context clues to figure out the meaning of an unfamiliar word	No

Materials:

- text
- *CCC Chart* (see cccchart.pdf)
- *CCC Word Mat* (see cccwordmat.pdf)
- *Clue Glue Word Cards* (see clueglueword.pdf)
- Vocabulary Journal

Learning Phases

I

Select a word from a text that may cause students difficulty in understanding the meaning of the sentence or text passage. Demonstrate a variety of ways students may use the context to figure out the meaning of the unfamiliar word using text structures (e.g., definition or description clues, linked synonym clues, compare and contrast clues). Read a sentence that uses the word in a different context but keeps the same meaning for the word.

We

Distribute the *CCC Chart* to show students some methods for using context. Ask students to share clue words (e.g., *means, is, describes*) and categorize these words according to how they support the text structure (e.g., definition/description).

Chart these words as "clue glue" words for each category of contextual clues. (See Figure 3.4 below for a sample of clue glue words.) Find clues in a text to support reasoning. **Suggested Teacher Talk:** *What clue glue words within the sentence help support the meaning of_____?*

Figure 3.4 Sample Clue Glue Words for Context Complex Clues

Definition/ Description	Synonym/ Compare	Antonym/ Contrast	Cause and Effect
means	like	differ	because
is	as if	not	due to
describes	same as	different	if...then
states	and	unlike	consequently

With You

Distribute *Clue Glue Word Cards* (one set for a group of students, partners, or an individual student) and one *CCC Word Mat* per team or student. Have students read the set of clue glue words/phrases and determine what kind of clue word it represents.

Instruct them to use their Vocabulary Journal and a clue word/phrase in the same sentence(s). For example, if the vocabulary word is *expedition* and the glue clue word/phrase being demonstrated is *due to* under the category of Cause and Effect, the student may respond with "The *expedition* was cancelled *due to* the weather hindering the team's journey." If they picked up the clue glue card *is* under the category of Definition using the same vocabulary word, they may respond with "A journey or voyage taken by a group of people for a specific purpose *is* an *expedition*."

By You

In their independent writing, have students use clue glue words to strengthen their support for the text structure they are creating (e.g., cause and effect or definition) by linking words or phrases to connect opinion and reasons. **Suggested Teacher Talk:** *Describe how you used the word in context.*

Differentiation

Provide students with different types of context clues, clue glue words (e.g., *therefore, due to, means*), and vocabulary words depending on their instructional or independent level.

Go Figure

Purpose:	ELL Technique:
To recognize and interpret figurative language (i.e., idioms, similes, metaphors)	No

Materials:
• text • *Go Figure Idiom Cards* (see gofigurecards.pdf) • figurative language phrases • chart paper

Learning Phases

I

Use a text that includes multiple examples of figurative language (e.g., the Amelia Bedelia book series). Read aloud a section to highlight figurative language in context. Record and omit a word within the phrase.

Use the probability of the choice of word to complete or finish the phrase (e.g., a [chip] _____ on the shoulder). Examine how the word was used in context, and interpret the meaning of the phrase. Discuss how figurative language gives us a creative way to compare thoughts and has double meanings.

We

Have students share figurative language phrases they have heard and record on a chart titled "Go Figure." Determine the difference between literal and figurative based on several examples given on the list. For example, "Does it really rain cats and dogs?"

Categorize the examples given by the various types of figurative language. Figure 3.5 demonstrates examples of types of figurative language and possible examples students may give. **Suggested Teacher Talk:** *What does this literally mean? What does this really mean?*

Vocabulary
Contextualizing

Figure 3.5 Sample Types of Figurative Language

Sample Types	Description	Examples
Simile	Compares two unlike entities using the words *like* or *as* to connect the thoughts.	*She eats like a bird.* *He is busy as a bee.*
Metaphor	Contains an implied comparison which carries over a direct thought to make one entity mean another without the words *like* or *as*.	*She is the apple of my eye.* *You are what you eat.*
Idiom	Contains peculiar language that normally would not be joined together for true meaning.	*He is pulling my leg.* *It's raining cats and dogs.*
Adage	Well-known phrase that expresses something noticed and believed to be true, usually more metaphorical than a proverb.	*A mind is a terrible thing to waste.* *Better late than never.*
Proverb	An adage that expresses common sense and wisdom.	*Haste makes waste.* *Knowledge is power.*

With You

Distribute a *Go Figure Idiom Card* to each pair of students. Have one partner read the idiom and omit the underlined word. The other partner determines the omitted word based on the familiarity with and understanding of the phrase.

Have students compare and contrast the discovered word (i.e., underlined word) for its positive or negative meaning. Have partners record their explanations or their definitions on the cards. Then, have them create sentences or illustrations to describe literal and figurative meanings of the idiom on the back of their cards. **Suggested Teacher Talk:** *Justify your placement of the phrase within your created sentence.*

By You

Have students review the class "Go Figure" chart, and select a phrase to apply in their independent writing. Encourage them to embed the new figurative speech into their everyday conversation to practice authentic use.

Differentiation

Select various types of figurative speech (similes, metaphors, idioms) depending on student instructional or independent levels.

Extension

Visit online resources to support figurative language development (e.g., http://www.idiomsite.com and http://www.readwritethink.org).

Vocabulary Strategy: Categorizing

Categorizing is a strategy that actively engages students and encourages them to organize new concepts and experiences in relation to prior knowledge about the concept. This strategy usually enlists the use of graphic organizers as visual representations of relationships. Graphic organizers such as concept maps, webs, semantic maps, and Venn diagrams make thinking visible to students (Fogarty 1997; Johnson and Pearson 1984; Olson and Gee 1991; Schwartz and Raphael 1985; Stahl and Nagy 2006; Taba 1967) As Stull and Mayer (2007) note, "the limits of the learner's cognitive capacity should be addressed in the design of graphic organizers" (818). Students can also gain cognitive knowledge by properly designing their own graphic organizers as they process the text.

Word sorting allows students to use their word knowledge to organize words (e.g., phonological, orthographic, and meaning-based features) (Henderson 1990; Bear et al. 2011; Zutell 1998). Categorizing features of vocabulary words enables students to use higher-order thinking and promotes cognitive word awareness in a visible manner. To categorize successfully, students need to be able to internalize the patterns under study and begin to make connections (Miller and Eilam 2008, Sousa 2010, Strickland, Ganske, and Monroe 2002). Categorizing vocabulary words gives students an opportunity to develop an understanding of the essential attributes, qualities, and characteristics of a word's meaning.

Appropriate text that best supports the application of the categorizing strategy has a variety of words in the text suitable for sorting according to features and noticeable patterns.

To support Categorizing while reading, a set of skills is required to effectively implement this reading strategy. The synchronized application of several reading strategies results in making meaning while reading a text. The skills, additional integrated reading strategies, and their reading components found in corresponding chapters are listed below.

Focus Skill(s):

- Classifying
- Organizing and sorting
- Patterning

Integrated Strategies:

- Analyzing Sounds (Chapter 2)
- Associating; Analyzing Words; Personalizing (Chapter 3)

Accountable Teacher Talk for Categorizing

Following is a list of suggested Teacher Talk that encourages readers to think strategically as they employ the Categorizing strategy. To effectively increase levels of thinking, these suggestions incorporate Bloom's Taxonomy's higher-order questioning (Anderson and Krathwohl 2001) and Webb's Depth of Knowledge (2002).

Remembering and Understanding (Recall)

- Explain how using a word map helps you.
- How do you know that a particular word belongs with this group?

Applying (Skill/Concept)

- Describe how you categorized your words.

Analyzing (Strategic Thinking)

- What features do these words have in common? What connects all these examples together?

Evaluating and Creating (Extended Thinking)

- How do the words you are studying relate to the story? Explain your reasoning.
- Gather and investigate ways to organize the words in a meaningful way. Create a criteria chart to determine how to systematize (arrange) your words. Describe how you categorized your words.

Behavior Indicators for Categorizing

As you assess students' ability to categorize. Do students exhibit these behaviors never, rarely, often, or always?

❑ Describe the attributes, qualities, and characteristics of a word's meaning

❑ Choose and sort concepts or words by specific features

❑ Connect common ideas to form the meaning of words

Techniques for Categorizing

Academic Word Walls

Purpose:	ELL Technique:
To focus attention on academic words and have multiple exposures to these words posted to acquire and use accurately	Yes

Materials:

- selected words for word wall

- designated space for word wall

- file folders or sheet of construction paper (optional)

- Vocabulary Journals

- *Word Relationship Web* (see relationshipweb.pdf)

- online resources: (e.g., http://padlet. com, http://en.linoit.com, and http://www.wordle.net)

- dry-erase board and colored markers, or construction paper, or cardstock (optional)

Learning Phases

I

Select and add approximately five academic words to be displayed as a word wall for all to view. Write words on dry-erase board, strips of construction paper, or colored cardstock and place them on the wall according to the categories (e.g., alphabetical order, first and last names, theme words, rime wall, homophone word wall).

Integrate daily how to actively find, write, discuss, and understand these technical words (i.e., Tier Three words). Add vocabulary in an organized display through various formats (e.g., photographs, drawings, mind mapping). **Suggested Teacher Talk:** *How do you know that word belongs with this group? How can you use the word wall as a resource to help you daily?*

We

Work the words with a variety of activities (e.g., clapping words, rhyming words, reviewing endings, making sentences, playing Bingo, word sorting, doing a cheer).

Engage students in conversations, noticing the features of how the words sound, look, what they mean, and how the words they chose connect to other words they know. **Suggested Teacher Talk:** *What features do these two words have in common, and what are their distinct differences? Give examples of their application.*

With You

Have students work in pairs or small groups to articulate, cluster, and identify similarities and differences among words. Use the *Word Relationship Web* (adapted from Ellery and Rosenboom 2010; Hyerle and Alper 2004) as a graphic word organizer to promote higher-order reasoning.

Ask students to choose several words from the word wall and record them on the *Word Relationship Web* as a guide. Then, have them record descriptors, attributes, words, and phrases about how the two words chosen connect. On the outer circles, instruct students to note attributes that are only specific for the particular word.

By You

As students read and write independently, have them interact with the class word wall to strengthen their word knowledge.

They can also create their own individual word wall using a large file folder or sheet of construction paper. If desired, students could also use alternative resources to create their own digital word wall.

Sample online versions that allow students to arrange sticky notes, pictures, and video support are Padlet™ (http://padlet.com) and Lino™ (http://en.linoit.com). Encourage students to identify real-life connections between words and their use and explain their thoughts and applications in their Vocabulary Journals.

Differentiation

Use a range of grade-appropriate general academic and domain-specific words (e.g., science, mathematics, social studies) for this technique, depending on students' instructional levels.

Extensions

- Create a portable wall by using trifold display boards for ease in moving around the room. These walls are great for content-related words at a center or workstation (e.g., math center with math concepts and symbols, science exploration area with words related to theme). Students can also place words in their word jars (see the Word Jars technique in this chapter).

- Brainstorm definitions, adjectives, and synonyms for words. Invite a student to be the class "Wordle Recorder," typing into the Wordle creator found on http://wordle.net, along with the key word. Display the created "Wordle" so that students may have a contextual reference of the class vocabulary.

Picture and Word Sorts

Purpose:	ELL Technique:
To sort and define words by category features	Yes

Materials:

- pictures, items, or words from texts that relate to a unit of study
- index cards
- online resources for word sorting

Vocabulary Categorizing

Learning Phases

I

Collect and place 10–12 objects, pictures, or word cards that represent a unit of study on display. For example if you are studying weather, you might have a raincoat, thermometer, snow boots, and a rain gauge. Model how the displayed items are alike (e.g., raincoat, rain gauge) and how they may differ (e.g., raincoat, snow boots) in several ways.

We

Have students assist as you begin to group the like items together. Justify your placement of each item. Once all items are placed in a group, decide on a title for the group of items. Figure 3.6 shows how items from a weather unit could be sorted.

Figure 3.6 Sample Weather Sort

Clothing	Types	Items Affected by Weather	Measuring Instruments
coat	wind	orange (food)	thermometer
snow boots	snow	leaves (plants)	rain gauge
sunglasses	rain	nose (people and animals)	wind vane

With You

With teams or partners, have students select 15 to 20 words from a selected text. Have them write the words on note cards for word sorting. (Optional: words may be selected prior to start of the technique and given to students for categorizing.) Have students work together to discuss the features of each word and put the words into different categories by their similarities or differences.

You may determine the categories in advance (a closed sort), or students may discuss the common features of the words and then determine for themselves how to categorize them (an open sort). **Suggested Teacher Talk:** *Check with a partner to see if you both agree with the categories.* After students place the words within appropriate categories, have a class discussion to allow them to justify their sorting criteria. Provide an opportunity for students to edit their sorts if they like after the discussion.

Have students revisit the text and review the vocabulary words in context. Use online tools for various individualized word-sort practice such as WordSift (http://www.wordsift.com) or Read Write Think (http://www.readwritethink.org/materials/wordfamily/). **Suggested Teacher Talk:** *What features do these words have in common?*

Differentiation

- Use a range of grade-appropriate general academic and domain-specific words, and vary the types of words used to sort (e.g., word parts, concept words, word patterns) for this technique, depending on students' instructional or independent levels.

- For visual learners, especially English language learners, consider using picture cards instead of word cards for sorting.

Extension

Create a "human" class graph by passing out picture or word cards relating to the concept of study and having students walk around finding their like partners. Take a picture of the class graph, and place the picture at the "Vocab Lab" (a vocabulary station where students study words). Have students examine the words and the categories in the class photo and discuss their overall findings.

Alphaboxes

Purpose:	ELL Technique:
To activate prior knowledge or collect newly acquired vocabulary by sorting words or concepts using an alphabetic graphic organizer	Yes

Materials:	
• *Alphabox Chart* (see alphaboxchart. pdf)	• picture cards related to unit of study
• text	• objects related to unit of study
• highlighter or sticky notes	• basket

Learning Phases

I   Collect a basket of items and pictures, or create a list of content words related to a unit of study. These items or pictures should begin with as many different letters of the alphabet as possible. Display the basket of items or content words list. Model how to sort these items or words alphabetically and describe how each item relates to the content/unit being studied.

We

Distribute the picture cards that relate to a text you are reading, one per student or pair of students. (Picture cards can be created using copyright-free images from websites e.g., http://www.clipart.com, if needed.) As you read the text, pause on selected words. Have students listen to the word and then decide if the picture card or object they have begins with that same sound or letter.

Students then place their pictures on the large *Alphabox* (Hoyt 2008) class chart. Once complete, place the chart with pictures and the text at the literacy center/station for students to utilize as they reread and write about the text.

With You

Have students work in pairs or small groups to discuss and think of words that reflect important points from the text they are reading. **Suggested Teacher Talk:** *How do the words you selected relate to the story?* Chart student responses.

Distribute copies of the *Alphabox Chart*. With the whole group or in pairs, have students decide which words to write in which boxes, according to the words' beginning letters. **Suggested Teacher Talk:** *Why did you place this word in this box?*

By You

Have students return to the text and highlight or mark with sticky notes the words selected for the alphaboxes.

Vocabulary Categorizing

Differentiation

Use words based on the characters, places, themes, or concept words for each letter. There can be a range of grade-appropriate general-academic, or domain-specific words according to students' instructional or independent levels.

Extensions

- Have students create sentences using the words from their *Alphabox Chart*.

- To provide students with further practice, use online alphabet word-sort resources such as Read Write Think (http://www.readwritethink.org/files/resources/interactives/alphabet/).

List/Group/Label/Reflect

Purpose:	ELL Technique:
To organize and connect word attributes, images, and descriptions of words through semantic grouping and labeling	Yes

Materials:

- text
- chart paper
- *List/Group/Label/Reflect Chart* (see listgroupchart.pdf)
- *List/Group/Label Form* (see listgroupform.pdf)
- online resources

Learning Phases

I

Determine a content-related topic or concept based on what the class is studying and reading. Explain that categorizing words is beneficial to helping organize new words using prior knowledge and thinking about how words relate to one another.

Share how proficient readers are constantly perceiving new words and creating a pattern network to process the new words and synthesize meaning. Model a few words and how you would group them, and why.

We

List: As a class, brainstorm words that relate to the chosen topic or concept and record the words. Visually display the generated words in a list form or around an oval containing the central concept.

With You

Group: Have students work in teams or with partners to decide how these brainstormed lists can be classified according to their meaningful connections, and share their reasoning with the whole group.

Label: Have students create a label or a title that best describes each newly formed category and signifies why the words have a shared relationship. **Suggested Teacher Talk:** *Gather and investigate ways to organize the words in a meaningful way. Describe how you categorized your words.* As a class, discuss if there are any words that could be eliminated, and if so, solicit reasons why.

By You

Reflect: Have students reflect on the categorizing process to examine words. Have students choose a vocabulary word from a self-selected text that they wish to examine. Invite them to use the *List/Group/Label/Reflect Chart* or other graphic organizers as a visual representation of and a way to form a definition of the studied topic/concept. **Suggested Teacher Talk:** *How does the format help you to connect and generate meaning of the focused words?*

Differentiation

Depending on student instructional or independent levels, use a range of grade-appropriate, general-academic, and domain-specific words for this technique.

Extensions

- Have students create graphical representations of their word choices using online tools such as WordSift (http://www.wordsift.com/).

- Have students use the *List/Group/Label/Reflect Form* to select one word from the class-generated list and investigate its deeper meaning. The goal is for them to have their "light bulb" turn on with the new knowledge gained from their investigation. The Group section allows students to design subcategories within three types of associations: class (What is it?—the broad category of things the concept fits into), properties (What is it like?—the attributes that define the concept), and examples (What is like it?—illustrations/examples of the concept).

Vocabulary Categorizing

Vocabulary Strategy: Visual Imaging

Visualizing vocabulary words enables students who are stronger in spatial rather than in verbal intelligence to find or draw pictures that illustrate the definitions of words, facilitating both vocabulary development and comprehension across the curriculum (Silver, Strong, and Perini 2001; Tate 2010; Williams 2008). Visual imaging is also referred to as mind, mental, or concept imagery.

"The visual image is pervasive in the newer forms of literacy. Meaningful images may be defined partially by their boundaries, the information that is in an image, and that which might have been included, but is not present" (Lapp, Fisher, and Frey 2012, 23). A student creates an image that represents the definition of the word and calls up this image whenever encountering the word. This strategy assists readers in assessing understanding of vocabulary knowledge, learning word meaning, interpreting point of view, making predictions and inferences, and concept acquisition.

When students use visual imaging, they think of a word that looks or even sounds like the word they are learning. The more vivid the imagery, the more likely they will be able to connect and mentally recall the vocabulary word to its meaning. Different types of art activate different parts of the brain (Burmark 2008; Jensen 2000, 2005), and this sensory connection is the bond for visual learners. Visual learners draw on the images present to help simplify the content and understand the point of view given. Linking verbal and visual images increases students' ability to store and retrieve information (Ogle 2000; Gary 2012). "Transforming ideas from reading into artwork, poetry, etc., is an evaluative, interpretive act that reveals students' level of understanding" (Collins 1993, 3).

Appropriate text that best supports the application of the visual-imaging strategy has a variety of words in the text suitable for creating vivid mental images. Also, note that graphic genre is a cross between a novel and comics and is a valid reading tool in a world dominated by digital games and high-tech movies.

To support Visual Imaging while reading, a set of skills is required to effectively implement this strategy. The synchronized application of several reading strategies results in making meaning while reading a text. The skills, additional integrated reading strategies, and their reading components found in corresponding chapters are listed below.

Focus Skill(s):

- Sensory connections
- Spatial awareness
- Point of view

Integrated Strategies:

- Personalizing (Chapter 3)
- Predicting; Inferring and Drawing Conclusions; Questioning (Chapter 5)

Accountable Teacher Talk for Visual Imaging

Following is a list of suggested Teacher Talk that encourages readers to think strategically as they employ the Visual Imaging strategy. To effectively increase levels of thinking, these suggestions incorporate Bloom's Taxonomy's higher-order questioning (Anderson and Krathwohl 2001) and Webb's Depth of Knowledge (2002).

Remembering and Understanding (Recall)

- Try to visualize the meaning of the word _____. Describe what you see.

- How does your illustration help you remember the new word?

Applying (Skill/Concept)

- Which word goes with _____? Why does that word go with _____? Explain the relationship.

Analyzing (Strategic Thinking)

- What image/movement do you see when you think of the word _____? Explain your interpretative connection. Explain why you chose that movement to represent the word _____.

Evaluating and Creating (Extended Thinking)

- Based on the performance, what part of the pantomime helped you to imply that the word might be _____?

- Propose an alternative image that demonstrates meaning. Explain your interpretation.

Behavior Indicators for Visual Imaging

As you assess students' ability to use visual imaging, use the following behaviors as a guide. Do students exhibit these behaviors never, rarely, often, or always?

❑ Create a mental image of a word through a variety of media

❑ Draw inferences from a visual image to determine the meaning of a word or a phrase

❑ Give examples and nonexamples of what the word is like or not like

❑ Question and hypothesize for meaning of the image (purpose and context)

Techniques for Visual Imaging

Museum Walk

Purpose:	ELL Technique:
To imprint visual meaning by creating a representation of a word	Yes

Materials:

- text
- balls of clay
- online resources *(optional)*
- highlighters or small sticky notes
- Vocabulary Journal
- note cards *(optional)*

Vocabulary
Visual Imaging

Learning Phases

I

Select a word or phrase out of a current text or unit of study. Demonstrate the idea of "forming" meaning, using a ball of clay. Then introduce the selected vocabulary word. Form a visual image of what the word means out of the clay.

Explain how when reading, our minds create images of the written text similar to the way you formed meaning of the word out of the clay.

We

Elicit from the class other ways the selected word/phrase could have been demonstrated, using the clay to convey similar meaning. Have a few volunteers use additional clay to create the additional images. Display the newly formed images and read the word/phrase from the selected text in context.

With You

Distribute a ball of clay to small groups of students, and assign each group a different word. Have each team create a visual image of its word, using the clay, and then share it with the class. Display the images around the room, and have students do a word "museum walk" to view the visual forms of the different words, recording in their Vocabulary Journal their interpretations of the formed concepts.

Students may also draw images in the Vocabulary Journal for future reference on the meaning of words or concepts. **Suggested Teacher Talk:** *Try to look at all the clay forms and create a definition of the word _____.*

Ask students to explain how their forms relate to the meaning of the word they were assigned in their small group.

Revisit the text, and have students highlight or mark with sticky notes the words they formed. **Suggested Teacher Talk:** *How would you adapt _____ to create a visual image that would make sense within the context of what you are reading?*

Differentiation

Use a range of grade-appropriate general academic and domain-specific words according to students' needs.

Extensions

- Have students provide explanations of their clay by folding a note card to make a table tent. On one side, have students write the name of their creation. On the other side, instruct students to write about how they would categorize the image.

- Have students use a computer graphics program to create picture cards for their words. The graphic should be a pictorial representation of the meaning of the word and the object that matches their clay form.

- Invite students to create forms of images physically (i.e., pantomime, skit, charts, music) to convey meaning. Have students present the way they improvised to the other students and develop a logical interpretation of what word or phrase might best represent the performance. **Suggested Teacher Talk:** *In determining which words to verbally include in the drama, think about how the specific words chosen can enhance the viewers' development of meaning for the undisclosed word.*

Four Corners

Purpose:	ELL Technique:
To visualize the meaning of a word in multiple ways	Yes

Materials:	
• text	• pictures from magazines
• chart paper	• glue
• pencils or markers	• scissors
• highlighters or sticky notes	• *Four Corners Form* (see fourcornersform.pdf)
• music player (e.g., CD player, MP3 with docking station, and speakers)	

Learning Phases

I

Divide a sheet of chart paper into fourths. Select a key vocabulary word from a familiar text or concept. Write the key vocabulary word in the center of the chart paper.

- In the top-left corner, draw a picture that represents the opposite meaning of the key vocabulary word.

- In the top-right corner, draw a picture that represents an example of the key vocabulary word.

- In the bottom-left corner, draw a picture that represents a personal connection to the key vocabulary word.

- In the bottom-right corner, draw—using the letters in the word—a picture that illustrates the meaning of the key vocabulary word.

Vocabulary Visual Imaging

We

Select a different key vocabulary word with the group. Ask students to share the pen with you by assisting in writing and creating ideas (antonyms, synonyms, connections) to illustrate the word. Create a class Four Corners chart of the new word. **Suggested Teacher Talk:** *What is the word _____ like? How does it remind you of that word? Which word goes with _____? Why does that word go with_____?*

With You

Divide students into groups of four. Provide each group with a large sheet of paper divided into fourths with a key vocabulary word written in the middle. Ask each student to be responsible for one square on the paper. Starting with the top-left square, have students talk as a group to generate ideas for illustrations that would connect with the key vocabulary. Allow students time to discuss all four squares.

Have students draw or cut out pictures from magazines to complete the team Four Corners chart. Then, have each team share their Four Corners project with the class, explaining their reasoning for each corner. If possible, have students use text evidence to support their explanations. Once each presentation is complete, return to the text and highlight or sticky-note the words students studied.

By You

Provide students with the *Four Corners Form* and a key vocabulary word. Ask students to complete the form independently.

Differentiation

- Use a range of grade-appropriate general-academic and domain-specific words according to students' instructional levels.

- Allow students to select a key vocabulary word from their reading instead of providing a word for them so that they may choose a word that is challenging and interesting to them personally.

Extensions

- After reading a text, provide students with a completed Four Corners illustration minus the bottom-right square and the key-vocabulary word. Ask students to determine the key-vocabulary word based on the illustrations they have. Have them justify their reasoning for which vocabulary word is represented, based on text evidence, and complete the bottom-right square.

- Select five key vocabulary words from a text that all students are reading. Create a Four Corners Form for each word, and cut it into the four squares. Give one piece to each student. While music plays, ask students to mix around the room and search for three pieces that coincide with their piece to create a group Four Corners of a key vocabulary word. Once the five puzzles are together, ask students to justify their reasoning for why the pieces go together using evidence from the text.

Eye Spy With My Eye

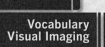

Purpose:		ELL Technique:
To enter imaginatively into the picture; to question and hypothesize for meaning of the image, its purpose, and its context		Yes

Materials:	
• texts	• Vocabulary Journals
• magnifying glass	• display options (chart paper, dry-erase boards, interactive whiteboard)

Learning Phases

I

Select a text with compelling graphics, and cover up the text to only show students the pictures. Hold up a magnifying glass to illustrate that you are going to investigate the images provided to extract meaning. Demonstrate drawing literal (exact/right there details) and inferential (suggested/not right there details) information from the image.

We

Ask students to look at the picture and describe what they see. Record and display their responses for all to view. **Suggested Teacher Talk:** *Spy with your eye who is in the picture. What do you think they are thinking or saying?* Examine each response, and determine if it is a literal or an inferential response.

Read a part of the text that correlates with the picture, and have students try to make predictions as to what they think happened before the scene depicted in the picture. Ask students to try to "solve the scene" by inferring what they think will be the rest of the story, based on the graphic they spied.

With You

Divide the class into two groups, one side representing the "Literal Team" and the other side representing the "Inferential Team." Display an image, and have students record their representations based on the type of team they represent.

Solicit responses from both sides, and analyze with the entire class whether it was classified correctly. Decide if the response gives enough information to determine the meaning of what is taking place in the text.

By You

While reading a selected text, have students create several images that are literal, and think of words with the text or an illustration for which they have to infer meaning. In their Vocabulary Journals next to the images, have them connect to a personal experience and describe or illustrate the connection.

Extension

Have each student convert the images from the text into a storyboard for a comic to share. Students can work independently or in small groups.

Vocabulary
Visual Imaging

Comic Connections

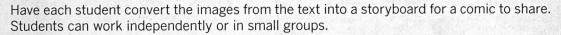

Purpose:	ELL Technique:
To enter imaginatively into the picture; to inspire empathy and curiosity, and to give voice to an image by creating a comic	Yes

Materials:

- texts (e.g., comics and graphic novels)
- storyboards
- online resources to create comics *(optional)*

Learning Phases

I

Display a sample of comic books and graphic novels. Discuss how this type of genre supports the reader by tapping into their visual intelligence. **Suggested Teacher Talk:** *What do your eyes do when viewing this text?*

We

Engage students in a conversation about the concept of "sequential art." Examine how we can view a series of illustrations in specific order to tell a story.

Distinguish the point of view, and discuss the power in comics to make connections to first, second, and third person, demonstrating different narrative points of view.

With You

In pairs, have students analyze a comic or a graphic novel for its specific features that enhance comprehension. For example, discuss how the expression of the character's face gives information so that the reader can derive meaning and understand the author's point of view. **Suggested Teacher Talk:** *Analyze and explain the difference between watching a movie and reading a novel. Describe the similarities and differences between these two in relation to a comic and/or graphic novel.*

Have students search for other examples in which the viewpoint from the visual representation is vital to bringing meaning to the comic or novel as they are abstracting what is happening.

By You

Have students read a comic or sections of a graphic novel and write an analysis based on the information and images with the text. Or, have students create a comic or begin a storyboard of a graphic novel during their independent writing experience. If desired, students could choose to use an online resource to create a comic strip.

Vocabulary Visual Imaging

Extension

To enhance students' ability to create comics or graphic novels as a class, examine the basic conventions within the format of a comic or a graphic novel:

Speech balloon—Assigns ownership of a character's words and thoughts, makes distinctions between speech (thought, exclamation), and declares the dialogue order. The font also can bring meaning (i.e., convey emphasis, diction).

The panel—This is the basic frame, capturing one segment of the story. The size, shape, and placement of the panels advances the reader.

The gutter—This is the empty space between panels where the human mind can use imagination to bridge to the next panel. Even this can be used to convey meaning.

Vocabulary Strategy: Analyzing Words

Students use the Analyzing Words strategy to examine the structure of words they are studying. Analyzing the structure, or word parts, is a way to determine the meaning of a word. There are three main word parts: prefixes, suffixes, and roots. Studying the morphemes of words (the smallest meaningful unit in language) allows students to acquire information about the meaning, phonological representation, and parts of speech of new words from their prefixes, roots, and suffixes contributing to reading comprehension (Deacon, Benere, and Pasquarella 2013; Nagy, Diakidoy, and Anderson 1991; Mountain 2005; Raskinski et al. 2014). These word parts help to contribute to the meaning of the word. "Morphological awareness should play a more prominent role in decoding morphologically complex words because it helps beginning readers parse strings of letters at the right syllable boundary (e.g., *mis-handle* vs. *mi-shandle*)" (Kuo and Anderson 2006, 172).

According to Nilsen and Nilsen (2003), spending class time on frequently used morphemes is a good teaching practice because it helps students establish structural connections among words. "Students need to learn to use word parts strategically, cautiously, and thoughtfully" (Stahl and Nagy 2006, 159). Implementing techniques that support the connections between the structural-analysis concepts and the basic definition will help students in understanding the word. Appropriate text that best supports the application of the analyzing strategy has a variety of words suitable for a specific structural concept.

To support Analyzing Words while reading, a set of skills is required to effectively implement this reading strategy. The synchronized application of several reading strategies results in making meaning while reading a text. The skills, additional integrated reading strategies, and their reading components found in corresponding chapters are listed below.

Focus Skill(s):

- Structural (morphemic) analysis (prefix, suffix, root and base words)

- Parts of speech (verb, noun, adjective, adverb, pronoun)

Integrated Strategies:

- Analyzing Sounds (Chapter 2)

- Personalizing (Chapter 3)

- Predicting; Questioning (Chapter 5)

Accountable Teacher Talk for Analyzing Words

Following is a list of suggested Teacher Talk that encourages readers to think strategically as they employ the Analyzing Words strategy. To effectively increase levels of thinking, these suggestions incorporate Bloom's Taxonomy's higher-order questioning (Anderson and Krathwohl 2001) and Webb's Depth of Knowledge (2002).

Remembering and Understanding (Recall)

- What does the prefix _____ do when added to the start of the word _____?

- Try to cover up part of the word (e.g., the prefix). What word do you have left?

Applying (Skill/Concept)

- What is the meaning of the prefix [or suffix] in the word _____?

Analyzing (Strategic Thinking)

- If you know what the root word for _____ means, what do you think _____ means?

Evaluating and Creating (Extended Thinking)

- Determine the changes you would need to make to the word _____ to have it mean _____. Explain your changes and how it gives the word a new meaning.

- Investigate the root in the word _____. Based on your determination of the meaning of the root, think of another word that can derive similar meaning. Explain your process and how these words relate. Create a list of other words with the same root, based on your new knowledge.

Behavior Indicators for Analyzing Words

As you assess students' ability to analyze, use the following behaviors as a guide. Do students exhibit these behaviors never, rarely, often, or always?

- ❑ Locate morphemes in a word, and examine their meaning
- ❑ Demonstrate how prefixes affect words and their meaning
- ❑ Decipher how words derive meaning from root words

Techniques for Analyzing Words

Playing with Plurals

Purpose:	ELL Technique:
To analyze the structure of a word to determine if it is singular or plural	No

Materials:

- text
- various items for demonstrating the (more than) plural concept
- highlighter
- shoebox (*optional*)
- crackers or grapes
- tray
- Vocabulary Journals
- glue (*optional*)

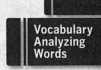

Vocabulary
Analyzing
Words

Learning Phases

I

Bring in several items where you visually highlight the meaning of the concept plural. Examples: shoe/shoes, key/keys, or book/books. Hold up the one item and say its name orally, and write the word visually demonstrating the singular noun.

Hold up two or more of the same item and say the items' names emphasizing the plural /s/ sound. Write and display the words representing the items, and highlight the letter s or es, if necessary, at the end of each of the words to denote when there are more than one.

We

Display a tray of crackers, and have students describe what you have in your hand. Their response may be "crackers." Go around the room, and ask students if they would like a cracker or crackers.

You can also use grapes and ask if they want a grape or grapes. **Suggested Teacher Talk:** *I will listen to the end of your word to determine what to give you.*

Discuss with students how listening to the ending of their word would help you determine the amount to give. Hold up items, and have students decide if the corresponding word is singular or plural (e.g., ball or balls). You can have two trays, one with singular items and one with plural. Have students compare and contrast the trays.

With You

During a read-aloud, have students listen for plural words and record them in their Vocabulary Journals. Have them review their lists and look for patterns, and then share their discoveries with a partner and create a chart of a variety of plural examples. Students should try to verbalize and record any patterns they find (e.g., if the word ends in *s*, *x*, *ch*, or *sh*, add an *es* to make it plural).

By You

Have students search for words in their independent reading or their personal writing that denotes the use of plurals.

Differentiation

Provide students with text that uses irregular plurals, and ask them to investigate types of regular and irregular plurals.

Extension

Go on a "plural walk" outside. Have students collect items (e.g., leaves, rocks, flowers) and also notice items (e.g., birds, clouds) that are plural. Place collected items on display, and create a label with the letter *s* highlighted. Students may put their collections in small shoeboxes or glue on paper as their plural collections.

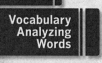

Vocabulary
Analyzing
Words

Vocabulary Tree Notebook

Purpose:	ELL Technique:
To identify morphemes within a word	No

Materials:	

- text
- display options (chart paper, dry-erase boards, interactive whiteboard)
- index cards
- *Vocabulary Tree Template* (see vocabularytree.pdf)
- small three-ring binders or clasp folders
- paper leaves (*optional*)

Learning Phases

I — Discuss the correlation of trees and words (e.g., both have parts, words can grow from base and root words just like trees grow from their roots). Use the *Vocabulary Tree Template* (adapted from Bear et al. 2011) to explain how you can draw leaves to record words that correlate with the specific word part of the designated tree branches.

We

Use the *Vocabulary Tree Template,* or draw three bare trees to display (e.g., on chart paper, a dry-erase board, an interactive white board) for all students to see. Label one tree *prefix,* one *suffix,* and the last *root.* Record sample prefix, suffix, and root words on individual index cards.

Pass out word card examples and have a few students stand under their appropriate trees. Read a sentence aloud, which includes one of the highlighted words in context.

Have the student that matches the word share their word part and explain the meaning of the word, based on the context and his or her word part. **Suggested Teacher Talk:** *Try to take the word apart and determine on which tree it will go.*

With You

Distribute the *Vocabulary Tree Template,* and have students begin to create Vocabulary Tree Notebooks (small three-ring binders or clasp folders), designating one page in their notebooks for each morpheme (e.g. root, prefix, or suffix) they study.

On each tree, teams would then label each branch a different type. For example, the prefix tree could have four branches, each labeled with a different prefix (e.g., *re, un, tri*). Have students create words that correspond to each specific prefix, record them on the leaves, and place them on the specific branch.

Have students share their vocabulary trees with a partner and discuss why the words on a particular tree are related. **Suggested Teacher Talk:** *How are all these words alike?*

By You

Have students locate the words they studied in their independent reading. Whenever students encounter a word with that part (e.g., *-ing*), have them write it on the appropriate tree and note where the word was encountered. Students can add to their vocabulary trees as they encounter specific tree elements in their reading and writing.

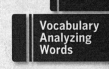

Vocabulary Analyzing Words

Extension

Create a matching game. Record a variety of root words on paper leaves, and cut them apart. Place the leaves at a station with different types of trees (e.g., specific prefix or suffix). Have students read the leaf and analyze its parts to determine on which tree to place the leaf.

Flip-a-Chip

Purpose:	ELL Technique:
To mix and match four meaningful word parts to make four words	Yes

Materials:	

- texts
- round chips (or circles cut from tag board)
- chart paper (*optional*)

- sentence strips
- Vocabulary Journals

Vocabulary Analyzing Words

Learning Phases

Select two words that can be interchangeable with their word parts (e.g., verbs: *laugh* and *start*) and two inflectional endings (e.g., -ing and -ed). Record the chosen word parts on two round chips. One chip represents the two words, with one word recorded on each side. The other chip represents the inflectional endings.

Model the Flip-a-Chip technique for students, using the two chips (adapted from Bear et al. 2011). Flip and connect chips together to form a word.

Record the newly formed word for display. Continue to flip the chips until you have created four different words (e.g., *laughing, laughed, starting, started*). (See Figure 3.7.)

Figure 3.7 Sample of Flip-a-Chip

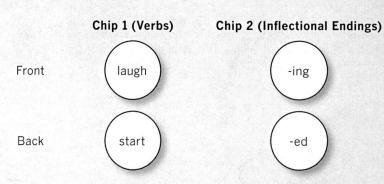

	Chip 1 (Verbs)	Chip 2 (Inflectional Endings)
Front	laugh	-ing
Back	start	-ed

We

Create sentences embedding the Flip-a-Chip words into the context prior to modeling the technique. Record these sentences on strips, omitting the Flip-a-Chip word.

Distribute sentence strips to volunteers or a table group. Have the volunteers or table groups select one of the words from the chart that would best complete their sentence.

Ask students holding the sentence strips to come up to the front of the room. Have them determine the order of the sentences to create a paragraph (story) that would make sense.

Sample Sentences: *The movie was _____, so I took my seat. After the first scene _____ in the movie, I knew it was going to be good. At the funny part, I _____ out loud. I kept _____ all the way through the movie.*

With You

Give each set of partners a different Flip-a-Chip set (prefix chip and root-word chip) to collaborate on forming words. **Suggested Teacher Talk:** *What does the prefix _____ do when added to the start of the word _____?* Have students flip the chips to form a word, and then continue this process to form all four words.

Have the partners record their results in their Vocabulary Journals. Rotate, giving all the partners time to work with each set of chips. **Suggested Teacher Talk:** *How are all these words alike?*

By You

Have students create their own Flip-a-Chip combinations, and demonstrate where their Flip-a-Chip word is located in their independent-reading texts.

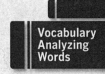

Vocabulary Analyzing Words

Differentiation

Depending on students' readiness levels, use various structural-analysis combinations: verbs with inflectional endings, adjectives with suffixes, nouns with plural and possessive endings, prefixes, and roots. See Figures 3.8 and 3.9 for lists of commonly used prefixes and suffixes.

Extensions

- Have partners write a paragraph with blanks. These blanks represent where the newly formed words on the chips would best complete the sentences. Then, students place the newly formed paragraph in a bag, with the corresponding chips. In centers or literacy stations; other students can work to complete the paragraph using the chips.

- Have students use word-sorting techniques (see the Categorizing strategy, this chapter, for more ideas) to further examine the concepts of prefixes and suffixes. Students also can use word walls, journals, and word study to reinforce the analysis of prefixes and suffixes.

Figure 3.8 Commonly Used Prefixes

Prefix	Meaning	Examples
auto-	self	automatic, autograph, automobile
bi-	two	biweekly, bicycle, bilingual
de-	reverse action, remove, away	deflate, detach, deodorize
dis-	apart, negative, away	dislike, disagree, disappear
in-	not, free from, out	inactive, invisible
mis-	wrong	misspell, miscount, misfortune
pre-	before	preview, prepay, prepare
re-	back, again	redo, recall, repaint
tri-	three	triangle, tricycle, trilogy
un-	not	undo, untold, unhappy

Vocabulary Analyzing Words

Figure 3.9 Commonly Used Suffixes

Suffix	Meaning	Examples
-tion	being, act, process (forms noun)	mention, vacation, location
-er	person connected with (forms noun)	runner, teacher, speaker
-less	without (forms adjective)	speechless, breathless, thoughtless
-ing	verb form (forms present participle)	running, singing, swimming
-ness	state of, condition of (forms noun)	likeness, forgiveness, happiness
-s, -es	plural	boys, girls, boxes
-ly	characteristic of (forms adverb)	lovely, happily
-est	comparative (forms adjective)	happiest, funniest, craziest
-ful	full of (forms adjective)	playful, helpful, grateful
-ed	verb form (forms past tense)	played, relaxed, rehearsed

Rootin' Root Words

Purpose:	ELL Technique:
To delve deep into the morphological analysis of a word and derive the conceptual meaning from the root word or base	No

Materials:

- text
- *Rootin' Root Tree Template* (see rootintree.pdf)
- *Rootin' Root Leaves Template* (see rootinleaves.pdf)
- chart paper
- Vocabulary Journal
- dictionaries
- highlighter

Learning Phases

I

Use the leaves from the *Rootin' Root Tree and Leaves Template* to demonstrate thinking about roots and producing words that incorporate the highlighted root for study. Record each of these generated words on a leaf that correlates with the word at the base of the *Rootin' Root Tree*.

Choose 2–3 leaves to analyze this foundational part of a word (root) and apply them in sentences, focusing on the meaning of each word. Model how attending to the root helps to determine a word's origin and history, which will make the word more memorable.

We

Assign a Latin and a Greek root word for students to work in teams to investigate the meanings and purposes, using the assigned roots. Ask teams to search for other words with the same root, and research the meaning of the root words.

Instruct teams to compare and contrast their root word choices and demonstrate how the root word is embedded in all the other words they were able to discover and how these words are similar in some part of meaning because of their roots.

With You

Have students work with partners to create a *Rootin' Root Tree* to collect common content-specific roots and sample words related to the text they are reading or the unit of study. Have students utilize their Root Tree to design a rap (see Rappin' With Roots in Word Study Chapter) from several leaves related to a specific root to bring meaning to the text or topic of study. **Suggested Teacher Talk:** *What information can you gather to support your idea about the parts of the words you are studying? Test your hypothesis on several words, draw a conclusion about the parts you are analyzing, and place your examples in a lyrical format.*

Vocabulary
Analyzing
Words

By You

Have students generate a set of new words by adding affixes (prefixes and suffixes) to the root words. Have them write these new words in their Vocabulary Journal. **Suggested Teacher Talk:** *What is the root word of_____?*

Lead students in a discussion on how these words all relate and can be categorized. Have students return to the text and highlight the words they studied. Instruct students to maintain their *Rootin' Root Tree* notes in their Vocabulary Journals.

Differentiation

Have students apply various phonics elements within their rap (e.g., phonograms, vowel patterns, suffixes, and various grade-appropriate root words according to their instructional or independent levels).

Extension

Create circle roots (Ellery and Rosenboom 2010; Vacca and Vacca 2008) by dividing a circle into quarters and writing a word in each section that has the same root within the word. Have students orally, or in print, identify and describe the relationship that exists among the words and use these words to create a rap, song, or poem.

Vocabulary
Analyzing
Words

Vocabulary Strategy: Personalizing

Students gain a sense of ownership of a word when they can transfer a new vocabulary word to their writing and speaking in a meaningful way (Routman 2000). Personalizing, also known as word awareness and word consciousness, is a strategy that brings one's thinking about the usage of a word to an application level and brings ownership to word learning. Effective readers acquire up to seven new vocabulary words each day. To enhance vocabulary, students need to have a desire to know words and gain "enjoyment and satisfaction from using them well and from hearing them used well by others" (Graves 2000, 127).

When students know a word, they are demonstrating their metalinguistic awareness. They are able to use that word in communication (written or oral) and to understand the word in text when it appears. Word-conscious students know and use many words, and they are aware of the subtleties of word meaning and the power words can have (Graves, Juel, and Graves 1998; Graves and Watts-Taffe 2008; Lane and Allen 2010). Applying the Personalizing strategy is a natural, motivating way to support students while they are building their vocabulary and increasing their comprehension.

To support Personalizing while reading, a set of skills is required to effectively implement this reading strategy. The synchronized application of several reading strategies results in making meaning while reading a text. The skills, additional integrated reading strategies, and their reading components found in corresponding chapters are listed below.

Focus Skill(s):

- Concept of a word
- Metalinguistic awareness

Integrated Strategies:

- Recognizing (Chapter 2)
- Expressing (Chapter 4)
- Activating and Building Schemas; Synthesizing (Chapter 5)

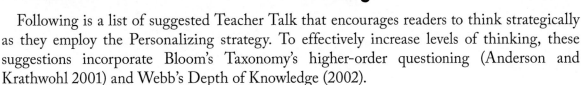

Accountable Teacher Talk for Personalizing

Following is a list of suggested Teacher Talk that encourages readers to think strategically as they employ the Personalizing strategy. To effectively increase levels of thinking, these suggestions incorporate Bloom's Taxonomy's higher-order questioning (Anderson and Krathwohl 2001) and Webb's Depth of Knowledge (2002).

Remembering and Understanding (Recall)

- How can you find out more about a chosen word?
- What do you know about the word _____?

Applying (Skill/Concept)

- How often did you use your chosen word in your journal writing?

Analyzing (Strategic Thinking)

- How did being aware of one word help you to learn about that new word?

Evaluating and Creating (Extended Thinking)

- Do you feel confident to use the word _____ in a conversation or in your writing? Why? Why not?
- How would you use the new word for proper application? Design a plan to self-monitor the use of your new words.

Behavior Indicators for Personalizing

As you assess students' ability to personalize, use the following behaviors as a guide. Do students exhibit these behaviors never, rarely, often, or always?

- ❏ Gain ownership of words by applying new words in everyday conversations
- ❏ Transfer a new vocabulary word to their writing
- ❏ Indicate levels of knowledge of words

Techniques for Personalizing

Word Jars

Purpose:	ELL Technique:
To examine words in their environment and use new words in real-life connections	Yes

Materials:

- text
- *Word Jar* (see wordjar.pdf)
- *Donavan's Word Jar* (Degross 1994) (optional)
- plastic jars (optional)

- sticky notes (optional)
- highlighters
- Vocabulary Journals

Learning Phases

I Discuss what it means to have a collection of something (e.g., baseball cards, books) and how items that are collected have value to the collector and can be traded. Select a text about collections to share, or read *Donavan's Word Jar* to students and discuss how Donavan shares his encounters with a variety of people and their reactions to his word jar collection.

We Distribute the *Word Jar*, or give each student a plastic jar for collecting words. Discuss the value in being aware of the words we use. Share with the class a word that you have added to your vocabulary recently, why you chose to add it, and how you have been using it.

With You Have students select a word from their word jar that they would like to use throughout the week in their conversations. In small groups, have students share their word selection, how they are using it, and why they chose each word. Encourage students to swap words or get ideas from other's word awareness.

By You Invite students to create their own word jar and have them search for words to add to the jar each day. Have students keep a daily vocabulary log, and during independent writing time, write how they used their vocabulary word in context for that day. Encourage students to have at least five entries per word before adding a new vocabulary word.

Vocabulary Personalizing

Differentiation

Vary the words selected for the word jars based on students' interest and instructional and independent levels.

Extensions

- Have students write their selected word on a sticky note and wear it on their clothes. Each time that a student uses his or her chosen word in conversation, the listener should add a tally mark to the sticky note. Read a text, and have students highlight the words they chose to study as they discover their word within context.

- Have students periodically use their word jars to categorize their words and add them to their Vocabulary Journals or a word wall.

- Have students share their words from their jars in teams and have a word-card trading day.

Journal Circles

Purpose:	ELL Technique:
To express an awareness of words in writing and participate in collaborative conversations	Yes

Materials:	
• text	• Vocabulary Journals
• chart paper	

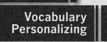
Vocabulary Personalizing

Learning Phases

I   Share a journal entry from one of your journals with students. Share how when you write in your journal, it is an opportunity for a free-flowing expression of your thoughts about a particular event, topic, or experience.

We   Compare journal writing to writing in a diary. Have students share diaries or journals they have read or heard about (e.g., Anne Frank). Create a list of various types of ways to journal (e.g., two-entry notes, academic journal, free-write journal).

Establish a daily journal writing time and have students agree to make an effort to use vocabulary words they are currently studying when they write in their Word Power Journals.

Practice having a conversation through multiple exchanges, using an agreed-upon class journal discussion procedure (e.g., listening to others with care, speaking one at a time about the topics).

When writing time is complete, ask students to join journal circles in which small groups of mixed or similar ability level students take turns sharing their daily entries and noting the word choices they used in their writing. This can be called "Journal Jive Time" or "Circle Time." It gives students a chance to try out sharing how they used words in context. **Suggested Teacher Talk:** *When you are sharing with your group today, try to incorporate orally one of your new applied words.*

After hearing each student orally read his or her journal entry, have the other team members make comments, ask questions, and compliment the reader regarding his or her word choices and overall journal entry.

Read a text, and have students point out what words they heard in the text that they have used in their journal entries.

Extension

Read aloud stories and create a class chart, using words from the text that are important or interesting for students to know. Have students sign their names on the vocabulary chart next to the vocabulary word identified for them to use. Place a tally mark beside the student's name each time he or she uses the assigned word in a meaningful way orally or in their journals.

Knowledge Rating

Vocabulary Personalizing

Purpose:	ELL Technique:
To identify the level of knowledge of a word	No

Materials:

- *Knowledge Rating Matrix* (see knowledgerating.pdf)
- text
- Vocabulary Journals

Learning Phases

I

Present students with a list of vocabulary words related to a topic you are studying. Use a range of grade-appropriate general academic and domain-specific words.

Read a word from the list, and model your thinking about how much knowledge you have of the word (e.g., not sure what the word means, can define the word and use it).

We

Have students analyze their familiarity with the chosen words, and ask them to share their level of word knowledge by holding up their fingers to represent their familiarity with the word (1 = I don't know the word, 2 = I have heard the word, and 3 = I use the word). **Suggested Teacher Talk:** *Try to rate the word according to how much you know about it.*

With You

Ask students to discuss with partners what they know about the list of words, and select words to focus on during the upcoming reading on the unit of study or the instructional-text selection. **Suggested Teacher Talk:** *What do you know about the word _____?* Read the text, and have students listen for the new words they are studying and think about how they are used in context.

By You

Distribute copies of the *Knowledge Rating Matrix* (Blachowicz 1986). Before reading, have students use the rating matrix to record newly selected words and to rate them according to their level of knowledge of each word.

After reading, have students reflect on their rating matrix and determine whether their knowledge of certain words changed. Have students place an X in the appropriate column of the matrix to represent any changes.

Ask students to keep their rating charts in their Vocabulary Journals and review them periodically, making adjustments of words that are becoming more familiar to them.

Vocabulary Personalizing

Extension

Create a class word knowledge matrix by having students physically line up across the room in order according to their knowledge of a selected word. Pair up students that acknowledge that they know a lot about the word with students that know little. Have partner discussions to enhance word knowledge.

Quick-Writes

Purpose:	ELL Technique:
To utilize background knowledge to formulate meanings of words and write routinely over extended time frames for a range of specific tasks, purposes, and audiences	Yes

Materials:	
• text	• Vocabulary Journals
• chart paper or document camera	

Learning Phases

I

Present one new vocabulary word to students prior to reading a text selection. After presenting the vocabulary word, use chart paper or a document camera to model writing about the word (whatever background knowledge that can be activated) for a few minutes in front of students.

This writing may include a definition of the word, a synonym or an antonym for the word, or a response to a question you present using the word or about the word. **Suggested Teacher Talk:** *What do I know about the word _____?* After modeling your Quick-Write, read a section from the text and then revisit your Quick-Write to add any information you have learned from the text or even questions you may have now.

We

Select a topic related to a unit of study and create a group Quick-Write soliciting student responses to open-ended questions or selected prompts that allow opportunity for opinions and ideas to be stated. Have students share the pen as you collectively write quickly but think deeply. **Note**: Writing mechanics and grammar are not assessed at this time.

With You

Have students participate in a Quick-Write, and then share in groups their Quick-Write responses, and discuss similarities and differences among the responses.

Have groups discuss their ideas about the word, helping one another to put new concepts into their own words. **Suggested Teacher Talk:** *How did being aware of the word today help you learn about that word?*

Vocabulary Personalizing

By You

Read the text and emphasize the vocabulary word within the context of the selection. Ask students to revisit their written responses and make any adjustments necessary to correspond with the way the word is used in the context of the text.

Differentiation

Depending on students' readiness levels, use different levels of Quick-Write prompts.

Vocabulary Strategy: Wide Reading

Wide Reading is a strategy that fosters vocabulary development through a variety of opportunities for students to read. Students need at least 20 minutes of daily reading to help increase their vocabulary list by 1,000 words per year (Nagy, Anderson, and Herman 1987). This daily exposure is a natural way to increase vocabulary. "Children learn new words by reading extensively on their own. The more children read on their own, the more words they encounter and the more word meaning they learn" (Armbruster, Lehr, and Osborn 2001, 35).

Encountering words in reading passages or speaking them in context multiple times is one of the best ways to commit words to long-term memory. Students will benefit from techniques geared toward rehearsing and talking about some of the words and concepts in a variety of genres as they gradually shape their word knowledge (Calkins 2001; Fountas and Pinnell 1996; Fountas and Pinnell 2012; Marzano 2004; Miller and Anderson 2009). Wide Reading gives students an opportunity to build background knowledge. The more exposure students have, the more opportunities they have to "augment their vocabularies and improve their reading" (Marzano and Simms 2013, 8).

To support Wide Reading, a set of skills is required to effectively implement this strategy. The synchronized application of several reading strategies results in making meaning while reading a text. The skills, additional integrated reading strategies, and their reading components found in corresponding chapters are listed below.

Focus Skill(s):

- Genres (text types)
- Sustainability
- Oral and written communication

Integrated Strategies:

- Recognizing (Chapter 2)
- Contextualizing; Personalizing (Chapter 3)
- Rereading; Expressing (Chapter 4)
- Activating and Building Schemas; Predicting; Questioning (Chapter 5)

Accountable Teacher Talk for Wide Reading

Following is a list of suggested Teacher Talk that encourages readers to think strategically as they employ the Wide Reading strategy. To effectively increase levels of thinking, these suggestions incorporate Bloom's Taxonomy's higher-order questioning (Anderson and Krathwohl 2001) and Webb's Depth of Knowledge (2002).

Remembering and Understanding (Recall)

- What are some of the interesting vocabulary words the author uses?
- What kind of words are common in this specific genre?

Applying (Skill/Concept)

- How have you used some words from your vocabulary journal in your everyday conversation?

Analyzing (Strategic Thinking)

- What pattern do you notice the author using for word choice?

Evaluating and Creating (Extended Thinking)

- Investigate the words you heard while listening to the read-aloud. Which words did you find interesting? Why?
- Develop a plan to have multiple exposures to a variety of genres. How have you used some words from your current independent reading in your everyday conversations?

Behavior Indicators for Wide Reading

As you assess students' ability to widely read, use the following behaviors as a guide. Do students exhibit these behaviors never, rarely, often, or always?

- ❑ Listen and absorb vocabulary from hearing and reading text
- ❑ Imitate author's words in conversation
- ❑ Investigate a range of text types for specific purpose

Techniques for Wide Reading

Accountable-Talk Read-Alouds

Purpose:	ELL Technique:
To listen to and absorb the vocabulary from a chosen text and support meaning from textual evidence	Yes

Materials:

- text
- note cards (*optional*)
- chart paper
- sticky notes

Learning Phases

Read aloud from a narrative or informational text rich with academic vocabulary, exposing students to complex language with support. Texts need to be on topics that allow students opportunities to generate in-depth vocabulary knowledge. Plan some areas in the text to stop and ponder, thinking aloud about your cognitive awareness while reading, and model using accountable talk to interact with a variety of text.

Read orally to the class while students listen during the read-aloud and try to absorb the vocabulary from the chosen text, and how you used evidence in the text to support the meaning of the chosen vocabulary words.

Sample Accountable-Talk Read-Aloud stems that support close reading:

- What does the text say about _____, and what does that mean?

- Based on the text, describe the meaning of _____.

- When the text says _____, I can visualize that it means...

- The clues I used from the text to determine the meaning of the word are...

- I (think, predict, speculate, infer) _____ about this word because...

- Based on the evidence in the text, I know that _____ means...

- What specific vocabulary did the author use to convey the meaning of _____?

We

Hold structured conversations in response to the written text that was read aloud, allowing students the ability to analyze interesting words and form thoughts on what they heard. Support students in how to make connections and relate the text by personalizing it.

Invite students to use the Sample Accountable Talk Read-Aloud stems above to support their understanding of the words they found interesting. **Suggested Teacher Talk:** *Tell me about some interesting words you heard while listening to the read-aloud. Why are these words interesting to you? What textual evidence supported the meaning of your chosen words?*

With You

Place the text that you read in an area in the classroom where students can reread it with a team or partners, or otherwise revisit it on their own. Ask students to create questions on sticky notes, and place them on a chart by the text. Encourage students to try to answer the generated student questions based on the textual evidence and place the sticky notes in the book for others to check for understanding.

By You

Keep a class chart of all the titles read aloud each month. Have students discuss and record their reflections on the texts on this chart and periodically compare previously noted connections with new connections (e.g., text-to-text connections, text-to-self connections).

Extension

Write selected words from the story on note cards, and pass them out to students before the read-aloud. As students are listening to the story, have them hold up their word cards when they hear the words in the story. After the read-aloud, have students share how each word was used in the story and how they applied the Accountable Talk Read-Aloud stems to support bringing meaning to their words.

Vocabulary
Wide Reading

Author Study

Purpose:	ELL Technique:
To participate in research on specific authors and imitate authors' words in oral and in written form	No

Materials:	
• multiple texts by the same author	• chart paper
• sticky tabs	• materials for students to create their own written versions

Learning Phases

I

Create an area in the classroom to display the books and other information about an author you are studying (e.g., an Awesome Author center). Display the author's books with sticky tabs on pages where you have identified specific words to be studied. Encourage students to visit the author center frequently.

We

Read several books by a particular author. During this author study, have students look for key words the author uses frequently in his or her writing. List the author's name at the top of a sheet of chart paper and have students list interesting words the author uses. **Suggested Teacher Talk:** *What pattern do you notice the author using for his or her word choice?*

With You

Have small groups of students select a particular book from the class-author study. Then, have students in each group participate in shared research to compare and contrast themes, settings, and plots, make connections, locate artifacts that relate to the author's style, and search online for author's blogs and other resources by the author.

By You

Encourage students to imitate the author by using the author's words in their everyday conversations. **Suggested Teacher Talk:** *What are some of the vocabulary words the author uses that are interesting to you?*

Extensions

- Have students imitate the featured author by creating their own versions of the stories at the writing center/literacy station, allowing the author being studied to be a "writing mentor."

- Compare and contrast two or more versions of the same story written by different authors (e.g., "Cinderella" or "The Story of the Three Little Pigs").

Vocabulary Wide Reading

Book Talks and Trailers

Purpose:	ELL Technique:
To identify vocabulary words that support the meaning of a book	Yes

Materials:	
• text	• Vocabulary Journals
• online resources (http://digitalbooktalk.net, http://www.booktrailersforreaders.com)	• poster board *(optional)*
	• art materials *(optional)*

Learning Phases

I

Select a book on which to give a book talk, enticing students to want to read the book. You can visit http://digitalbooktalk.com or other online resources that demonstrate digital book trailers to help provide you with ideas for your own book talk. Explain to students that a book talk is like a commercial for the book, and you are advertising the basic storyline.

We

Encourage students to read a variety of narrative and informational text. Explain that they will be giving book talks or creating book trailers using vocabulary from each story to introduce classmates to a particular book. Create a class rubric to assess the quality of the book talks and trailers.

With You

Work collaboratively with a partner to research key details and create a book talk or a book trailer. **Suggested Teacher Talk:** *How did you select your words for your book talk?*

By You

As students are reading, have them write in their Vocabulary Journals interesting vocabulary words that help them relate to the meaning of the book. Have students use the words they found interesting in their own created book talks to share with the class.

Extension

Have students create a poster that illustrates their book talk and display these at the classroom library area with the books to entice others to read them.

Vocabulary
Wide Reading

Genre Study

Purpose:	ELL Technique:
To identify similarities and differences among vocabulary words within genres	No

Materials:	
• texts in a variety of genres	• materials for creative writing
• chart paper	• highlighters

Learning Phases

I

Select a variety of genre samples to share with the class. Expose students to several different genres (e.g., historical fiction, fantasy, science fiction). Explain that a *genre* is a category, text type, or class of literature or informational text.

We

During this genre study, keep a chart of specific vocabulary words that correlate with each particular genre. Figure 3.10 provides some examples.

Create a group list of genre characteristic traits. **Suggested Teacher Talk:** *What kinds of words did you notice that are common in the specific genre?*

Figure 3.10 Sample Genre Vocabulary Words and Phrases

Genre	Description	Vocabulary Words and Phrases
Fantasy	Fiction that contains elements that are not real, such as magical powers and animals that talk	Wizard, magical, hero, powers, imagine, supernatural, journeys and quests, mythical
Mystery	Narrative fiction that contains suspense, foreshadowing, mysterious, detective	Secret, classified, investigation, discover, clue, evidence, witness, suspects, suspense
Folk tale	Literature story passed on from one generation to another by word of mouth	Once upon a time, This is the story of, Long ago, There once was
Fable	Narrative fictitious story meant to teach a lesson; characters are usually animals	Responsibility, moral, courage, freedom, noble, kindness
Science fiction	Narrative story that often tells about the future, incorporates technology, what if, infinite possibilities, imagination	Aliens, encounter, outer space, scientific, time travel, consequences, theories, dimension
Biography	Nonfiction expository text about life of an individual, historical figures, third-person point of view	Accomplishment, achievement, failure, contribution, influential, environment, he or she
Technical text	Informational text on how to perform a task; execute or solve something; give directions	Procedural steps, academic/content-related words, sequential words (*first*, *next*, *last*)

Vocabulary Wide Reading

Have students frequently discuss the similarities and differences among the vocabulary words and formats within the various genres. **Suggested Teacher Talk:** *In what genre would you most likely find these words: ____?*

 Have students keep a log of the various genres and book titles they read. Have them place tally marks to denote a specific genre. Set genre requirements for students to have a vast array of wide reading.

Differentiation

- Create a class reading blog to highlight the wide range of genre being demonstrated by your readers.

- Using the genre chart, have students select a genre and create a writing piece using at least 10 words that indicate strongly their genre choice. Have partners read the writings and decide the chosen genre and highlight the words that correlate with the genre.

Vocabulary
Wide Reading

Vocabulary Strategy: Referencing

Referencing is a strategy that allows readers to use resources to bring meaning to an unknown word. Students simply select a resource to search for the meaning of the word. However, teachers and students can overly rely on this traditional strategy. "Definitions alone can lead to only a relatively superficial level of word knowledge. By itself, looking up words in a dictionary or memorizing definitions does not reliably improve reading comprehension" (Nagy 2003, 5). Instruction for students should focus on how these resources can aid in learning meanings of words in the appropriate context. The quality of the definition is also an important factor in being able to use the dictionary as an aid to understanding text (McKeown 1993; Nist and Olejnik 1995).

Teachers need to work with students in selecting the definition that best supports the meaning of the chosen word. "To make deriving the meaning from the dictionary definitions most effective, it needs to be modeled for students and practiced in a scaffolded way" (Beck et al. 2008, 47). Several techniques are possible, including using a book's glossary, a dictionary, a thesaurus, a resource buddy, or online search engines. "When readers activate their ability to reference a word, they are using a resource indicator that orients them to bring clarification and meaning" (Ellery and Rosenboom 2010).

To support Referencing while reading, a set of skills is required to effectively implement this reading strategy. The synchronized application of several reading strategies results in making meaning while reading a text. The skills, additional integrated reading strategies, and their reading components found in corresponding chapters are listed below.

Focus Skill(s):

- Organizational sense
- Clarification

Integrated Strategies:

- Analyzing Sounds (Chapter 2)
- Analyzing Words (Chapter 3)

Accountable Teacher Talk for Referencing

Following is a list of suggested Teacher Talk that encourages readers to think strategically as they employ the Referencing strategy. To effectively increase levels of thinking, these suggestions incorporate Bloom's Taxonomy's higher-order questioning (Anderson and Krathwohl 2001) and Webb's Depth of Knowledge (2002).

Remembering and Understanding (Recall)

- Explain how a dictionary helps you to figure out the word. Select words to examine and record the ones that are of interest to you.

- How do you use a thesaurus, a glossary, or a dictionary to help you understand the meaning of a word?

Applying (Skill/Concept)

- Think about the word _____. Which word means _____? How did you find the meaning of the word?

Analyzing (Strategic Thinking)

- What feature of the online program helps you understand the word better? How does it help you?

Evaluating and Creating (Extended Thinking)

- How does the communication tool used determine the degree of information received?

- Formulate a definition of the word based on how it is used in context. Elaborate on the reason for your definition of the word. Use a variety of resource tools to support your thinking.

Behavior Indicators for Referencing

As you assess students' ability to reference, use the following behaviors as a guide. Do students exhibit these behaviors never, rarely, often, or always?

❏ Analyze resource indicators to determine meaning for unknown words

❏ Use glossaries, dictionaries, thesauri, and various online tools to determine meaning of words

❏ Select meaning of a word that best supports the use of the word in context

Techniques for Referencing

Resource Buddies

Purpose:	ELL Technique:
To work with a partner to analyze unknown words for meaning	Yes

Materials:

- text
- chart paper
- online resources (*optional*)

- reference materials (e.g., dictionaries or glossaries)
- Vocabulary Journals or index cards

Learning Phases

I

Share a time when you had to call another teacher, a friend, or a family member to assist you with something you did not know. Discuss how getting help from others can be a great resource to support you when trying to figure out something you are studying.

We

Have students think about times when they needed to ask someone to help them do something. Create a class list of their responses on chart paper, and analyze each one by how the buddy was a resource to support the student in need.

With You

Assign each student in your class an older student from a different classroom to be his or her resource buddy. Once each week, have students get together with their resource buddies to analyze unknown words. **Suggested Teacher Talk:** *Try to tell your "buddy" what you think the word means. Discuss it together.*

Working in pairs, have students confirm or modify their predictions through analysis of the words in a dictionary, a glossary, and/or a thesaurus. Allow students time to note the definitions (from the glossary or dictionary), synonyms, and antonyms on index cards or in Vocabulary Journals. Encourage students to use online dictionary and thesaurus resources, if desired. When applicable, encourage students to include a visual representation to enhance their understanding.

By You

Throughout the week, have students keep track of words from their reading for which they need assistance to understand the meaning. Have students write these unknown words in their Vocabulary Journals and include any information the buddy shares about the words. **Suggested Teacher Talk:** *How did your buddy help you understand the unknown word?*

Vocabulary Referencing

Extension

Create vocabulary word cards and definition cards, or use an online resource such as Quizlet™ (http://www.quizlet.com). Laminate, cut apart, and distribute one card, either a word or a definition, to each student. On your signal, have students walk around the room trying to find their match. When a match is found, have students line up and share their word's meaning with the group. Resource buddies can create a definition page for a class dictionary for content-area study. Optional: use online dictionary and thesaurus resources (e.g., http://www.dictionary.com or http://www.thesaurus.com).

Defining Moment

Purpose:	ELL Technique:
To explore the dictionary features to sum up the meaning of a word	Yes

Materials:

- *Defining Moment Feature Cards* (see definingmoment.pdf)
- *Four Corners Form* (fourcornersform.pdf)
- index cards
- dictionaries
- online dictionary resources
- text
- notebook paper or chart paper

Learning Phases

I

Model the process for Defining Moment, using a sample content word. Using a print or an online dictionary, locate the sample word, and read aloud each of the dictionary resource features noted on the *Defining Moment Feature Cards*.

Select four of the cards as focus areas to create a *Four Corners Form* (see the Visual Imaging strategy in this chapter) on notebook paper, chart paper, or an index card. Use a think-aloud to demonstrate how each feature provides the reader with a deeper understanding of the word.

We

Guide students in a reflective discussion on how the multiple features presented in a print and/or an online dictionary support readers in extending their understanding beyond a definition. Sample dictionary support features:

Guide Words—The first and last words defined on a page

Pronunciation—Separated by syllables, which syllable to stress

Parts of Speech—Usually abbreviated to denote the function of a word in a sentence

Definition—Meaning of word

Vocabulary Referencing

With You

Divide students into small groups and assign each group one of the focus content vocabulary words from a unit of study or a text. Then, have students collaborate and use the *Defining Moment Feature Cards* and locate their focus word, using a print or an online dictionary resource.

Instruct students to use the information on their assigned card(s) as a guide for sharing their word feature(s) with the group. Groups will need to determine four of the *Defining Moment Feature Cards* that would support understanding of the focus vocabulary to create their Four Corners model. Encourage students to be creative by using diagrams, models, or illustrations to share their focus vocabulary term.

By You

Encourage students to self-select their Defining Moment Feature vocabulary in any text they are reading.

Extension

Deepen students' word associations by having them each craft an acrostic poem using the letters from their word.

Glossary and Thesaurus Use

Purpose:	ELL Technique:
To utilize a glossary and/or a thesaurus to help identify the definitions of key words	Yes

Materials:	
• texts with glossaries	• dictionary
• thesaurus	• sticky notes

Vocabulary Referencing

Learning Phases

I

Select several words from a text to examine, using a glossary. Show students how to use a thesaurus to look up multiple words to represent the chosen word. Model how you can get a better understanding of what the word means by reviewing the choices from the thesaurus about the chosen word.

Select several words from an informational text you are currently reading in class, and demonstrate that informational texts often have glossaries of the terms used throughout the text. Remind students how words that appear in the glossary are often boldfaced or italicized in the text.

We

Have students look up a few selected words in the text's glossary to determine their definitions. As a class, discuss how students can see several words listed together in a thesaurus that all have similar usages in a sentence. Discuss how this also helps them determine meaning or give alternatives for word choice.

Display a sentence from a class text and put a sticky note over a chosen word you want students to reference. Have students predict other words they could substitute for the word that is covered up in the class text that would still make sense in the text. Invite them to use the generated list to infer the meaning of a particular word.

With You

Have students look for a word in the glossary. After reading the definition from the glossary, ask students to retell the definition to a partner and point out where that chosen word is in the text. **Suggested Teacher Talk:** *What feature helps you to know if a word will be in the glossary?*

Have students compare and contrast the thesaurus to a dictionary. Students can work with partners to examine and identify the various parts of a dictionary (e.g., guide words, parts of speech, definitions, etymologies).

By You

Ask students to look up the word in a thesaurus and compare the word they chose to the ones that are under that entry in the thesaurus. **Suggested Teacher Talk:** *How do you use a thesaurus?* Students can put a check mark by the words that are both on their sticky notes and in the thesaurus.

Differentiation

Use a range of grade-appropriate general-academic and domain-specific words at students' instructional and independent levels.

Extensions

- Have students create an illustrated glossary for visual support.

- Have students use an online thesaurus (e.g., http://www.merriam-webster.com) to highlight a chosen word and then search for some word choices that correspond with the original word. **Suggested Teacher Talk:** *What feature of the online program helps you understand the word better? How does it help you?*

Vocabulary Referencing

Start Your Engines

Purpose:	ELL Technique:
To navigate Web search engines for informational literacy	Yes

Materials:

- Internet access
- Vocabulary Journals
- variety of search engines

Learning Phases

I

Examine the use of keywords and phrases as a starting point that might lead to necessary topical information when conducting a search online.

Explain how online search engines deliver multiple results from technology and that the information might be found in any one of the results that come up after a key word or key phrase search. **Suggested Teacher Talk:** *How does the type of communication tool determine the degree of information received?*

We

Investigate the various types of search engines and their functions (e.g., page rank, statistic bar, dictionary definitions, search results). Below are a few recommended search engines for vocabulary development:

- **Google Wonder Wheel™:** A graphical representation of related search items (http://www.googleswonderwheel.com)

- **Visuwords™:** A site that creates a word map of connections and word families (http://www.visuwords.com)

- **Eyeplorer:** A colorful wheel that arranges topics by categories (http://www.vionto.com)

- **Shahi©:** A visual dictionary that combines Wiktionary content with Flickr images (http://www.blachan.com/shahi/)

With You

Have partners select keywords that are important to the topic they are searching. Invite them to investigate three search engines and try out the same topical search in each. As a class, discuss the process and results. **Suggested Teacher Talk:** *Describe which search engine provided the best response to your search and why. What keywords did you use to narrow your search?*

By You

Have students use search engines as they research information and record in their Vocabulary Journals the keyword or phrase that supported their connection to the necessary information.

Extension

Have students demonstrate their use of search engines by sharing how they found information from the search and incorporated that information into their independent-writing project (research, essay).

Word Power: Vocabulary Wrap-Up

Vocabulary is a key component of effective reading instruction. All other reading components, word study, fluency, and comprehension are affected by vocabulary knowledge (Flood et al. 1991; Stahl and Nagy 2006; Robb 1997). Vocabulary "is the glue that holds stories, ideas, and content together and that facilitates making comprehension accessible for children" (Rupley, Logan, and Nichols 1999, 5). Effective vocabulary instruction gives words the strength to transform oral communication or written print into powerful meaning-making machines. Oral conversation is key in the development of vocabulary and learning to make the transition from oral to written forms, whereas reading vocabulary is crucial to the comprehension processes of a skilled reader (Marzano and Simms 2013; NICHD 2000, 4–15).

The strategies, techniques, and Teacher Talk presented in this chapter support teachers in maximizing their readers' potential in becoming strategic readers. When teachers brush this stroke (techniques and Teacher Talk in vocabulary) across their canvases, they are adding another dimension to their masterpieces—strategic readers.

Vocabulary Referencing

#51185—Creating Strategic Readers 3rd Edition

Fluency

Pacing with Beam Reading Technique

Expressing with Express Yourself Technique

Fluency represents a level of expertise in combining appropriate phrasing and intonation while reading words automatically. Fluency is far more complex than attending to word-recognition skills. It is an essential component for reading and is embedded in the English Language Arts Standards of Reading (CCSS 2010) as part of the foundational skills, which are not an end to themselves. Fluency creates a reciprocal bridge between word study, vocabulary, and comprehension.

As one crosses back and forth on this fluency bridge, they will begin to see the river of meaning flow. Readers demonstrate proficiency through fluency strategies such as phrasing, rereading, pacing, and using prosodic features of language to bring meaning to the text. These fluency expectations can serve as outcome measures for reading proficiency as well as for acquisition of reading skills (Foster, Ardoin, and Binder 2013; Klauda and Guthrie 2008; NICHD 2000; Samuels and Farstrup 2006; Torgesen, Rashotte, and Alexander 2001). The ability to read efficiently brings self-assurance to a reader. Fluent readers are confident readers that apply the fluency strategies on their own while they become a habit of mind (Gaskins 2005). When readers are using all of their efforts to decode unknown words within the text, they begin to lose the meaning of what they are reading. Their confidence as readers diminishes with every moment that passes as they try to understand the intricate process that their brain is seeking to navigate. "Becoming a fluent reader has as much to do with constructing meaning as it has to do with attending to words on a page" (Forbes and Briggs 2003, 3).

This chapter features strategies students need to develop independence as readers. Having a repertoire of fluency tools readily available allows "the maximum amount of cognitive energy (to) be directed to the all-important task of making sense of the text" (Rasinski 2003, 26). Fluency strategies are essential to comprehension and serve as a proxy for reading proficiency (Fuchs et al., 2001; Pinnell et al., 1995; Rasinski 2006; Samuels and Farstrup 2006). The fluency strategies and their corresponding techniques detailed in this chapter are listed in Figure 4.1.

Figure 4.1 Fluency Strategies and Techniques in Chapter 4

Strategy	Corresponding Techniques in This Chapter	
Phrasing	Eye–Voice Span (page 184) Phrase Strips (page 185) Cluster Busters (page 186)	Pausing With Punctuation (page 188) Eye 2 Eye (page 189)
Assisted Reading	Shared Book Experience (page 193) Echo Reading (page 194)	Choral Readers (page 195) Read-Alongs (page 196)
Rereading	Listen to Me (page 199) One-Minute Repeated Reads (page 200)	Recorded Reading: Record/ Check/Chart/Repeat/Reflect (page 201)
Expressing	Express Yourself (page 205) Totally Tonality (page 206)	Interpretation/Character Analysis (page 207) Reader's Theatre (page 208)
Pacing	Beam Reading (page 213) Tempo Time (page 214)	Time/Record/Check/Chart (page 215) Sprints and Stamina (page 216)
Wide Reading	Book Baskets/Browsing Boxes (page 220) "Just Right" Books (page 221)	Book Clubs (page 222)
Accuracy	Use the strategies from Chapter 2 and 3: Word Study and Word Power	

To be effective when using the strategies and techniques presented in this chapter, teachers should allow ample time for teacher modeling and student application long before independent application is expected. Teachers should select and model reading appropriate text aloud to apply the techniques in a meaningful manner, which supports authentic learning for strategic reading. By using this process, students are able to see first the whole text (i.e., appropriate literature), then see the parts systematically (i.e., strategies and techniques), and finally, apply the parts back to the whole (i.e., become metacognitively aware of strategies while reading appropriate literature). Using quality text and promoting language development throughout the techniques will help to enhance students' development of the strategies. In addition, teachers can use the motivation and engagement feature within many techniques as an additional means (i.e., multiple intelligence standard) of motivating the whole child and creating 21st-century learners. Refer to Chapter 1 for a description of the whole child and Figure 1.1 for an illustration. This allows for differentiation within the technique as needed to educate the whole child.

Fluency Strategy: Phrasing

Phrasing is the ability to read several words together before pausing, as opposed to word-by-word reading. Strategic readers phrase words together to derive meaning rather than trying to use the meaning of each word independently. Reading word by word sounds choppy, and it can stifle the overall meaning of the passage the student is reading.

When a reader "chunks" the text into syntactically meaningful phrases (e.g., by grammar), the reading rate and comprehension improve. Cohesive chunking allows the reader to connect several words to make a meaningful phrase and promotes smooth-cadenced print processing (Gaffney and Morris 2011; Rasinski, Yildirim, and Nageldinger 2012). "Studying grammar fosters fluency because grammar alerts the reader to natural phrases in a sentence" (Blevins 2001, 18). The reader needs to have an understanding of noun phrases, verbal phrases, and prepositional phrases. This understanding of grammar will support readers as they appropriately chunk text (Blevins 2001; LeVasseur, Macaruso, and Shankweiler 2008; Miller and Schwanenflugel 2006).

The ability to connect important phrases into cohesive chunks is enhanced when the reader "learns that punctuation marks such as commas, semicolons, parentheses, and dashes signal the end of a phrase and require a pause in reading" (Strickland, Ganske, and Monroe 2002, 135). Strategic readers use this strategy of phrasing to make a conversational connection in their reading. The goal is to read phrases seamlessly, sounding as if the reader is holding a conversation. This permits the reading to flow, allowing the reader to concentrate on making sense of the reading.

Readers' perceptual spans dictate how much information they can take in from words in a single fixation of their eye movement (Drieghe et al., 2008; NICHD 2000; Paulson 2005). "There are well-known individual differences in eye-movement measures as a function of reading skill: Fast readers make shorter fixations, longer saccades (the jump of the eye from one fixation to another) and fewer regressions than slow readers" (Rayner 1998, 392). Readers need many opportunities to practice techniques that support their ability to make shorter fixations to strategically phrase appropriately. Appropriate text that best supports the application of the phrasing strategy has a variety of meaningful phrases throughout the text.

To support Phrasing while reading, a set of skills is required to effectively implement this reading strategy. The synchronized application of several reading strategies results in making meaning while reading a text. The skills, additional integrated reading strategies, and their reading components found in corresponding chapters are listed below.

Focus Skill(s):

- Parts to whole

- Concept of rint

- Syntactically meaningful phrases: (Grammar: noun, verbal, prepositional phrases)

Integrated Strategies:

- Blending and Segmenting Sounds; Analyzing Sounds (Chapter 2)

- Analyzing Words (Chapter 3)

- Expressing (Chapter 4)

Accountable Teacher Talk for Phrasing

Following is a list of suggested Teacher Talk that encourages readers to think strategically as they employ the Phrasing strategy. To effectively increase levels of thinking, these suggestions incorporate Bloom's Taxonomy's higher-order questioning (Anderson and Krathwohl 2001) and Webb's Depth of Knowledge (2002).

Remembering and Understanding (Recall)

- How does the punctuation help you when reading?

- Where are your eyes looking next? What words are you still holding in your mind but which are no longer presented for you to view?

Applying (Skill/Concept)

- What would happen if you paused after each word?

Analyzing (Strategic Thinking)

- Why does grouping the words together help you make sense out of what you are reading?

Evaluating and Creating (Extended Thinking)

- How does the number of fixations affect the reader's phrasing? Watch another reader's eyes and evaluate the flow for the number of fixations (jumps).

- Construct a sentence that demonstrates a seamless flow while reading. Explain how grouping the words helps to make sense out of what and/or why you are reading.

Behavior Indicators for Phrasing

As you assess students' ability to phrase, use the following behaviors as a guide. Do students exhibit these behaviors never, rarely, often, or always?

❏ Demonstrate the value of forward eye movements and fixations

❏ Use punctuation to support inflections

❏ Read seamlessly with a flow

Techniques for Phrasing

Eye-Voice Span

Purpose:	ELL Technique:
To recognize and demonstrate the value of forward eye movements when reading	No

Materials:

- text
- visual enhancer device (e.g., projector or interactive whiteboard)
- straw (*optional*)
- *Teacher Talk Phrase Strips 1* (see teachertalk1.pdf, *optional*)
- *Teacher Talk Phrase Strips 2* (see teachertalk2.pdf, *optional*)

Learning Phases

I

Demonstrate the difference between natural vision (i.e., seeing what is directly in front of us and what is within our peripheral vision), peripheral vision (i.e., seeing what lies outside the direct line of sight), and tunnel vision (i.e., seeing what is only within the direct line of sight), using a piece of text.

Hold up a piece of text and illustrate natural vision by pointing out what you can see as a whole on the page using your natural vision. Identify the peripheral vision by reading aloud and sharing in a think aloud what is going on with your eyes: "As I am reading aloud with my voice, my eyes are looking ahead, 'prereading' the next few words before I say them aloud."

Model proper phrasing and the left-to-right sweep demonstrated in the concept of Eye-Voice Span (Blevins, 2001). Select a passage to project for all to see.

We

With the class, begin to read aloud the text placed on an overhead transparency or a visual presenter where all students can see it. Just before you finish reading a sentence or a paragraph, turn off the projector or remove text from under the visual presenter. **Suggested Teacher Talk:** *Where were your eyes looking next? Did you push your eyes forward ahead of your voice and capture several words at a time with your eyes?*

Have students demonstrate how they can still say the next few words from the passage right after the text is removed. Discuss why this happens (e.g., students' eyes were ahead of their voices, reading ahead with your eyes).

With You

Have students work in A/B pairs (A = teacher role and B = student role). The A partner listens as the B partner begins to read from the text. Using the *Teacher Talk Phrase Strips*, partner A randomly places the strip over partner B's text and then flips the strip to model phrasing the Teacher Talk. Partner B responds to the Teacher Talk presented.

Have partners discuss the process and then reverse roles. **Suggested Teacher Talk:** *What words are you still holding in your mind but that are no longer presented for you to view?*

By You

Have students practice reading independently and trying to phrase chunks while thinking about the distance between their eye placement and their voice when reading.

Differentiation

- Use a variety of engaging genres at the independent or instructional level of students that will motivate and spark their interest while implementing the Eye-Voice Span technique.

- Use a straw to demonstrate tunnel vision by looking through the straw at one word or several letters at a time. Discuss the frustration of trying to gain meaning by only looking at one word at a time.

Phrase Strips

Purpose:	ELL Technique:
To read more words together seamlessly before pausing	Yes

Materials:

- texts
- *Phrase Strips Choices* (see phrasechoices.pdf)
- sentence strips
- pocket chart
- pipe cleaner
- transparency pens (*optional*)
- transparencies
- clay (*optional*)
- pencil or highlighter

Learning Phases

I

On sentence strips, list common phrases. Model reading them in a seamless flow without pausing between words, moving your body from left to right as you read. Place phrases in a pocket chart. Use the *Phrase Strips Choices* to get started.

We

Have students take turns selecting a strip and reading the phrase cued (e.g., *we like to*). Students may need to read the strip aloud several times before it can be read seamlessly. **Suggested Teacher Talk:** *What would happen if I paused after each word? Does the text make sense when I read just a word by itself? Why or why not?*

With You

With partners, students orally put the phrase into a complete sentence to bring meaning to the phrase (e.g., *On Saturday morning, we like to sleep late*).

Students record their sentences on a new sentence strip, highlighting the phrase within the newly formed sentence. **Suggested Teacher Talk:** *How did grouping the words together bring meaning to your sentences and sound more as if you are having a conversation?*

By You

Place the sentence strips in a literacy station or center. Have students reread the sentences and practice sounding seamless as they phrase the words together. They use words and phrases acquired through conversations, reading, and by having someone read to them.

Differentiation

- Use a variety of developmentally appropriate text and/or grade-level text to implement the Phase Strip technique. Emergent to Early-reader texts would have two to three word phrases, Transitional to Fluent-reader texts would have three to four word phrases.

- Use a variety of frequently occurring phrases to implement the Phrase Strip technique (e.g., conjunctions to simple relationships; adjectives and adverbs to describe; spatial and temporal relationship; precise actions, emotions, or states of being; signaling contrast, addition, or other logical relationships).

Cluster Busters

Purpose:	ELL Technique:
To recognize and demonstrate chunking text into syntactically meaningful phrases (e.g., noun, adjective, prepositional)	Yes

Materials:
• text • index cards • display options (chart paper, dry-erase boards, interactive whiteboard)

Learning Phases

I

Create a list of phrases (e.g., prepositional, verbal). Select one to read to the class, and model asking a question based on the phrase presented (e.g., = *on the field*; question = *Where did she sing?*).

Model taking the phrase and the response to the question and forming a complete thought (e.g., *Amy sang the national anthem on the field before the game*).

We

Share the list of phrases for all students to see. Ask a volunteer to be the "Class Cluster Buster." Have them select a phrase from the created list and generate a question as a springboard for the group to compose several related sentences that contain phrases that would answer *what*, *who*, *where*, *when*, *how*, and *why* questions.

From a stack of index cards, select a question card (*what*, *who*, *where*, *when*, *how*, *why*) and have students reflect back on the formulated sentences to find a phrase that would best answer the card. For example, if the card selected was *where*, then the phrase from the sentence above would be, *on the field*.

With You

Have partners analyze a section of text and underline the phrases. Each partner takes a turn selecting a question card from the stack and "busting" into the sentence to find a phrase that would support the particular question.

By You

Students practice reading and writing phrases during their independent literacy time, trying to read each of the phrases identified with a seamless flow.

Differentiation

- Use a variety of phrases (noun, adjective, prepositional) while implementing this technique.

- Record sentences and cut apart the sentence according to its phrases. With each part of the sentence, think of a question that aligns to the phrase (*what*, *who*, *where*, *when*, *how*, *why*). Students can also categorize the type of phrase (e.g., *noun*, *verb*, *prepositional*). For example, *My friend Amy went to the park and played ball.*

  My friend Amy = who

  went to the park = where

  played ball = what

Pausing with Punctuation

Purpose:	ELL Technique:
To demonstrate a command of punctuation to support appropriate pausing for meaning	Yes

Materials:

- texts
- display options (chart paper, overhead projector, sentence strips, interactive whiteboard)

Learning Phases

I

Select several sentences from a passage to model how to read using punctuation. Demonstrate through oral reading how punctuation may cause pausing in different parts of the text, which in turn can alter the meaning of the text.

Show a sentence for all students to see and that doesn't contain punctuation, to demonstrate not pausing. Example: *The man, saw the boy, with the binoculars. The man saw the boy with the binoculars.*

We

Ask a volunteer to read aloud these sentences without pausing. Have them try to determine and mark where punctuation should go, to encourage pausing. **Suggested Teacher Talk:** *Listen to someone read these two sentences. Which sounded better to you and why?*

Have students revisit the text read, pausing and marking where the proper punctuation should go to make the text more clear and easier to read.

With You

Have pairs practice reading sentences that do not have punctuation and determine where they think the punctuation should go based on their interpretation of the correct meaning of the text.

Have students return to the text and compare their versions to the original text with the proper punctuation marks. **Suggested Teacher Talk:** *Did your punctuation choices alter the meaning of the original text? Why or why not?*

By You

During independent reading time, have students notice punctuation marks and practice reading the text accordingly. **Suggested Teacher Talk:** *How does the punctuation help to bring meaning to what is being read?*

Differentiation

- Use a variety of punctuation to demonstrate a command of conventions (e.g., period, question mark, exclamation point, commas, quotation marks) to implement this technique.

- Have students create sentences or use the following sentences to demonstrate through oral reading how punctuation may cause pausing in different parts of the text, which in turn can alter the meaning of the text.

    I know a friend with a cat that has fleas.

    The boy fed Jack the big fat cat.

- Create an organization chart to demonstrate the use of punctuation. Ask students to search for examples in a text of the use of the highlighted punctuation. In one column, have them record highlighted punctuation. In the second column, record the example of how the punctuation was used in the text. In the final column, students can create their own sentences to represent the highlighted punctuation.

Eye 2 Eye

Purpose:		ELL Technique:
To identify eye movements when reading		No

Materials:	
• texts	• copy of the passage
• clipboards with sheets for tally marks	• colored markers
• pencil	• Vocabulary Journals

Learning Phases

  Discuss how commentators, newscasters, and reporters read their lines from a teleprompter. However, their goal is to make the audience believe they are just seamlessly talking to us, not reading. They are trying to have their eyes flow with the words on the teleprompter without too many stops (fixations) on the words, which would then make it sound as if they are reading.

We Invite students to view you reading and notice your eye movements. Demonstrate rereading to see if they can identify the moment when you begin to reread or when you get to the end of the line and need to do the return sweep.

Discuss their observations. **Suggested Teacher Talk:** *What do you do with your eyes when you read?*

With You

Ask students to each sit knee to knee with a partner. Have the first student read aloud 100 words from a passage while the partner observes the reader's eye movements. **Suggested Teacher Talk:** *Try to capture several words at a time with your eyes.* The observer should record a tally mark for each time the reader's eye "jumps." Or he or she may record a slash mark on the copied passage. Have the readers reread two more times, trying to phrase more words together (do fewer jumps with the eye). The observers should record eye movements all three times. If working from the copied text, have students use a different color pen each time. Have the partners switch roles and repeat the activity.

By You

During independent reading, have students be aware of their eye movement and record their thoughts in their Vocabulary Journals.

Extension

Video a reader's eyes. Have students view, observing for fixations, saccades (jump of the eye from one fixation to another), and regressions.

Fluency Strategy: Assisted Reading

Assisted Reading is a strategy used to provide the reader with support while building fluency. By listening to good models of fluent reading, students learn how a reader's voice can help text make sense (Kuhn and Stahl 2003; Wilson 2012). Many of the techniques used for assisted reading allow the teacher or modeler the opportunity to scaffold students' learning while they are gaining confidence as readers. Peers, parents, and teachers all can provide guidance and feedback on how fluent readers read and how they become aware of and correct their mistakes (Foorman and Mehta 2002; Shanahan 2002; Samuels and Farstrup 2006).

Scaffolding while the student is performing is critical to the development of fluency (Rasinski 1989, 2006). This "social reading"—engaging in conversations about the text being read—benefits the reader because he or she knows there is support when needed and has the ability to deepen meaning about the text he or she is reading. "Classroom practices that encourage repeated oral reading with feedback and guidance lead to meaningful improvements in reading expertise for students—for good readers, as well as those who are experiencing difficulties" (NICHD 2000, 3–3). Appropriate text that best supports the application of the assisted reading strategy has repetitive patterns, interesting characters, and dialogue.

To support Assisted Reading, a set of skills is required to effectively implement this reading strategy. The synchronized application of several reading strategies results in making meaning while reading a text. The skills, additional integrated reading strategies, and their reading components found in corresponding chapters are listed below.

Focus Skill(s):

- Listen attentively
- Concepts of print

Integrated Strategies:

- Synthesizing Sounds; Recognizing (Chapter 2)
- Wide Reading; Personalizing (Chapter 3)
- Activating and Building Schemas (Chapter 5)

Accountable Teacher Talk for Assisted Reading

Following is a list of suggested Teacher Talk that encourages readers to think strategically as they employ the Assisted Reading strategy. To effectively increase levels of thinking, these suggestions incorporate Bloom's Taxonomy's higher-order questioning (Anderson and Krathwohl 2001) and Webb's Depth of Knowledge (2002).

Remembering and Understanding (Recall)

- Read the text the same way you heard it.

- How does imitating what I read build your confidence as a reader?

Applying (Skill/Concept)

- Listen to the modeled reading. Demonstrate how understanding of the text is supported by the expression and pace used.

Analyzing (Strategic Thinking)

- Explain how hearing my voice reading assists you to read better.

Evaluating and Creating (Extended Thinking)

- After listening to the modeled reading, critique the necessary changes to your reading to sound more as if you were having a conversation.

- Design a fluency rubric based on the modeled reading features and assess your reading, making adjustments as needed.

Behavior Indicators for Assisted Reading

As you assess students' ability to read with assisstance, use the following behaviors as a guide. Do students exhibit these behaviors never, rarely, often, or always?

❏ Listen and observe modeled reading

❏ Engage in reflective conversations about their reading, and receive feedback

❏ Imitate modeled reading and self-monitoring

Techniques for Assisted Reading

Shared Book Experience

Purpose:	ELL Technique:
To listen and observe reading and build fluency confidence while confirming understanding of a text read aloud or information presented	Yes

Materials:

- text
- display options (chart paper, dry-erase boards, interactive whiteboard)
- pointer (*optional*)
- Vocabulary Journals (*optional*)
- writing paper

Learning Phases

I

Select an appropriate text that includes a focused area of learning (text feature, concept, strategy). Use a variety of engaging genres at the independent or instructional level of students that will motivate and spark their interest as they implement this technique. Display the text so that all students can easily view it, perhaps using a big book. Read aloud the text, highlighting the text itself and modeling the characteristics of a fluent strategic reader (i.e., pacing, expressing) during a *Shared Book Experience* (Allington 2001; Holdaway 1979). Over several readings, revisit the text to assist deeper comprehension.

We

Have students share the reading experience orally as they follow along with the rereading of the text. After the reading, engage students in a discussion of the text, allowing them to question and respond to, and at times retell, what they are reading. **Suggested Teacher Talk:** *Reread this part, using the pointer to guide your way. Respond in your journal to the book we just read.*

With You

Have groups select a "Recorder" to record stories that the team members dictate. Have him or her pause to clarify and reread the recorded transcription. **Suggested Teacher Talk:** *Try to remember what you said in the story and match your words to the print.* Students reread their words, maintaining ownership of the text and reflecting on what they are reading.

By You

Place these scripts at literacy stations or centers for further readings to increase fluency. **Suggested Teacher Talk:** *In what way is it easier for you to read a story that you have already heard or read aloud?*

Differentiation

Instruct using a variety of strategy lessons from the chapters of Word Study (Chapter 2), Vocabulary (Chapter 3), Fluency (Chapter 4), and Comprehension (Chapter 5).

Fluency Assisted Reading

Echo Reading

Purpose:	ELL Technique:
To gain confidence by listening to and imitating a strategic reader	Yes

Materials:
• texts   • audio recorder

Learning Phases

I
Explain to students that when you hear an echo, it is a repeat of an original sound. Say a sentence aloud with expression, and ask a student to repeat the sentence exactly the way you sounded. Discuss how we can imitate a reader and improve on our own reading ability by listening intently to the modeled version.

We
Ask a fluent reader to model a sentence or a paragraph, using all the strategies of a strategic reader. The other student rereads the modeled segment, striving to repeat exactly how the fluent reader modeled the reading. Gradually increase the speed and length of what is to be echoed. **Suggested Teacher Talk:** *How does imitating another reader make you feel more confident as a reader?*

With You
Pair students as reading partners. An option is to pair students so that one partner is a slightly stronger reader than the other partner. Have them take turns reading aloud to each other, and give instructional support as needed. **Suggested Teacher Talk:** *How might you use the same expression and pace as you extend the story, section, or chapter? What do you notice as you listen to the passage read aloud and/or preview the text?*

By You
Record a "modeled reading," leaving a pause after sentences or short paragraphs. This pause allows the student to "echo" the voice on the recording. Using the recordings gives the student privacy while they continue to gain the confidence and fluency needed to sound more like strategic readers. Use a variety of engaging genres that will motivate and spark interest with students.

Differentiation

If a student is struggling to echo while following the print because of lack of print concepts or visual distractions, remove the printed version. Have the student listen only and echo the modeling reader without the print. Use the print when the echo pattern is established.

Choral Readers

Purpose:	ELL Technique:
To monitor and practice oral reading in a risk-free setting	Yes

Materials:

- text
- three-ring binders
- songs, poems, charts, or excerpts from text

Fluency Assisted Reading

Learning Phases

I — Have students listen as you model the selection, using all of the strategies of a strategic reader. Give students a three-ring binder to use as their choral-reader notebooks. At the beginning of each week, insert a text selection into the choral-reader notebooks. These selections may be songs, poems, chants, or excerpts from texts that correspond with the topic or theme you are studying. You also can use these entries in the choral readers as the springboard for mini lessons from all five areas of reading described in this book.

We — After modeling the reading, echo-read the selection with students. Have students reread the modeled segment, attempting to repeat the reading exactly as it was modeled. Choral reading should follow as students gain confidence with the selection. **Suggested Teacher Talk:** *How was it helpful to have me beside you when you were reading?*

With You — Guide students in reading the selection together. Students should read aloud at the pace of the modeler, using all the appropriate expressions to bring the selection to life. Encourage students to rehearse the passages aloud, striving for seamless, fluent reading.

By You — Have students reread the previous selections together before beginning their assisted reading with the new selection. **Suggested Teacher Talk:** *How does rereading in your choral-reader notebook help you?* These choral-reader notebooks may periodically be sent home for students to show their fluent reading skills to family members.

Differentiation

- Use engaging genres at a variety of instructional and independent levels that will motivate and spark interest with students as they implement the choral-reading techniques.

- Have groups of students perform a choral reading of one of their favorite selections to an audience. Students can use a variety of ways to bring the text to life (e.g., clapping words while reading, whispering the rhyme, dramatic role play).

Read-Alongs

Fluency Assisted Reading

Purpose:	ELL Technique:
To gain confidence by listening to modeled reading and by reading along	Yes

Materials:

- texts
- audio books
- tape/MP3 player/CD player

Learning Phases

I

Make your own prerecorded book tapes, or purchase audio books according to the readers' level.

We

Have students listen to and follow along with MP3 players or computer-generated recordings. **Suggested Teacher Talk:** *How does reading along with the tape/MP3 player/CD player help you?*

With You

Ask a student to sit slightly in front of you or partner with a more-fluent reader, and begin a *Neurological Impress* (Heckelman 1969) by reading aloud a passage of text with the student. You should read a little louder and slightly ahead of the student to reinforce the natural flow of reading. **Suggested Teacher Talk:** *How does hearing my voice help you read better?* Track the words by smoothly running your forefinger under the words while reading.

Reread the passage several times together before going on to new sections of the text. As the student gains confidence, lower your voice and have the student take the lead as the reader. Gradually release the responsibility of tracking and reading to the student. Continue to speed up, challenging the student to keep the pace.

By You

Encourage students to note one-to-one correspondences between spoken words on the tape and the printed text. Students can practice this technique at a learning center or at home. **Suggested Teacher Talk:** *Try to find one-to-one correspondences with oral words and written words.*

Differentiation

Use engaging genres at a variety of instructional or independent levels that will motivate and spark interest with students to implement this technique.

Extension

After the reading, ask the partners to retell the text and discuss meaning or answer comprehension questions to demonstrate meaning.

Fluency Strategy: Rereading

Rereading is a strategy used to develop rapid, fluent oral reading. This strategy is one of the most frequently recognized approaches to improving fluency (NICHD 2000; Rashotte and Torgesen 1985). When students repeat their reading, their amount of word recognition errors decreases, their reading speed increases, and their oral-reading expression improves, potentially influencing higher-level comprehension (Samuels 2002; O'Connor, White, and Swanson 2007; Vadasy and Sanders 2008; Foster, Ardoin, and Binder 2013). An extensive opportunity for practice in pattern recognition is readily available through rereading text passages. When students acquire the rhythm within a predictable pattern book, they benefit from their desire to reread the text.

> *Just as a traveler going down a winding road for the second or third time begins to notice specific houses along the way, children on their second and third trip through a text will begin to focus on specific words—committing them to memory* (Morris 1992, 123).

Musicians, athletes, and actors also use this practice strategy to gain fluency; they rehearse the same aspect of their performance repeatedly until they gain independence and confidence. When students get an opportunity to rehearse their reading, they are able to gain confidence through repetition to ultimately provide a fluent read on a particular text. This type of commitment by students to improve the quality of their reading is vital.

To support Rereading, a set of skills is required to effectively implement this reading strategy. The synchronized application of several reading strategies results in making meaning while reading a text. The skills, additional integrated reading strategies, and their reading components found in corresponding chapters are listed below.

Focus Skill(s):

- Concepts of print

Integrated Strategies:

- Synthesizing Sounds; Recognizing (Chapter 2)
- Personalizing (Chapter 3)
- Questioning; Visualizing and Sensory Imaging; Inferring and Drawing Conclusions; Determining Importance; Summarizing; Synthesizing (Chapter 5)

Accountable Teacher Talk for Rereading

Following is a list of suggested Teacher Talk that encourages readers to think strategically as they employ the Rereading strategy. To effectively increase levels of thinking, these suggestions incorporate Bloom's Taxonomy's higher-order questioning (Anderson and Krathwohl 2001) and Webb's Depth of Knowledge (2002).

Remembering and Understanding (Recall)

- How does rereading help you make sense of the text?
- How does knowing the pattern of a text help you reread?

Applying (Skill/Concept)

- When you reread the text, try to add expression and pick up your pace just a little.

Analyzing (Strategic Thinking)

- Compare your first reading with your second or third reading. How did rereading the text affect your reading?

Evaluating and Creating (Extended Thinking)

- Examine the miscue that caused you to reread the sentence or passage for clarification.
- Create a criteria rubric for those who will listen as you reread the text. After receiving the responses from those who heard you reread the text, what changes would you make to continue to increase reading speed, read expressively, and bring meaning to what you have read?

Behavior Indicators for Rereading

As you assess students' ability to reread, use the following behaviors as a guide. Do students exhibit these behaviors never, rarely, often, or always?

❑ Analyze repetitive features

❑ Interact as a listener and a reader to gain confidence

❑ Self-assess and evaluate one's own reading

Techniques for Rereading

Listen to Me

Purpose:	ELL Technique:
To interact as a listener and a reader, and to give and receive feedback	Yes

Materials:

- texts
- *Reading Bookmark* (see readingbookmark.pdf)
- *Listen to Me Form* (see listentomeform.pdf)

- chart paper
- browsing boxes (*optional*)

Fluency
Rereading

Learning Phases

I

Model how you can apply the *Reading Bookmark* as you read to keep you focused on the reading skills before, during, and after reading. Focus on Rereading as a strategy.

We

Have students reflect and record on a class chart reasons why rereading is important (e.g., helps readers make sense of what is being read, helps readers better understand meaning, helps readers notice words that were skipped before, helps readers understand difficult words in context, helps readers read faster). **Suggested Teacher Talk:** *Why do readers sometimes need to go back and reread?*

Add *rereading* to a class chart of strategies readers use, and have students place their initials or tally marks by their name on the chart each time they apply the strategy.

With You

Have students practice reading aloud to several listening buddies in the classroom. These listening buddies can practice their active-listening strategies by leaning in toward the reader, keeping their eyes on the reader, and waiting until the reader is finished before speaking.

Students can use the *Reading Bookmark* as a reminder of the steps students can follow before, during, and after reading. Have students use the *Listen to Me Form* to score and give feedback on the reader's oral reading. **Suggested Teacher Talk:** *How was your reading, according to the* Listen to Me Form?

Have students select books at their independent level to read aloud to others. They also may use books made in class. After a student has had several practice reads with a book, send the book home with the student to read to three others.

Attach a *Listen to Me Form* to the book. The other listeners should sign the form and provide positive feedback on the student's reading. **Suggested Teacher Talk:** *What happens each time you read the text again?*

Extensions

- Use a variety of engaging genres at the independent or instructional level of students that will motivate and spark their interest while implementing the Listen to Me technique.

- Place the books being used in the student's independent reading basket or browsing box (see the Browsing Box technique found in this chapter) for him or her to return to during independent reading time.

One-Minute Repeated Reads

Purpose:	ELL Technique:
To increase the number of words per minute read with accuracy by successive readings	No

Materials:	
• texts	• stopwatch
• *Fluency Rubric* (see fluencyrubric. pdf)	• data-tracking paper
	• One-Minute Reader App (*optional*)

Learning Phases

I

Select a short, meaningful, and appropriate leveled passage for rereading. Discuss setting independent reading goals (see pacing strategy in this chapter for formula and graphs) for *One-Minute Reads* (Samuels 1979; Samuels and Farstrup 2006).

We

Select a passage to post where all students can see. Share with students that together you will examine the *Fluency Rubric*. Select four students at a time to model a reading feature and the particular descriptor that aligns with the 1–4 rubric scale.

Continue modeling each reading feature on the rubric, selecting different volunteers to model each behavior indicator for each numeric scale.

Discuss individually with each student a baseline for the number of words they should try to read per minute and establish goals. Have students read aloud a text that is slightly above their independent reading level.

Using a stopwatch, time students' reading for one minute and keep data on errors. After reading, discuss reading strategies for problem-solving the incorrect words.

Have the student reread the same passage while you time the reading with a stopwatch and record any errors again. Continue this process at least three times.

Record results each time, followed by a discussion of the results. **Suggested Teacher Talk:** *Compare your first reading with your second and third rereading.*

Students analyze the recording results and self-assess their reading, using the *Fluency Rubric* based on their reading and the data results from their reading.

Differentiation

- Use a variety of engaging genres at the independent or instructional level of students that will motivate and spark their interest while implementing this technique.

- To motivate and engage students via technology, download the One Minute Reader app by Read Naturally, Inc. to calculate students' pace while reading. It also has the ability to check for understanding of what is read with a comprehension quiz.

Recorded Reading: Record/Check/Chart/ Repeat/Reflect

Purpose:	ELL Technique:
To self-assess using a visible marking process, and to chart progress on successive readings	No

Materials:

- texts
- photocopy of text
- three different color pens
- video recorder (*optional*)

- audio recorder
- stopwatch
- reflective journals

Learning Phases

I

Select a short, meaningful, and appropriate leveled passage for rereading. Discuss the value of analyzing and assessing the process of successive readings and how to self-assess.

We

Have a volunteer read aloud a passage while you model the Record/Check/Chart/Repeat/Reflect procedure (Allington 2001):

Record: Have students record their own readings and replay the recording to check for errors.

Check: As students listen to their first readings, ask them to mark any misreads they hear on a photocopy of the text.

Chart: Ask students to read the text aloud for a second time into the recorder. Have them listen to the second recording, and, with a different color pen, have them mark the same photocopy of the text to show any mispronunciations of words read the second time. *What happens each time you read the text again?*

Repeat: Have students record a third reading into the audio recorder and mark a third round of misreads on the same photocopy of the text, with a third color.

Reflect: Have students tally the different color pens' markings. Generally, with each reading, the errors will decrease. **Suggested Teacher Talk:** *Compare your first reading with your second and/ or third reading. What do you notice?*

With You

Repeat the Record/Check/Chart/Repeat/Reflect procedures above with student partners who are paired based on academic abilities. Partners will monitor each other through the procedural steps.

By You

Students independently proceed through the Record/Check/Chart/Repeat/Reflect procedures.

Differentiation

- Use a variety of engaging genres at the independent or instructional level of students that will motivate and spark their interest as they implement this technique.

- Record a video or create a slideshow of a student reading aloud a selection from the text. Have the student watch the recording and reflect on the reading, using the Record/Check/Chart/Repeat/Reflect procedures.

Fluency
Rereading

Fluency Strategy: Expressing

Teachers need to incorporate reading with expression into the beginning stages of reading instruction. Thus, students will learn that through expressive reading that text comes to life and has meaning and purpose. Without expression, students' readings will be monotone, laborious, and incomprehensible. "Many times concepts appear in ambiguous, confusing language that students can read but do not understand" (Kinniburgh and Shaw 2007, 16). Applying the expressing strategy through techniques like Readers Theater enhances students' understanding that reading is a meaning-making process even in content-area reading. Speeches, poetry, journal entries, song lyrics, and scripts are all examples of texts that support the student to apply prosodic functions (Rasinski and Lenhart 2007).

When students concentrate on prosodic functions and forms when reading, they can indicate syntax and attitudes and can add appropriate stresses, pitch, and tone where needed to give a conversational sound to their reading. This allows the reader to convey the text's mood and meaning (Benjamin and Schwanenflugel, 2010). It is also important that students know the difference between just reading loudly when expressing themselves and reading with warm but firm voices (Dowhower 1994). Appropriate text that best supports the application of the Expressing strategy has a variety of words and phrases that allow for students to use their voices to bring the text to life.

To support Expressing while reading, a set of skills is required to effectively implement this reading strategy. The synchronized application of several reading strategies results in making meaning while reading a text. The skills, additional integrated reading strategies, and their reading components found in corresponding chapters are listed below.

Focus Skill(s):

- Prosody (pitch, tone, stress)
- Moods and emotions
- Syntax

Integrated Strategies:

- Contextualizing (Chapter 2), Analyzing Words; Personalizing (Chapter 3)
- Questioning; Inferring and Drawing Conclusions; Determining Importance (Chapter 5)

Accountable Teacher Talk for Expressing

Following is a list of suggested Teacher Talk that encourages readers to think strategically as they employ the Expressing strategy. To effectively increase levels of thinking, these suggestions incorporate Bloom's Taxonomy's higher-order questioning (Anderson and Krathwohl 2001) and Webb's Depth of Knowledge (2002).

Remembering and Understanding (Recall)

- What does a period (or other mark of punctuation) mean?
- What message can the volume of your voice send to the audience?

Applying (Skill/Concept)

- What feeling do you think the author wanted the character to have in this part? How do you know what the author wanted?

Analyzing (Strategic Thinking)

- Did you use the proper tone to convey the meaning? Why, or why not?

Evaluating and Creating (Extended Thinking)

- Examine the various tones characters can use, and determine which one to use for the specific character in text. How did the tone of your voice set the mood for your statement?
- How would the character say that line? Create a story line for the character that would make sense. Make your reading sound as if the characters are having a conversation.

Behavior Indicators for Expressing

As you assess students' ability to use expression, use the following behaviors as a guide. Do students exhibit these behaviors never, rarely, often, or always?

❑ Identify prosodic functions

❑ Demonstrate how text "comes to life" with voice and body language

❑ Convey the text's mood and meaning

Techniques for Expressing

Express Yourself

Purpose:	ELL Technique:
To demonstrate voice and body language as a form of expression to bring "life to reading"	No

Materials:

- *Express Yourself Emotion Cards* (see expressyourself.pdf)
- microphone (*optional*)
- note cards

Fluency Expressing

Learning Phases

I

Use note cards to create emotion cards, or cut out the cards from the *Express Yourself Emotion Cards*. Emotion cards should include an emotion that students will be asked to use as they read (e.g., surprise, sadness, wistfulness, anger). Create statement cards by selecting several simple statements (e.g., *Don't do that*) and write each of them on a card.

Select one emotion card and one statement card without revealing them to students. Model saying the statement while conveying the emotion on the card. Reveal the emotion to students.

We

Ask a student to select an emotion card and a statement card without revealing it to the class. If desired, the student may use a handheld microphone while performing. Act as a talk show host by saying, "Class, it is time to..." with the class responding, "Express Yourself!"

Have the selected student read the statement with the specified dramatic expression. For example, if the student draws an emotion card that says *surprise* and a statement card that says, *Don't do that*, the student would say to the audience, *Don't do that!* in a very surprised voice. **Suggested Teacher Talk:** *What expression do you think the reader was trying to share in his or her dramatic expression statement?* Have the audience respond with what kind of expression they think the student performed and ask the student to reveal the correct emotion.

With You

Place students in pairs based on their academic abilities. Supply partners with a set of emotion cards and statement cards. Have one partner select an emotion card and a statement card to read with expression. The other partner will listen and determine the emotion being expressed. Partners will reverse roles and repeat these steps.

By You

Place emotion cards, statement cards, and a microphone (if desired) in a reading center. Students may select a statement card and an emotion card and read the statement with the specified dramatic expression.

Differentiation

- Model sentences from a read-aloud, and have students show with their face what the character is feeling.

- Ask students to share with partners how they might use the expression sentence in the proper order and in a context that would make sense to them (e.g., *Oh, no! Don't do that! You might get hurt*).

Totally Tonality

Fluency Expressing

Purpose:	ELL Technique:
To adjust tone of voice appropriately to convey the text's mood and meaning	No

Materials:	
- texts	- note cards
- chart	- *Express Yourself Emotion Cards* (see expressyourself.pdf)
- highlighting tape (*optional*)	

Learning Phases

I

On a chart, write some words describing a variety of tones that readers can use to express an author's purpose (e.g., to persuade, entertain, or inform) or use the *Express Yourself Emotion Cards*. Point out that the tone of voice that a reader uses reflects the emotion the character is feeling and the mood of the text.

Select a sentence from a familiar text and a tone from the chart to convey as you read the sentence aloud. By supplying text evidence, orally justify whether the tone used matches the context of the text. Discuss how tones of voice can completely change the meaning of a text. For example, if a character says, "You are so funny" in a sarcastic tone, then he or she means someone is not funny.

We

On note cards, write some phrases from a familiar text that students can read and different tones of voice they can use. Separate the two types of cards, and ask a student to select a tone card and a phrase card to read aloud with the selected tone. Ask the class to verify if the tone used matches the context of the text. **Suggested Teacher Talk:** *Did you use the proper tone to convey the meaning? Why or why not?*

With You

Select 8 to 10 quotes from the text, and either write the sentences on note cards or locate them in the text and mark with highlighting tape. Distribute the text selections or the note cards to volunteers, and have them form a circle facing outward. Distribute tone cards with a variety of expressions, and have these volunteers find one person in the circle to stand opposite, so two circles are facing each other.

Ask the outside (tone) group to demonstrate their card with facial or body expressions only. The inside partner then decides the tone being demonstrated and begins to read the quoted sentence in the tone given. After the sentence is read with the outside partner's tone, the partners then reread the sentence in the context of the text and decide whether they used the proper tone to convey the meaning or if they change the meaning completely with the tone presented.

The partners exchange roles and cards. Instruct inside and outside circles to make a quarter right turn and tell them how many times to rotate to face a new partner and share tones and sentences. Continue the process for several rotations.

By You

After practicing reading with phrases, have students read sections from texts while using a chosen tone. **Suggested Teacher Talk:** *How did the tone of your voice set the mood for your statement?*

Fluency Expressing

Differentiation

Place a set of tone cards in a reading center. Students may select a sentence from a familiar text, select a tone card, and read the sentence conveying the chosen emotion. They will determine if the tone matches the context of the text.

Interpretation/Character Analysis

Purpose:	ELL Technique:
To interpret and portray the traits of character(s) in text	No

Materials:	
• texts	• numbered chips
• *Emotion Mat* (see emotionmat.pdf)	• microphone (*optional*)

Learning Phases

I   Select a text and analyze a dialogue between some of the characters. Explain your interpretations of the characters based on the dialogue and the importance of securing a correct analysis of the characters in context. This helps to keep meaning from being misconstrued.

We

Reread a section of dialogue from a text, asking for volunteers to form their own interpretations of how they should portray the characters' voices. Have a student perform the part of one of the characters, reading aloud with expression.

With You

Discuss with students any new insights they gain from analyzing the characters' voices after the performance. Copy and distribute the *Emotion Mat* and numbered chips, and then read aloud a selected text.

Have students listen and interpret the emotions of a chosen character by placing a numbered chip on the matching emotion while listening to the read-aloud. After the read-aloud, have partners share their retell or interpretation of the character(s) as they pick up the numbered chips in order.

By You

Ask students to think about the character(s) in the text they are reading and record a character analysis about each one. **Suggested Teacher Talk:** *What feeling do you think the author wanted the character to have in this part? How do you know what the author wanted?*

Fluency Expressing

Extension

Have students select a text with a specific character they would like to interpret. Allow students to practice and perform on a "live" syndicated radio talk show called "Radio Reading" (Stayter and Allington 1991). Have each student who will be the "radio reader on the air" prepare open-ended questions or provocative statements about their particular character. When the radio show is ready to "air," hold up a red sign to signal the beginning of the show. The radio reader reads the selection into a karaoke microphone, expressively and meaningfully, to capture the listening audience. After the performance, have the radio reader invite the listening audience into a discussion about the character, using the questions and statements generated previously to demonstrate if they derived meaning from the reading. **Suggested Teacher Talk:** *What message can the volume of your voice send to the audience?*

Reader's Theater

Purpose:		ELL Technique:
To explore language use through oral reading of scripts		Yes
Materials:		

- texts
- scripts
- microphone (*optional*)
- online resource (*optional*)

Learning Phases

I

Provide a dialogue-rich script of a story derived from text that may be prepared, selected right from a story, student generated, or one you created with dialogue. Students need to have a clear understanding of the types of adjustments made to change the text into a play.

Model and discuss with students the understanding of the text and the importance of the use of language. **Suggested Teacher Talk:** *How would the character say that line? Change your voice to sound like the character you are portraying. Try to make your reading sound as real as it can be.*

We

Assign characters to students. Give the option for students to read the original text and then the newly scripted version to help them compare and contrast the dramatization that they will need to perform the reader's theater (Ellery and Rosenboom 2010; Hoyt 1992; Sloyer 1982). Encourage reading with expression.

Remind them that they do not have to memorize their parts prior to the performance. They will be holding the script and reading directly from the text. It is the student's responsibility to bring the character to life with prosodic features.

With You

Invite groups of students to perform a dramatized presentation, *expressively* reading their parts in front of a live audience. Follow the performance, giving feedback on how students portrayed the characters with their expressions. **Suggested Teacher Talk:** *Did you use the proper tone to convey the meaning? Why or why not? How did the tone of your voice set the mood for your statement?*

By You

Invite students to adapt a piece of literature into a script for reader's theater. It may include characters, a narrator, scenes, and props needed.

Fluency Expressing

Extension

Use a variety of scripts to meet the needs of students. There are numerous websites with scripts available to download, such as Building Fluency through Reader's Theater (http://www.teachercreatedmaterials.com/reading/readersTheater) and readers-theater.com (http://www.readers-theater.com). These selections should contain interesting characters, appealing themes, and stimulating plots that enhance language.

Fluency Strategy: Pacing

Pacing is a strategy that develops through extensive exposure to reading. This strategy encompasses reading rate, which is the speed at which one reads, as well as reading flow and flexibility with the text to alter the pace as needed to comprehend. Figure 4.2 demonstrates the reading rate formula and correlates the rate to grade levels. The simple fact that slow reading requires readers to invest considerably greater amounts of time in reading tasks than classmates who are reading at a rate appropriate for their grade level should be a major cause for concern for all teachers (O'Connor et al., 2007; Rasinski 2000; Vadasy and Sanders 2008). However, reading too fast does not always constitute proficient strategic reading.

Figure 4.2 Oral Reading Fluency Target Norms for Words Read Correctly Per Minute (WCPM)

Grade	Percentile	Fall WCPM	Winter WCPM	Spring WCPM
1	90	0	60	103
	50	0	21	52
	10	0	7	20
2	90	95	125	140
	50	49	76	94
	10	15	30	49
3	90	125	151	168
	50	73	96	110
	10	30	50	57
4	90	142	167	180
	50	94	114	124
	10	48	66	75
5	90	169	184	189
	50	117	131	137
	10	65	78	88

(Adapted from Beaver and Carter 2006; Hasbrouck and Tindal 2006)

Note: To figure rate formula: words per minute = # of words in passage divided by reading time (in seconds) × 60 seconds.

In trying to increase fluency, educators need to be cautious not to create word callers, who have increased in speed but fail in developing meaning. Pacing permits a reader to be flexible when interacting with the text; the proficient reader is capable of slowing down and speeding up when necessary to construct meaning. Depending on the tasks, readers may need to adjust their reading and focus on the flow of their reading to bring meaning to the text. "Show me a thoughtful reader who adjusts his pace according to prior knowledge and text structure, and I'll show you a real reader" (Marcell 2010, 1).

Appropriate text that best supports the application of the pacing strategy needs to be at the student's independent or instructional reading level. Leveling percentage can vary. A student's independent reading level is the level at which he or she has an accuracy rate of 96 percent or better at word recognition; it is considered the "level at which a student can read a text without the teacher's assistance" (Blevins 2001, 23). The instructional level is the level at which a student should be able to read the text with some assistance. (See figure 4.3 for a formula to figure out students' accuracy rates.)

Figure 4.3 Reading Levels and Accuracy Formula

Level	Accuracy Rate
Independent	96–100% (able to read without assistance)
Instructional	90–95% (able to read with some assistance)
Frustration	89% and below (unable to read even with assistance)

Note: To figure accuracy rate:
# of words minus # of errors divided by the # of words read = word accuracy rate

To support Pacing while reading, a set of skills is required to effectively implement this reading strategy. The synchronized application of several reading strategies results in making meaning while reading a text. The skills, additional integrated reading strategies, and their reading components found in corresponding chapters are listed below.

Focus Skill(s):

- Flexible rate
- Punctuation

Integrated Strategies:

- Recognizing; Embedding (Chapter 2)
- Analyzing Words, Contextualizing; Personalizing (Chapter 3)
- Phrasing; Expressing; Rereading (Chapter 4)
- Determining Importance (Chapter 5)

Accountable Teacher Talk for Pacing

Following is a list of suggested Teacher Talk that encourages readers to think strategically as they employ the Pacing strategy. To effectively increase levels of thinking, these suggestions incorporate Bloom's Taxonomy's higher-order questioning (Anderson and Krathwohl 2001) and Webb's Depth of Knowledge (2002).

Remembering and Understanding (Recall)

- What is reading rate?
- How does increasing or decreasing your rate help you?

Applying (Skill/Concept)

- Do you have to reread a sentence often? Why?

Analyzing (Strategic Thinking)

- How does hearing yourself read and tracking how long it takes you to read help you to pace better? Explain.

Evaluating and Creating (Extended Thinking)

- How do you determine if you are pacing appropriately? How effective is your rate of reading?
- Formulate a plan to adapt your pacing as you read.

Behavior Indicators for Pacing

As you assess students' pacing ability, use the following behaviors as a guide. Do students exhibit these behaviors never, rarely, often, or always?

- ❑ Distinguish appropriate rhythm in reading
- ❑ Adjust reading rate accordingly
- ❑ Track and observe the flow of their reading

Techniques for Pacing

Beam Reading

Purpose:	ELL Technique:
To track and observe reading rate using a beam of light	Yes

Materials:

- texts
- display options (chart paper, dry-erase boards, interactive whiteboard)
- visit http://www.ValerieEllery.com for colored Flow It Flashlights (*optional*)
- laser pens or handheld flashlights

Learning Phases

I   Display the text for all students to see. Use a laser pen or a flashlight to shine a light on the words as you model reading aloud, tracking the flow at which you are reading. Move the light along the words at a steady pace.

We   Encourage students to follow along with the light as they choral-read the text aloud. The rate at which you shine the light on the words should increase with each rereading of the text selected. **Suggested Teacher Talk:** *Try to keep up with the light to increase your reading rate.*

With You   Have students practice this technique with partners, taking turns using the light and practicing keeping the pace of the light. **Suggested Teacher Talk:** *Is it easy or difficult for you to keep up with the pace being modeled?*

By You   Place small handheld flashlights for students to use independently, or give one for all students to keep in their browsing boxes for independent reading. This allows the teacher to observe students' reading rate without their knowing that they are being observed. This creates a risk-free environment.

Differentiation

Based on students' preferences or behavioral needs, select a color beam (e.g., blue and green for calming and ease on the eyes) for students to choose in order to support the Beam Reading technique.

Fluency Pacing

Tempo Time

Purpose:	ELL Technique:
To distinguish rhythm in reading and maintain the reading pace with a predetermined rhythm while reading orally	No

Materials:

- texts (preferably poetry or pattern books)
- musical instruments (e.g., maracas)
- nursery rhymes
- Vocabulary Journal

Learning Phases

I

Model using maracas or other musical instruments to beat out a tempo. The reader's ability should determine the tempo, and the tempo can increase as the reader improves. **Suggested Teacher Talk:** *What is happening as you hear the tempo in the background?*

We

Ask students to listen to the tempo that you provide and begin to read, trying to keep up with the tempo time. **Suggested Teacher Talk:** *Is it easy or difficult for you to keep up with the tempo?*

Use predictable nursery rhymes while tapping out a predetermined rhythm as students follow along with their maracas. For example, display the words to "Twinkle, Twinkle Little Star" and shake the maraca to match one to one with the word as it is read together orally. Change the tempo periodically for students to practice a variety of reading paces.

With You

Have partners listen to each other read. One partner holds a musical instrument and tries to create a rhythm of their partner's reading. Have partners discuss the process and what they noticed.

By You

Using a maraca, invite students to beat out their tempo as they read independently. Have students record their observations in their journals.

Fluency Pacing

Time/Record/Check/Chart

Purpose:	ELL Technique:
To increase reading rate and evaluate progress	No

Materials:

- texts
- photocopies of text
- stopwatch
- audio recorder
- graph paper
- voice-recording program such as Audacity® free software program (http://www.audacity.sourceforge.net) (*optional*)

Learning Phases

I

Discuss the importance of setting goals and evaluating progress. Read a couple of sentences at different paces, and have students determine which pace was more appropriate according to the meaning being derived from the text.

We

Demonstrate using Time/Record/Check/Chart (adapted from Allington 2001) with a volunteer.

Fluency Pacing

> **Time:** Have a student read aloud a text while someone (you or a volunteer) times the student with a stopwatch, measuring how long it takes the student to read the chosen text. Chart the time on graph paper. **Suggested Teacher Talk:** *Tell how increasing your rate will help your reading.*
>
> **Record:** Have the student record the same reading on an audio recorder and time his or her reading.
>
> **Check:** The student should replay the recording while following along using a photocopied version of the text.
>
> **Chart:** Chart the time for the second reading on graph paper. Have the student mark miscues on the photocopy. The student should compare reading times and continue the previous steps as needed.

With You

Have partners time each other and complete the steps. **Suggested Teacher Talk:** *How does hearing yourself read and tracking how long it takes you to read help you to pace better?*

By You

Have students reflect and self-assess the reading and the graphed results. Repeat the process two more times. Have students create self goals as they note their progressions.

Extensions

- Prepare an area for students to read aloud and record their reading to create a digital portfolio. Download a voice-recording program like Audacity®. Have students save their sample readings to create a digital portfolio or Efolio.

- Select an appropriate computer program such as QuickReads (Hiebert 2013) and REWARDS (Reading Excellence Attack and Rate Developing Strategies; Archer, Gleason, and Vachon 2006). Incorporate one of the computer-based fluency programs into your comprehensive literacy-based classroom to increase pacing.

Sprints and Stamina

Purpose:	ELL Technique:
To apply varied reading rates to correlate speed and increase endurance	Yes

Materials:	
- texts	- clipboard
- stopwatch	- Vocabulary Journals
- dictionary and translation dictionary	

Learning Phases

I

Model the difference between "*sprints*" *and* "*stamina*" (Ellery and Rosenboom 2010) as you read aloud. Explain to students that the sprint concept relates to running a short distance at a fast pace.

The goal of sprints is to get the students to practice reading as quickly as they can in a short time period. The range of time can be one-, two-, or three-minute increments.

Demonstrate how the reading is timed and recorded by word per minute (WPM) time. Explain that the goal is to increase speed while still maintaining a certain level of accuracy in comprehension. (The accuracy level can be moved based on specific ability but should be at least 70 percent.)

We

Demonstrate the sprint concept applied to reading by asking volunteers to use several strategies that support pacing their reading without sacrificing meaning of content. See Extensions for variations of "*sprints*" *and* "*stamina*."

Explain to students the concept of stamina by relating it to running a long-distance race. The goal of stamina is to help students endure longer reading passages and to be able to recall information from longer texts while still keeping at a certain pace. Passages for stamina need to be at least 500–750 words and can be up to 2,500 words. The amount of words is directly tied to how strong of a reader the student is and should increase over time. Model several stamina ideas applied to reading by asking students to use several strategies that support pacing reading without sacrificing meaning of content.

Students reflect in their Vocabulary Journals the various processes of Sprints and Stamina and reflect on how the technique has brought awareness to their reading pace.

Extensions

Apply a variation of Sprints and Stamina with students:

- **Relay Sprints:** Students are in a group of four. They read a short passage and when the one minute is up, they must pass the paper to the next person. By the end of four minutes, they discuss the four passages as a group, and work together to answer the list of questions without looking at the passages.

- **Interval Sprints:** Students read for one minute, then for two minutes, then for three, and then for four (and it can go back down). At the end of each, they have a brief "rest" and answer the questions. They then compare the WPM time and accuracy at each level.

- **Who/What/When/Where/Why Sprints:** Students read the passage as before, but instead of having predesigned questions, they must simply answer the Who/What/When/Where/Why questions from the passage to show they comprehended the meaning.

- **Vocabulary/Review Sprints:** Create a template with the vocabulary terms or characters that students need to study or remember. Rearrange them on a single sheet of paper so that they are in a varying order. Time students for one minute with the goal of reading as many of the terms as they can before time is called. After time is called, students rotate papers so that they have a new sheet in a different order. Repeat two to three times to help them study and increase reading speed.

- **Novel Stamina:** This can be done in class or at home. Students time themselves reading a chapter in a novel that is at an appropriate reading level. They can count four lines and then create an average based on the total number of lines. This may help them get through a book that they are having a hard time reading.

- **Low-Level Stamina:** These are shorter passages and are at a reading level one grade level below the student's actual ability. This is done to increase confidence in reading and to help them increase flow.

- **Prepared Stamina:** Students preview the passage and have the opportunity to skim the passage and look for any unfamiliar/unknown words before actually reading. They may use several resources to help guide them (dictionary, translation dictionary) before actually beginning the passage. Students are given a predetermined amount of "prep" time as needed.

Fluency Pacing

Fluency Strategy: Wide Reading

Students need many opportunities to read a variety of genres as they experience the many facets of Wide Reading. It is a powerful realization when students discover that the more they read and want to read, the more fluent they become as readers. Research by Nathan and Stanovich (1991) indicates that "[if students are] to become fluent readers, they need to read a lot. Our job as educators is to see to it that children want to read, that they seek new knowledge via written word and derive satisfaction and joy from the reading process" (79).

Providing the opportunities for students to read and to find enjoyment in their reading is the challenge for today's educators. The Wide-Reading techniques will support students on their journey to becoming fluent readers. It exposes the readers to a plethora of words, increasing word consciousness and allowing students to personalize more of the vocabulary found within rich texts.

To support phrasing while reading, a set of skills is required to effectively implement this reading strategy. The synchronized application of several reading strategies results in making meaning while reading a text. The skills, additional integrated reading strategies, and their reading components found in corresponding chapters are listed below.

Focus Skill(s):	**Integrated Strategies:**
• Genre	• Recognizing; Embedding (Chapter 2)
• Reading levels	• Associating; Personalizing; Contextualizing (Chapter 3)
	• Predicting; Activating and Building Schemas; Questioning; Inferring and Drawing Conclusions; Determining Importance (Chapter 5)

Accountable Teacher Talk for Wide Reading

Following is a list of suggested Teacher Talk that encourages readers to think strategically as they employ the Wide Reading strategy. To effectively increase levels of thinking, these suggestions incorporate Bloom's Taxonomy's higher-order questioning (Anderson and Krathwohl 2001) and Webb's Depth of Knowledge (2002).

Remembering and Understanding (Recall)

- How does your reading sound (in your head or aloud) when you are independently reading?

- Pick a book that interests you and meets your reading needs.

Applying (Skill/Concept)

- Describe indicators that tell when a book is too easy or too difficult for you.

Analyzing (Strategic Thinking)

- How do you know if a book is just right for you?

Evaluating and Creating (Extended Thinking)

- Examine the books in your browsing box. Why is it important to independently read books at your appropriate level?

- Create an organization chart of traits (i.e., features, supports, and structures) that you look for when selecting a text to read. How do you determine if the text is aligned to your reading level?

Behavior Indicators for Wide Reading

As you assess students' pacing ability, use the following behaviors as a guide. Do students exhibit these behaviors never, rarely, often, or always?

❑ Choose to read independently

❑ Self-select books based on reading level

❑ Determine purpose for reading

Techniques for Wide Reading

Book Baskets/Browsing Boxes

Purpose:	ELL Technique:
To self-select text and find enjoyment in reading	Yes

Materials:	
• baskets and boxes	• flashlight
• leveled texts of various interests and genres	

Learning Phases

I

Model selecting books for pleasure and purpose. Place multiple levels of texts (fiction and informational text) into baskets or browsing boxes. These may be books that were previously read during guided-reading time.

We

Have students at different stages of development browse through the book selections to choose one book that is "just right" for them. Students should select books from the baskets with which they are familiar and that are at their own independent reading level. **Suggested Teacher Talk:** *How do you feel when you are reading a book that is at your level?*

With You

Have students place their selections into their own browsing box (a box or a plastic bin that holds each student's collection of independent-level reading books).

By You

During independent reading time, have students read and reread texts from their boxes. Reading these books ensures quality time spent on reading at the appropriate level of each reader. **Suggested Teacher Talk:** *Has your reading rate improved each time you've read and reread books from your browsing boxes?*

Differentiation

Place a flashlight in each student's browsing box and have students follow along with their flashlights as they read silently. This gives students a guide as they are reading and allows the teacher to view each student's pace with the flow of the beam light. (See Beam Reading in this chapter for a more detailed explanation of this technique.)

Fluency Wide Reading

"Just Right" Books

Purpose:	ELL Technique:
To identify/select books at students' independent reading level	Yes

Materials:

- variety of leveled texts
- three chairs of different sizes
- "Goldilocks and the Three Bears"
- chart paper or blank poster

Learning Phases

I

Demonstrate how to choose a just-right book, and discuss the value of independently reading a book that fits the reader. Read aloud the story of "Goldilocks and the Three Bears." Line up three chairs: one too small, one too big, and one just right for students. Select three books for the demonstration: one that is too easy, one that is too hard, and one that is just right for students.

We

After modeling how to select a book that is just the right match, have the class generate three posters or charts.

Too-Easy Chart: List what makes a text too easy (e.g., your reading rate is too fast, you know all the words, you use less energy decoding).

Too-Hard Chart: List the traits of a text that make it too hard (e.g., your reading rate is too slow, you lose focus as you are reading, you have trouble understanding or decoding words).

Just-Right Chart: Show what type of book is just right (e.g., your reading rate is just right, you can read most of the words, you can get the meaning from the story).

With You

Post the charts in the classroom library area as a reminder for students when selecting their independent reading materials. **Suggested Teacher Talk:** *What are the signs that the book is too easy or too difficult for you? How do you know if a book is just right for you?*

By You

Have students list types of genres they prefer and why. Have them practice selecting text for their personal browsing boxes.

Fluency
Wide Reading

Extension

Have a school-wide poster contest in which students create visual displays about how to select just-right books. Students could then go on a "museum walk" around the school and discuss the various steps and ideas given to help select a book that is just right for them.

Book Clubs

Purpose:	ELL Technique:
To determine a purpose for reading, and to develop an interest in sharing books with others	No

Materials:
• a variety of texts (four to six copies of the same title)

Learning Phases

I — Display a variety of book sets. Each book title should have at least four additional copies on display. **Suggested Teacher Talk:** *Try to pick a book that interests you for your book club selection.*

We — Have students select a book that is at their independent reading level and is interesting to them, and sign them up to be in a book club. Each student will be in a book club with students who are reading the same selection.

With You — Have the groups meet and plan how much reading they will do independently before they get together to share and discuss the book. Each week, the clubs should meet to share their ideas, feelings, questions, concerns, and general comments about what they read.

By You — Continue the process with new book selections and new clubs being formed. **Suggested Teacher Talk:** *How does being in a book club help your reading?*

Fluency Wide Reading

Differentiation

Select a variety of text sets to meet students' needs for the various book clubs that may form. These sets may address different reading levels, content, genres, or student interest.

Extension

"Market the books" by periodically featuring selected content text resources. Use teacher modeling to highlight books and resources by reading a dramatic text excerpt and/or sharing illustrations. Students can replicate this process to market the books and feature books and titles they found particularly interesting.

Fluency Strategy: Accuracy

Students who read fluently read with accuracy. The accuracy strategy focuses on being able to identify and apply the graphophonic cueing system (i.e., the relationship between letters and sounds) with ease and precision. In order for students to accurately read, they need to use the phonemic awareness and phonics strategies described previously (see Chapters 2 and 3). Gaining independence at their developmental reading level in these two areas of reading will ensure a higher level of automaticity and accuracy as students read.

Research indicates that the brain devotes only a limited amount of attention to any given cognitive task (LaBerge and Samuels 1974). The more attention a reader devotes to trying to decode an unknown word, the less time and energy he or she has to cognitively gather meaning from the text. Teachers need to assess students' accuracy by using oral-reading inventories (e.g., running records, analytical reading inventories, informal reading inventories). (See Figure 4.3 for a formula to help calculate a student's accuracy rate.) This type of assessment can be used to analyze what the student's specific needs are within the cueing system. It is important to note that this is only one strategy for helping students to read fluently.

McEwan (2002) explains that "students who make no errors but read very slowly have as little likelihood of comprehending what they read as students who read very quickly but guess at and misidentify many words" (54). There must be a balance for the student to read with both fluency and comprehension. Accuracy is a vital link to reading with ease. However, teachers must keep in mind that reading is an art, with many facets that fuse together for a proficient reader to evolve.

The techniques found in Chapters 2 and 3 are appropriate for building accuracy, especially the techniques for teaching sight word recognition (i.e., recognizing) and decoding (i.e., analyzing). The techniques for teaching the rereading strategy found in this chapter also are appropriate for promoting accuracy.

Fluency
Wide Reading

Fluency Wrap-Up

Fluency instruction extends beyond word recognition. It is the bridge from Word Study and Power to Comprehension. The fluent reader recognizes words automatically and can now attend to comprehension. The strategies, techniques, and Teacher Talk presented in this chapter support teachers in maximizing their students' potential in becoming strategic readers. Fluency is yet another medium by which teachers can create their masterpieces—strategic readers.

Chapter 5

All Roads Lead to Meaning

Comprehension

Determining Importance with Chapter Tours Technique

Summarizing with Summary Ball Technique

Comprehension is the essence of reading. Therefore, teachers should weave comprehension strategies into the fabric of all instruction across the curriculum. In fact, teachers need to begin teaching these strategies in pre-kindergarten experiences. "To delay this sort of powerful instruction until children have reached the intermediate grades is to deny them the very experiences that help them develop the most important of reading dispositions" (Pearson and Duke 2002, 248). These emerging readers are able to begin using higher-order critical-thinking skills to bring meaning to the text. The ability to comprehend is far from being passive. "Comprehension occurs when a reader is able to act on, respond to, or transform the information that is presented in written text in ways that it demonstrates understanding" (Brassell and Rasinski 2008, 18).

Comprehension as a strategic process enables readers to make connections and move beyond literal recall. Strategic readers will need to read with intent and purpose. It will be vital for them to use textual evidence to support their conclusions of the meaning of what is being read (CCSS 2010). "Citing evidence from the text can be a challenge for students who have become accustomed to stating their thoughts and opinions without referring back to the text" (Fisher and Frey 2013, 40). Teachers need to remember that good comprehension instruction needs to be taught explicitly and strategically. With every technique, it is vital that teachers explain and explicitly demonstrate, guiding students on how the technique builds the corresponding comprehension strategy (Boulware-Gooden, Carreker, Thornhill, and Joshi 2007; Fisher, Frey, and Lapp 2009; Hilden and Pressley 2007; Israel and Duffy 2009; NICHD 2000, Pressley 2002). Comprehension instruction requires making "the strategy a part of our unconscious reading process, so that students are able to combine any number of strategies to problem solve before, during, and after they read" (Routman 2003, 129). This transactional approach has been proven to support readers to becoming active, independent readers who bring meaning to reading (Brown 2008).

The Comprehension strategies and their corresponding techniques detailed in this chapter are listed in Figure 5.1.

Figure 5.1 Comprehension Strategies and Techniques in Chapter 5

Strategy	Corresponding Techniques in This Chapter	
Previewing	What I Know...What I Wonder... (page 230) Text Traits: Getting to Know the Text (page 231)	Skim and Scan (page 232) Constructing Structure (page 233)
Activating and Building Schemas	Connect and Reflect (page 237) Anticipation/Reaction Guides (page 239)	Think Sheet (page 240) Carousel Brainstorming (page 241)
Predicting	Walking Closely Through the Pictures (page 244) Story/Concept Impression (page 245)	Journaling (page 246) Two-Column Note Prediction (page 247)
Questioning	Ripple Effect (page 250) Question–Answer Relationships (QARs) (page 251) Question Logs: 3Rs (page 253)	Survey, Question, Read, Recite, Review (SQ3R) (page 254) Questioning The Author (QtA) (page 255)
Visualizing and Sensory Imaging	Sketch to Stretch (page 259) Wordless Picture Books (page 260) Frame This (page 261)	Drama (page 262) Sensory Impressions (page 263)
Inferring and Drawing Conclusions	Interpreting Text (page 266) Save the Last Word for Me (page 267)	Talk Show (page 268) Scenarios With T-Charts (page 269)
Determining Importance	Picture This (page 272) Chapter Tours (page 273)	Main Idea Wheel (page 274) Highlighting the Highs (page 275)

Strategy	Corresponding Techniques in This Chapter	
Summarizing	Detail/Retell (page 279) Summary Ball (page 280)	Informational Text and Narrative Pyramid (page 281) Somebody/Wanted/But/So (page 282)
Synthesizing	Creating a Play (page 286) Mind Mapping (page 287) Rewriting a Story (page 288)	Say Something: Text Talk (page 288) Synthesizing Target (page 289)

To be effective, the strategies and techniques presented in this chapter should allow ample time for teacher modeling and student application long before independent application is expected. Teachers should select and model reading aloud of appropriate text to apply the techniques in a meaningful manner, which supports authentic learning for strategic reading. By using this process, students are able to see first the whole text (i.e., appropriate literature), then see the parts systematically (i.e., strategies and techniques), and finally, apply the parts back to the whole (i.e., become metacognitively aware of strategies while reading appropriate text).

Using quality literature and informational text while promoting language development throughout the techniques will help to enhance students' development of the strategies. In addition, teachers can use the motivation and engagement feature within many techniques as an additional means (i.e., multiple intelligence, standard) of motivating the whole child and creating 21st-century learners (refer to Chapter 1 for a description of the whole child and Figure 1.3, for an illustration). This allows for differentiation within the technique as needed to educate the whole child.

Comprehension Strategy: Previewing

Previewing motivates students to want to read the text. It enables readers to examine text features, skim to get a sense of what the text is about, and identify the organizational structure. While previewing, readers begin relating to what they already know—their schema—and form several opinions about the text they are reading (Snow and O'Connor 2013). Previewing is one of the best strategies for evoking relevant thoughts and memories relating to the text. It allows readers to get their minds ready to read a particular type of text, and "teachers should examine their texts carefully to identify features that might either support or intrude on meaningful understandings" (Risko 2011). When they use this strategy, students have a better understanding of what they know about the text, what they would like to learn from the text, and what they anticipate might happen as they read.

To support Previewing, a set of skills is required to effectively implement this reading strategy. The synchronized application of several reading strategies results in making meaning while reading a text. The skills, additional integrated reading strategies, and their reading components found in corresponding chapters are listed below.

Focus Skill(s):

- Structure of a text (informational and literary)
- Concepts of print

Integrated Strategies:

- Associating (Chapter 3)
- Activating and Building Schemas; Predicting; Questioning (Chapter 5)

Accountable Teacher Talk for Previewing

Following is a list of suggested Teacher Talk that encourages readers to think strategically as they employ the Previewing strategy. To effectively increase levels of thinking, these suggestions incorporate Bloom's Taxonomy's higher-order questioning (Anderson and Krathwohl 2001) and Webb's Depth of Knowledge (2002).

Remembering and Understanding (Recall)

- Are you familiar with the topic of the text?
- The title makes me think the book will be about_____. The illustrations help me to_____. This picture makes me think about _____.

Applying (Skill/Concept)

- I noticed that the pictures are helping to tell the story because_____. What do you notice about the captions?

Analyzing (Strategic Thinking)

- The pictures may provide clues about_____. What else do you notice about the pictures?

Evaluating and Creating (Extended Thinking)

- Use the text traits to examine the text features, supports, and structures and gain an awareness of the text. How is the text structured? What features help you when previewing the book?

- Reflect on the significance of the title and how it relates to the meaning of the text. Create an alternative title and explain your thinking.

Behavior Indicators for Previewing

As you assess students' ability to preview, use the following behaviors as a guide. Do students exhibit these behaviors never, rarely, often, or always?

- ❑ Augment background knowledge
- ❑ Initiate mental images
- ❑ Use text traits (features, support, and structures) to determine purpose

Techniques for Previewing

What I Know...What I Wonder...

Purpose:	ELL Technique:
To activate background knowledge to preview a text	Yes

Materials:

- text
- display options (chart paper, dry-erase boards, interactive whiteboard)
- journals
- marker
- Hula-Hoops™
- sticky notes

Learning Phases

I

Create a two-column graphic organizer on chart paper (or other display options). Label the left column "What I Know" and the right column "What I Wonder." This can be done with a read-aloud or during independent reading (one-to-one conferring).

Through class discussions, activate students' prior personal experiences that are pertinent to the text you are about to read. **Suggested Teacher Talk:** *What comes to your mind as you view this text? Think about the connection between what you see and what you know.*

We

Begin to build with students any necessary background knowledge they might need for studying this text (for ideas, see the activating and building background knowledge strategy and its techniques in this chapter). **Suggested Teacher Talk:** *Ask yourself, "Have I heard about this topic before?"*

With You

Have students reflect on what they wonder as they preview a text. Have students use sticky notes to record their thinking in print or with illustrations and align with the column titles. **Suggested Teacher Talk:** *What are you thinking? What are you wondering about? I am wondering_____.*

By You

Students can create two columns in their journals and respond to the heading *What I know_____* and *What I wonder_____.*

Extension

Place two differently colored Hula-Hoops™ on the floor to represent *What I Know_____* and *What I Wonder_____*. Have students model their thinking as they step into each hoop.

Text Traits: Getting to Know the Text

Purpose:	ELL Technique:
To identify and use text features, supports, and structures to help determine the purpose of a text	Yes

Materials:

- text
- *Text Traits* and *Text Trait Bookmark* (see traitsbookmark.pdf)
- index cards

Learning Phases

I

Before reading a chosen book, preview a specific text trait (i.e., features, supports, or structure) that will support students' ability to determine the purpose of the text. **Suggested Teacher Talk:** *How is the text structured? What text features help you preview the book?*

We

Provide a "Text Trait" mini-lesson. Use *Text Traits* to examine the text traits (features, supports, structure). For example, select one text trait (headings) and have a student demonstrate reading the headings in a text and predicting what they think the text will be about based on the headings. Continue exploring several text traits with the class.

With You

Have students work with partners to make predictions about a particular text. **Suggested Teacher Talk:** *Based on the text features, what do you think the story is about? Which details or clues from the text did you use to make your prediction?*

Have students pause throughout the reading of the text and use text features to make further predictions as well as to confirm or change their previous predictions.

By You

Give each student a *Text Trait Bookmark*. Remind them to tap into the traits as they preview the text to get a sense of what they are reading and begin to set their minds for the reading purpose.

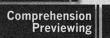

Differentiation

- Use a variety of engaging genres at the independent or instructional level of students that have a variety of text features, supports, and structures.

- Give each student a *Text Trait Bookmark* (examples of text traits or the text trait terminology). Have students match their *Text Traits Cards* in a large-group activity. With their matched partners, share how their text traits can help them as readers. Have the partners locate an example of their particular text traits from a text and share their findings. They can create a scavenger hunt for the various text traits.

Skim and Scan

Purpose:	ELL Technique:
To stimulate interests, implant vocabulary, and initiate mental images while making first impressions about a text	Yes

Materials:
• text   • chart paper

Learning Phases

I

Before reading a chosen text, model how to briefly examine to see what the text is about, key concepts of the text, and new vocabulary. Eliciting vocabulary and then identifying a few of those words directly within the text helps to implant the words in students' minds.

We

Have students skim the text they are about to read, noting their first impressions. **Suggested Teacher Talk:** *I noticed that the author_____.* Encourage students to scan the lead-ins, subheadings, diagrams, pictures, and any other portions of the text that give them a feel for the text they will be reading. Ask students to use these first impressions to begin selecting strategies that they will need to comprehend the text.

Post these strategies in the classroom so students can identify them and they are more readily accessible to students. **Suggested Teacher Talk:** *How can skimming and scanning be helpful? When would you use it?* Discuss and record a variety of purposes for skimming and scanning.

With You

Encourage students to think aloud with a partner or in a small group, describing their reactions to the illustrations and the text. **Suggested Teacher Talk:** *What does the text seem to be about? Maybe the pictures will provide clues about_____.* Have them preview some of the pictures in the book as a source of information.

By You

Have students create an introduction about themselves, highlighting some of their key traits. Have them stand and introduce themselves to the group.

During a one-to-one conference with the student, dialogue how the key traits support their independent reading and interact using specific information they found to help them to get to "know" each other better through the introductions. Compare this technique to using a book introduction to preview the book.

Extension

Distribute to teams a scenario to bring to "life" (e.g., you need a job, you want to bake a cake, you want a new video game). Invite students to select a resource to skim and scan for their scenario. Have students describe how the resource supports the purpose. Have teams act out their scenario results.

Constructing Structure

Purpose:	ELL Technique:
To generate and augment background knowledge to prepare students for successful reading	Yes

Materials:	
• text	• highlighters or small sticky notes
• print or online content text	• *Constructing Structure Form* (constructing.pdf)

Learning Phases

I

Initiate the *Constructing Structure* (Ellery and Rosenboom 2010) process by identifying a nonfiction text or portions of texts that include examples of the author's use of text supports.

We

Guide students in developing their *Constructing Structure Form*. Students independently skim the title, illustrations, and headings to determine what they think they will learn from the selection. In their notebooks or journals, ask students to list three to five things they might learn.

With You

Encourage students to share their ideas with a partner. Guide students to use the title, headings, and subheadings to create three prediction questions to be answered while reading the text. **Suggested Teacher Talk:** *How does the text help you question the author prior to reading? When you finish reading, what new information might you learn? How does this information support what you have learned before?*

By You

Revisit the text, focusing students on subheadings, signal words, text layout, graphs, charts, and illustrations. After revisiting the text, students record the title, heading, subheadings, and other text supports on their *Constructing Structure Form* or notebook.
Suggested Teacher Talk: *What do you notice about the layout of the text? What are the signal words that give you clues about what this text will explain?*

Differentiation

As a whole-group or a small-group process, list, organize, and label categories of information students know about the topic and questions they would like to have answered.

Comprehension Strategy: Activating and Building Schemas

Proficient readers bring their prior knowledge to a text to help them discern the meaning of what they are reading. When readers are thinking about what they already know, they are using their schemas to better understand the text. This frontloading process allows readers to evoke relevant thoughts and memories relating to the text. When text is read in isolation from these relevant thoughts, information is dismissed and considered unimportant. For assimilation of information to occur, readers must call on existing knowledge (Tovani 2000).

Strategic readers add to alter their thinking as they encounter new ideas and information from the text. "It is probably impossible to suppress the process of using existing knowledge schemas when reading, so readers with more relevant background knowledge will automatically comprehend a text more readily" (Snow 2013, 4). It is critical that teachers not only activate their students' knowledge of topics that they are reading about but also are aware of situations in which students have little or no background knowledge so that they can build, through scaffolding, essential understandings before their students begin reading (Fisher et al. 2009; Jensen and Nickelsen 2008; Risko 2011; Strickland et al. 2002). Harvey and Goudvis (2013) state the case for having strong background knowledge instruction in today's classrooms: "Recently, Pearson (2012) quipped, 'Asking kids to read without using background knowledge is like asking people to breathe without using oxygen.' We concur. Supporting readers to connect their prior knowledge to new information is at the core of learning and understanding" (437).

To support Activating and Building Schemas, while reading, a set of skills is required to effectively implement this strategy. The synchronized application of several reading strategies results in making meaning while reading a text. The skills, additional integrated reading strategies, and their reading components found in corresponding chapters are listed below.

Focus Skill(s):

- Access schema
- Connect information or events

Integrated Strategies:

- Wide Reading; Expressing (Chapter 4)
- Previewing; Predicting; Questioning; Inferring and Drawing Conclusions (Chapter 5)

Accountable Teacher Talk for Activating and Building Schemas

Following is a list of suggested Teacher Talk that encourages readers to think strategically as they employ the Activating and Build Schemas strategy. To effectively increase levels of thinking, these suggestions incorporate Bloom's Taxonomy's higher-order questioning (Anderson and Krathwohl 2001) and Webb's Depth of Knowledge (2002).

Remembering and Understanding (Recall)

- What do you think of when you hear the word (or phrase) _____ ?
- What do you already know that will help you understand the information in this section?

Applying (Skill/Concept)

- What personal connection did you make with the text? Which details from the text connected to your own experiences?

Analyzing (Strategic Thinking)

- Try to read and confirm whether your answer to the statement is true or false. Examine the text and refer to details in the text that support your thinking.

Evaluating and Creating (Extended Thinking)

- Explain how you supported your thinking—with the text, background knowledge, or both. Based on your prior knowledge of the topic, what questions do you have?
- Create a list of what you think of when you hear the words_____ and _____. What do the words _____ and _____ mean to you?

Behavior Indicators for Activating and Building Schemas

As you assess students' ability to activate and build background knowledge, use the following behaviors as a guide. Do students exhibit these behaviors never, rarely, often, or always?

❑ Make connections to self, text, and the world

❑ Confirm or change predictions

❑ Expand background knowledge

Techniques for Activating and Building Schemas

Connect and Reflect

Purpose:	ELL Technique:
To associate text with self, another text, and other aspects of the world	No

Materials:

- text
- *Connect and Reflect Puzzle Pieces* (see connectreflect.pdf)
- sticky notes (optional)
- globe *(optional)*
- mirror *(optional)*

Learning Phases

I

Explain that a text-to-self connection is made when something in the story reminds you of something in your life. Provide an example of a supportive text-to-self connection (Keene and Zimmermann 2007; Harvey and Goudvis 2007). **Suggested Teacher Talk:** *This reminds me of a time when_____. I have made a text-to-self connection in this story because_____.*

We

Use large-size puzzle pieces from the *Connect and Reflect Puzzle Pieces* for text-to-text connections (i.e., related books, characters, and so forth), text-to-world connections (i.e., a broader connection to people and places around us through newspaper articles, magazine interviews, and so forth), and text-to-self connections (i.e., personal experiences). Use the following questions for students to respond to text they have read.

Text-to-self

How does this relate to my life?

What does this remind me of in my life?

What is this similar to in my life?

Has something like this ever happened to me?

Text-to-text

Have I read about something like this in another book?

What does this remind me of in another book I've read?

How is this text similar to other things I've read?

How is this different from other books I've read?

Text-to-world

What does this remind me of in the real world?

How did that part relate to the world around me?

How is this text similar to things that happen in the real world?

How is this different from things that happen in the real world?

With You

Distribute the *Connect and Reflect Puzzle Pieces* and have students find a partners to complete their puzzles. One can illustrate or write the event from the text on one piece, and how they connect to the text might be on the other puzzle piece. **Suggested Teacher Talk:** *What made the event so memorable?* Have students share the connections and display puzzle pieces for future discussions.

By You

Students can use their puzzle piece as a reminder to make connections with the text they have read independently.

Extension

Bring in tangible objects to represent each "text to..." area (e.g., globe = world, book = text, mirror = self). Place the objects in an area in the room near chart paper or place sticky notes next to the objects. Ask students when they "catch" themselves making a connection in one of these areas to add their initials by the appropriate connection or on a sticky note and place directly on the designated object. During class meeting time, select a student to share the connections he or she made during reading time.

Anticipation/Reaction Guides

Purpose:	ELL Technique:
To confirm or change predictions about text based on support in text	No

Materials:

- text
- *Anticipation/Reaction Guide* (see anticipation.pdf)
- notebook paper

Learning Phases

I

Identify the main topic or concept of a text prior to meeting with students. Create three to five statements that will challenge or support students' beliefs or that may reflect common misconceptions about the subject, topic, or concept. Record these statements on the *Anticipation/Reaction Guide* (adapted from Herber 1984).

We

Have students read each statement and note whether they agree (+) or disagree (–). **Suggested Teacher Talk:** *Do you agree or disagree with the statement presented? Why or why not? Try to read and confirm whether your answer to the statement is true or false.*

With You

Encourage students to generate an evidence-based prediction, as some content-area statements may be more challenging. Discuss their predictions and their justifications in small groups. Invite students to change or confirm your thinking based on the discussions.

By You

Have students return to the statements after they have read the text and engage in a discussion on how the textual information supported, contradicted, or modified their first opinions. **Suggested Teacher Talk:** *Which key words or statements in the text support your ideas? Justify your thinking as you confirm or reassess your original response to the statement.*

Extension

Create statements about the subject, topic, or concept before the class read-aloud and then have students decide what they think they know about the statements with signals (e.g., thumbs up, thumbs down). Then, listen to the read-aloud and share reactions to previous statements.

Think Sheet

Purpose:	ELL Technique:
To activate prior knowledge related to the information and events in a text	No

Materials:

- text
- *Think Sheet* (see thinksheet.pdf)
- paper for making a foldable booklet (*optional*)
- nail, hammer, piece of wood (*optional*)

Learning Phases

I

Choose a text to study and write the text's main topic for all to see. Display a lightbulb image and a question mark. Demonstrate prior knowledge you have about the main unit of study and record it next to the lightbulb image. Ask a question you may have about the topic and record it next to the question mark.

We

On the side of the sheet with the lightbulb, list ideas that students may have about the main topic based on their prior knowledge. Record any questions students have about the main topic on the side of the sheet with the question mark. **Suggested Teacher Talk:** *Based on your prior knowledge of the topic, what questions do you have?*

With You

Copy the *Think Sheet* and distribute it to each student. Have students read the text in small groups and discuss what they have recorded on their *Think Sheet* to guide their reading of the text.

By You

Have students reread the text. As they locate information related to their original prereading ideas and questions, have students write the information beside their corresponding original statements. **Suggested Teacher Talk:** *What evidence in the text supports your thinking?*

Extensions

- Make a two-fold flip book and record on one side the lightbulb thoughts (prior knowledge). On the other flap, record questions about the topic that need to be "lit up" to bring understanding to light.

- As students locate information in the text that supports their thinking and begins to answer their questions, have them take a hammer and nail and tap on the top of the nail to represent going deeper in the text. Make a connection to how as the nail goes deeper in the wood, it becomes stronger and more sealed and is not falling over. The same can be true for their learning; as they go deeper into the text, their comprehension becomes stronger and meaning is sealed.

Carousel Brainstorming

Comprehension
Activating and
Building
Schemas

Purpose:	ELL Technique:
To activate prior knowledge related to the information and events on a unit of study	Yes

Materials:

- text
- charts
- recording device
- different color markers
- clipboards or SmartPads (*optional*)

Learning Phases

I

Select a number of key phrases, critical-thinking questions, or vocabulary about a topic of study (the same number as the amount of groups you intend to form) for you to introduce. Write each phrase/question/vocabulary word on separate charts and assign a different color to each chart. Display the charts around the room. Divide your students into groups that will carousel around the charts for *Carousel Brainstorming* (Lipton and Wellman 1998).

We

Have each group meet in front of one of the charts and select a group recorder to hold the team's different-color marker. Each group can have a different color marker. Groups begin to think and record as many brainstorm thoughts as possible in a certain amount of time (estimated time 2–3 minutes). When time is up, ask each group to rotate to the next chart.

With You

Begin the rotation and continue until all of the groups have made it to each chart. Once a the group is back to its original chart, invite it them to read through all the class brainstorming thoughts. Ask each group to select its top three responses given to support the text information (e.g., key phrase, question, vocabulary). Students will need to revisit the text for evidence-based support when selecting their top three choices.

By You

Have students do a "walk-about" or a gallery walk around the class carousel charts and record key information in a study log.

Extensions

- Students can use the generated list to create group summaries or extend to their writing projects.

- Instead of chart paper, put questions on clipboards or SmartPads and pass the boards/pads for students to record, or speak into the recorder to capture their responses.

Comprehension Strategy: Predicting

Predicting is a strategy that helps readers set expectations for reading, connect early with the text for meaning, and decide what they think will happen. Strategic readers make predictions before reading and while reading based on a number of skills and strategies like previewing, activating background knowledge, and asking questions (Block, Rodgers, and Johnson 2004; Fisher et al. 2009; Kelly and Clausen-Grace 2013; Jiang 2009; Robb 1996). "When readers make predictions about what they'll learn, they activate their schema about the topic and what they know about the type of text they are about to read" (Miller 2002, 145). Predictions can be based on clues in the title, the illustrations, and the details within the text. These organizational structures are the blueprints that show the author's plan for presenting information to the reader (Strickland et al. 2002).

During reading, readers may predict what content will occur in succeeding portions of the text. Readers can describe what they think will be revealed next, based on what they have read so far and based on the personal background knowledge which they bring to the text. After reading a portion of the text, readers can confirm whether their predictions were accurate and adjust them as needed.

To support Predicting while reading, a set of skills is required to effectively implement this reading strategy. The synchronized application of several reading strategies results in making meaning while reading a text. The skills, additional integrated reading strategies, and their reading components found in corresponding chapters are listed below.

Focus Skill(s):

- Access schema
- Connect information or events

Integrated Strategies:

- Expressing; Wide Reading (Chapter 4)
- Previewing; Activating and Building Schema; Questioning; Inferring and Drawing Conclusions (Chapter 5)

Accountable Teacher Talk for Predicting

Following is a list of suggested Teacher Talk that encourages readers to think strategically as they employ the Prediction strategy. To effectively increase levels of thinking, these suggestions incorporate Bloom's Taxonomy's higher-order questioning (Anderson and Krathwohl 2001) and Webb's Depth of Knowledge (2002).

Remembering and Understanding (Recall)

- I wonder if _____? I want to know _____.

- Based on the text features, what do you think the story is about?

Applying (Skill/Concept)

- What makes you think _____ is going to happen? Why? Which details or clues from the text helped you make your prediction?

Analyzing (Strategic Thinking)

- What do you think the text is going to tell you? What makes you think so? What evidence supports your prediction?

Evaluating and Creating (Extended Thinking)

- How did you formulate your prediction? Have you read or heard of something like this before to be able to come up with your prediction?

- Justify your hypothesis. How did the process of predicting and modifying your predictions enhance your motivation before, during, and after reading?

Behavior Indicators for Predicting

As you assess students' ability to predict, use the following behaviors as a guide. Do students exhibit these behaviors never, rarely, often, or always?

❑ Analyze illustrations within text and observe clues about topic or events

❑ Forecast what a text will be about

❑ Compose, confirm, or modify predictions

Techniques for Predicting

Comprehension Predicting

Walking Closely Through the Pictures

Purpose:	ELL Technique:
To use illustrations within a text to make predictions; extracting essential information from text	Yes

Materials:

- text

Learning Phases

I
Lead students in a discussion about understanding the concepts, key words, or key phrases from the text based on the illustrations. **Suggested Teacher Talk:** *How do the pictures help you to predict what the story will be about?*

We
Have students peruse a text briefly with a key question in mind, looking at the pictures and trying to answer the question they think will be essential to their understanding of the text.

Ask students to use the pictures to make predictions. **Suggested Teacher Talk:** *Looking at the picture on the cover, what do you imagine the answer to this question will be?*

With You
Have students discuss the predictions or answers they made based on the information extracted from the picture walk while reading the text with a partner.

By You
Students can select a text to create key questions for others to think about prior to "Walking Closely Through the Pictures."

Extension

Have students go on a nature walk to represent a picture walk. Have students predict what will happen on their nature walk before they begin and as they are in the process.

Story/Concept Impression

Purpose:	ELL Technique:
To compose, check, and modify predictions	Yes

Materials:	
• text	• chart paper

Learning Phases

I

Select seven key words that relate to significant information from the text you are studying and display the chain of words in the order in which they appear in the text for all students to see. If reading a literary text, these words should reflect the following story elements: main characters, setting, problem, events, and solution.

If reading an informational text, these words should reflect seven key concepts within the text. **Suggested Teacher Talk:** *Try to imagine what is going on in the text based on the key words presented here.*

We

Have students work in teams to predict a story line or key concepts based on the keywords given for the *Story Impression* (McGinley and Denner 1987). Invite teams to create a story or idea using all seven words after they have had time to discuss their predictions.

One student in the class can be the recorder and write the teams' story or idea on chart paper. **Suggested Teacher Talk:** *Present your story or idea to the entire class. Which details or clues from the selection did you use to make your prediction?*

With You

After all the teams have shared their versions of the story, have groups read the text and compare and contrast their text to it. Rereading for clarification may be necessary.

By You

Students select a text and search for key words to create their own Story/Concept Impression to submit to the class. Each word chosen needs to have a reason why it is essential to the main idea.

Differentiation

Have students create a Venn diagram to compare and contrast their story predictions with the original story.

Journaling

Purpose:	ELL Technique:
To predict in written form what a text will be about and close read to find what it is really about	Yes

Materials:

- text
- journals

Learning Phases

I
: Share an entry from your journal where you recorded a prediction prior to reading a text. Discuss how after you read the text, you were able to confirm your prediction or change your response based on the information you discovered while reading the text.

We
: Have students write or draw in their journals what they think a text will be about and justify their predictions. **Suggested Teacher Talk:** *What will happen? I think I know what is going to happen. What do you think the text is going to tell you about _____? What makes you think so? What evidence supports your prediction?*

With You
: Have students sit knee to knee and make predictions about the text. **Suggested Teacher Talk:** *What will happen next? I think I know what is going to happen.*

Have students listen to their partners' predictions to help support any additional predictions. This process encourages more reluctant readers to contribute their predictions.

By You
: Read the text and have students confirm or change their predictions in comparison to the actual events in the text.

Differentiation

Scaffold sentence stems in written form based on student needs (e.g., *I think the following questions might be answered based on _____ . My prediction is _____ . After seeing _____ , I am wondering _____ .*).

Two-Column Note Prediction

Purpose:	ELL Technique:
To record and justify predictions	No

Materials:

- text
- *Two-Column Note Prediction Form* (see twocolumnnote.pdf)
- online resources (freeology.com; scriblink.com) *(optional)*
- individual whiteboard *(optional)*

Comprehension Predicting

Learning Phases

I   Copy the *Two-Column Note Prediction Form* (adapted from Miller 2002) and model making predictions and locating key details in the text to support your prediction.

We   Give one side of the room a key word and have them predict why they think that word is related to the unit of study. The other side of the room is given a main idea from which they will create a question. Have students share responses and explain the reasoning behind their prediction and created question.

With You   Distribute to each student a *Two-Column Note Prediction Form*. Have students record their predictions about key words or concepts from a text on the left side of the form.

On the right side, have students elaborate their thought processes behind these predictions. **Suggested Teacher Talk:** *What makes you think _____ is going to happen? Why do you believe _____ is going to happen?* Have students share their predictions with partners.

By You   Students then read the text to see whether their predictions were correct. **Suggested Teacher Talk:** *Which predictions were confirmed by the text?*

Extension

Students can use online resources to take notes on their own interactive whiteboard such as Scriblink™ (http://www.scriblink.com) or Freeology (http://www.freeology.com).

Comprehension Strategy: Questioning

Questioning is a strategy that helps readers to review content and relate what they have learned to what they already know. Generating and asking questions also helps students to identify issues and ideas in all content areas, construct meaning, enhance understanding, discover new information, clarify confusion, and solve problems (Kinniburgh and Shaw 2009; Raphael, Highfield, and Au 2006; Lewin 2010; Marzano 2010). Asking questions before reading allows readers to set purposes for reading and helps them to determine what they want to learn while reading.

Strategic readers move from general questions to text-dependent questions during their interaction with the text, and they integrate information from different segments of text. When the text becomes unclear, strategic readers formulate questions and then continue reading to find details that may later help answer those questions and make sense of the text. Asking and answering questions encourages readers to notice pieces of information within the text that support the main idea. This process of asking and answering questions allows readers to think actively as they read. According to Fisher and Frey (2013) there are six types of questions (general understanding; key details; vocabulary and text structure; author's purpose; inferences; and opinions, arguments, and intertextual connections) that require readers to use evidence from the text. "These questions represent a progression of increasingly more complex understandings, with literal-level knowledge forming the foundation as they move toward inferential meaning and critical analysis" (Fisher and Frey 2013, 40).

To support Questioning while reading, a set of skills is required to effectively implement this reading strategy. The synchronized application of several reading strategies results in making meaning while reading a text. The skills, additional integrated reading strategies, and their reading components found in corresponding chapters are listed below.

Focus Skill(s):

- Ask a question
- Set a purpose for reading
- Think actively
- Integrate information

Integrated Strategies:

- Embedding (Chapter 2)
- Contextualizing; Wide Reading (Chapter 3)
- Rereading; Expressing; Wide Reading (Chapter 4)
- Previewing; Activating and Building Schema; Predicting; Inferring and Drawing Conclusions; Determining Importance; Synthesizing (Chapter 5)

Accountable Teacher Talk for Questioning

Following is a list of suggested Teacher Talk that encourages readers to think strategically as they employ the Questioning strategy. To effectively increase levels of thinking, these suggestions incorporate Bloom's Taxonomy's higher-order questioning (Anderson and Krathwohl 2001) and Webb's Depth of Knowledge (2002).

Remembering and Understanding (Recall)

- Why do we ask questions while reading?
- How does forming a question about the text help you comprehend it?

Applying (Skill/Concept)

- What questions did you have while you were reading this text? What questions did you have about the story after reading it? How can you answer your questions?

Analyzing (Strategic Thinking)

- What differences of opinion between _____ and _____ (name two characters) did you notice?

Evaluating and Creating (Extended Thinking)

- What is the author's purpose in writing this section of the text? What is he or she trying to convince us of? The author's message is _____.
- Compose questions that will support comprehension of the text. While you are reading, try to find the answers to your questions.

Behavior Indicators for Questioning

As you assess students' ability to question, use the following behaviors as a guide. Do students exhibit these behaviors never, rarely, often, or always?

- ❑ Establish a purpose for reading by asking questions
- ❑ Generate questions to discover new information
- ❑ Use questions for clarification and problem solving

Techniques for Questioning

Ripple Effect

Purpose:	ELL Technique:
To activate questions and stimulate thinking based on the generated questions	Yes

Materials:	

- text
- small inflatable pool or fishbowl
- colored pebbles
- colored construction paper
- large, blue butcher paper for pond

Learning Phases

I

Select a text, a theme, or a concept to introduce to the class. Bring in a child's small inflatable pool or a fishbowl, and place for all to see. Hold a few small colored pebbles in your hand. Demonstrate the rippling concept that occurs when you throw a pebble into water and there is a splash. You may even hear the pebble hit the water.

Remark how you notice concentric circles rippling out from the entry point. There may even be other effects when the pebble enters the water (e.g., scare a fish, hit another rock, frighten someone near it). By throwing the pebble into the water, you have caused change through the ripple effect.

We

Engage in conversation with the class about how to connect the concrete demonstration to what happens in your head as you think about a story or an idea.

The pebble can represent a question that you form and toss "out there" into the sea of the unknown. A ripple of thoughts (wave of thinking) begins to spread and expand from the point of origin.

During a read-aloud, hold some colored pebbles in your hand, and when a thought or question occurs in your mind, stop and toss the pebble into the water. Share the question and let the "wave of thinking" ripple into the conversation about the text.

With You

Have students ask comprehension questions relating to the content passage. Focus on the varied levels of questions by providing access to the Questioning Matrix found in the QAR Technique in this chapter.

Model the process of generating questions by crafting a question from the text passage, justifying the type of question as well as your thinking process. Use the ripple lines to demonstrate the expansion of thinking in which these questions can take a reader.

By You

After reading a text, create leveled questions to submit to the Ripple Effect area in the classroom based on the level of thinking (literal, interpretive, evaluative, critical). **Suggested Teacher Talk:** *Reflect on your thinking as you generate questions. Justify your choice of question starters (question words) to align with the levels of questions.*

Differentiation

Create a class pond from construction or chart paper by drawing circles representing the waves moving out from the center. Use colored construction paper pebbles as a visual tool for students to record their questions and place on the class pond. The pond can be labeled based on the text you are reading or the concept you are studying. You can also draw ripple waves and record students' thoughts on each wave.

Comprehension Questioning

Question–Answer Relationships (QARs)

Purpose:	ELL Technique:
To determine various questioning techniques to aid in comprehension of the text	Yes

Materials:	
• *QARs* (see qars.pdf)	• notebooks
• text	• note cards (*optional*)

Learning Phases

I — Introduce the four QAR (question-answer relationships): Right There, Think and Search, Author and Me, and On My Own (Raphael et al. 2006). Explain that these four question-answer relationships can be categorized into the two ways the reader derives the answers:

In the Text (Text-based)—This type of question requires students to remember exactly what the author said and to return to the text to find where the author said it. **Suggested Teacher Talk:** *Search and find the exact words in the book to support your thinking.*

- **"Right There"** questions ask readers to respond at the literal level; words from the question and words from the answer will usually be found exactly stated in the text very close to each other. Key Words: *who, what, when, where, identify, list, name, define*

- **"Think and Search"** questions are inferential ones that require readers to derive the answer from more than one sentence, paragraph, or page. Key Words: *compare and contrast, explain, tell why, find evidence, problem and solution, cause and effect*

In My Head—These questions are not found in the book; they require readers to utilize their background knowledge and understanding of what they are reading to answer the questions.

- **"Author and Me"** questions are inferential; the words from the book are in the question, but these questions also require input from readers' own prior knowledge to connect with the text and derive an answer. Key Words: *in what ways, how is the author using, what might happen based on, what is the author's message*

- **"On My Own"** questions require application from readers' background knowledge and experiences. Key Words: *in your opinion, this is what I think, I derived, I feel, I believe it will, I already know that*

We

After discussing the four types of questions, ask students to practice answering the different types of questions, which should be produced beforehand. Have students determine the question–answer relationship of each question and record and justify their answers in their notebooks. **Suggested Teacher Talk:** *Where do you find answers to your questions?*

With You

Partners or teams could practice generating their own questions for each other to answer.

Have students share their responses and then reread the text to verify their accuracy.

By You

Students work independently to present examples of *Open Questions* (Ellery and Rosenboom 2010; Small 2010) or a broader question that encourages choice and varied levels of responses. Provide students with answers to the content question, and students will respond with the questions. The following are examples of open questions:

- The answer is _____. What might the question be? (The answer is C-Squared. What might the question be?)

- How are _____ and _____ alike? How are they different? (How are immigration and relocation alike? How are they different?)

- Initiate a one-minute conversation using the concepts of _____, _____, and _____. (Initiate a one-minute conversation with your partner using the concepts of mean, median, and mode).

Comprehension Questioning

Differentiation

Assign four corners of the classroom one type of question (i.e., Right There would be in a corner, Think and Search in another corner). Write questions from a familiar text on note cards and distribute them to students. The same question may be written several times, if desired. Once students have read their questions, ask them to go to the corner that describes the types of questions in their hands. For example, if the question on the note card is a Right There type of questions, the student will go to the Right There corner. Once students arrive in their corners, ask them to explain to a partner the type of question they have and why that type of question is based on evidence from the text.

Question Logs: 3Rs

Purpose:	ELL Technique:
To bring meaning to the text by recording, reacting, and reflecting to questions	Yes

Comprehension Questioning

Materials:

- text

- *Question Logs: 3Rs Form* (see questionlogs.pdf)

- question logs (binders for recording)

Learning Phases

I During a read-aloud, model asking questions and record your thinking aloud for all to see. Demonstrate the process of readers asking a question to give their mind a springboard to jump off by "reacting, responding, and reflecting" deeply in order to bring meaning to the text.

 We Create three columns to form a question log, and label them to record questions (1R), reactions (2R), and reflections (3R).

Record: Have students record questions that they think or wonder about before and during reading in the (1R) column.

React: Have students note their reactions in the (2R) column as they continue to read the text. **Suggested Teacher Talk:** *What did you wonder about while you were reading this text?*

Reflect: Have students use the final column to reflect, make connections, or note any other thoughts that help bring meaning to the text. **Suggested Teacher Talk:** *What questions do you have about the story after reading it?*

With You

During small-group instruction while using a leveled text, post the *Question Logs: 3Rs Form* and provide students opportunities to go through the process of Question Logs: 3Rs with support by the group.

By You

Have students emphasize the value of composing questions along the path of the reading process and record their thinking pattern in their reading response journals. Have students create their own Question Logs: 3Rs with a text they are reading independently.

Extension

Have students create a three-tab folder by dividing the top part of a folder into thirds. Cut each third section from the bottom of the top folder to the fold, creating three flaps. Label the first flap with the heading *Record*, on the second flap *React*, and the final flap *Respond*.

Survey, Question, Read, Recite, Review (SQ3R)

Purpose:	ELL Technique:
To establish a purpose for reading by asking questions	No

Materials:
• text • *SQ3R Chart* (see sq3r.pdf) • journals

Learning Phases

I

Model surveying the text material by looking at the title, headings, illustrations, graphics, and key terms. Use the questions in the far-left column of the *SQ3R Chart* (adapted from Miller 2002; Robinson 1961) to guide students through this survey process.

We

With the class, apply the SQ3R structure to establish purpose for questioning.

Survey: Invite students to skim and scan the text traits before reading to survey what they are about to read.

Question: Ask students to think about how each of these items might relate to the text, and have them ask questions about the text to establish a purpose for reading. Encourage students to turn the title, heading, and pictures into questions. Have students write their questions in the middle column of the *SQ3R Chart*. **Suggested Teacher Talk:** *Think about the title. What do you know about this subject? What do you want to know? Turn the title into a question. While you are reading, try to find the answers to your questions.*

Copy the *SQ3R Chart* and distribute to each student. Continue the process with teams or partners.

Read: Have students read the text to search for answers to their questions, and have them discuss the columns of the SQ3R sheet.

Recite: Have students recite or write answers to the questions, looking away from the text to recall what was read. Students may need to reread the text for any remaining unanswered questions.

Review: Have students review the information learned by applying it to another context. Examples may be creating a graphic organizer that depicts the main idea, role-playing parts of the text, drawing a flow chart, summarizing, and participating in group discussions.

Ask students to write their thoughts about questioning in a reflective journal. Have students share their journal responses during one-to-one conferencing. Example prompt: *How were your questions answered? Were some questions answered through making an inference? What examples can you share?*

Comprehension Questioning

Extension

Discuss with students some possible answers to the following questions and allow time for students to think about them before responding: What do we know about asking questions? How does asking questions help a reader? How do readers figure out the answers to their questions? Write students' answers on a chart in separate columns.

Questioning the Author (QtA)

Purpose:	ELL Technique:
To ask questions and deeper queries to determine the author's purpose	No

Materials:

- text
- journals

Comprehension Questioning

Learning Phases

I

Select a passage of text to create deeper discussions about the author's point of view. Determine a purposeful stopping point to "Question the Author" (Beck et al. 1997, 2006). Create questions that spark critical thinking. **Suggested Teacher Talk:** *What is the author's purpose in this section of the text? What is the author trying to convince us about? The author's message is _____ .*

We

Discuss with students the concept of questioning: *What do we know about asking questions? How does asking questions help you as a reader? How do you figure out the answers to your questions?* Record students' answers visually for future reflection.

With You

In small groups, have students read to predetermined logical stopping points. Ask and answer open-ended "queries" to support in understanding the author's intended purpose for the meaning of the concept while interacting with the reading process. **Suggested Teacher Talk:** *This part of the text is about _____ . The point the author is making here is _____ . Why is the author telling us this part now?*

By You

Have students record in their reading journals how they uncovered the author's point of view through "questioning the author" while reading. Have them create alternative ways to present the information. **Suggested Teacher Talk:** *What would you say differently from what the author said to present the information? How could the author have presented the information more clearly to support your understanding?*

Comprehension Strategy: Visualizing and Sensory Imaging

Visualizing is a strategy that enables readers to make words on the page of a text real and concrete (Keene and Zimmermann 2007). This strategy helps readers engage with the text, strengthens their relationship to the text, and stimulates imaginative thinking, which aids in comprehension. The reader visualizes by creating a picture in his or her mind based on descriptive details within the text to assist understanding. Before and after reading, sensory language helps readers form appropriate mental images in their heads about what is happening in the text. Visual literacy is the ability to think visually. "Learners are most able to build connections between verbal and visual representations when text and illustrations are actively held in memory at the same time" (Avgerinou and Pettersson 2011, 11).

Visualizing provides a springboard for memory recall and retention and makes reading an active process by stimulating the mental interchange of new ideas and experiences. "Visualizing personalizes reading, keeps us engaged, and often prevents us from abandoning a book" (Harvey and Goudvis 2000, 97). Creating sensory images equips readers to draw conclusions, bring to mind details, and create interpretations of the text. Forming these images during reading seems to increase the amount readers understand and recall (Fisher et al. 2009; Irwin 1991; Johnston, Barnes, and Desrochers 2008; Sprenger 2005).

Using drama is another way to explore a story and its content in a visual way. A research study on drama by McMaster (1998) found that vocabularies presented in a drama content provided students with the opportunity to acquire the meanings visually. "Drama for language learning not only provides a whole learning experience but brings language learning to life" (Robbie, Ruggierello, and Warren 2001, 2). Using drama appeals to all the senses and encourages the use of sensory imaging as a strategy for acquiring meaning of text. Appropriate text that best supports the application of the visualizing strategy needs to have words and phrases that provoke thinking and are full of images for the mind.

To support Visualizing and Sensory Imaging while reading, a set of skills is required to effectively implement this reading strategy. The synchronized application of several reading strategies results in making meaning while reading a text. The skills, additional integrated reading strategies, and their reading components found in corresponding chapters are listed below.

Focus Skill(s):

- Create mental images
- Interpret sensory language

Integrated Strategies:

- Wide Reading; Categorizing; Visual Imaging (Chapter 3)
- Expressing; Rereading (Chapter 4)
- Previewing; Activating and Building Schema; Predicting; Questioning; Inferring and Drawing Conclusions (Chapter 5)

Accountable Teacher Talk for Visualizing and Sensory Imaging

Following is a list of suggested Teacher Talk that encourages readers to think strategically as they employ the Visualizing and Sensory Imaging strategy. To effectively increase levels of thinking, these suggestions incorporate Bloom's Taxonomy's higher-order questioning (Anderson and Krathwohl 2001) and Webb's Depth of Knowledge (2002).

Remembering and Understanding (Recall)

- In my head, I can see _____.
- What images did you see in your mind as you read?

Applying (Skill/Concept)

- Describe how the setting looked in your mind. What pictures came to your mind as you read? What sounds did you hear as you read?

Analyzing (Strategic Thinking)

- What words or phrases did the author use to help you create an image in your mind?

Evaluating and Creating (Extended Thinking)

- Analyze and explain the difference between watching a movie and reading. Describe the similarities and differences between these two in relation to the story line.
- Create a movie in your mind. What sensory details did the author use to help you create an image of the text in your mind?

Behavior Indicators for Visualizing and Sensory Imaging

As you assess students' ability to visualize, use the following behaviors as a guide. Do students exhibit these behaviors never, rarely, often, or always?

- ❏ Record mental images of text
- ❏ Create illustrations to support meaning of a text
- ❏ Use senses to attend to story details

Techniques for Visualizing and Sensory Imaging

Sketch to Stretch

Purpose:	ELL Technique:
To sketch visual images of text to aid in memory and recall of the story	Yes

Materials:

- texts
- drawing paper
- markers or colored pencils
- music (*optional*)

Learning Phases

I

Introduce *Sketch to Stretch* (Short, Harste, and Burke, 1996) by demonstrating how to sketch a scene, a thought, or idea of what the text means after you finish reading or listening to it. **Suggested Teacher Talk:** *What words or phrases did the author use to help you create an image in your mind?*

We

Determine the most important scene from a class read-aloud and discuss why students think that image needs to be highlighted graphically. Have a volunteer begin to draw parts of it where it is visible to everyone. As the student begins to "sketch," ask the rest of the class to discuss symbols, words, and phrases that can be added to stretch the concept and bring deeper meaning of the text.

With You

Arrange students in heterogeneous groups. Have students take turns sharing their sketch-to-stretch compositions, and have group members tell their interpretations of the sketches. When everyone in the group has given his or her version of the sketch, the student who drew the picture describes his or her interpretation of the illustration. **Suggested Teacher Talk:** *What images did you see in your mind as you were sketching?* Repeat this process until all members of the group have shared their sketches.

By You

Have students reread the text and reflect on the words or phrases that were sketched as they reacted to the text.

Extension

Have teams add all the sketches together to create a sequential mural of their version of the text and share with the class.

Wordless Picture Books

Purpose:	ELL Technique:
To create illustrations that support the meaning of a text	Yes

Materials:

- text
- drawing paper
- TV show theme songs or instrumentals
- CD player

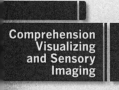

Comprehension Visualizing and Sensory Imaging

Learning Phases

I

As you read a text with students, discuss how to create mental pictures of it. **Suggested Teacher Talk:** *What picture comes to mind as you read the text? Here's what I picture....*

We

After reading a text, have students describe images that would create pictures of the parts of the text that were not illustrated.

With You

Ask students to draw the "missing parts" that they created in their minds and share their drawings with a small group. **Suggested Teacher Talk:** *Try to imagine the setting. What does it look like?* Compile students' drawings to create a picture book.

By You

Have students reread the original text, reflecting on the illustrations they drew to capture the mental images.

Differentiation

Use similes appropriate for students' needs to create mental images by attaching the known to the unknown. For example, the icicle was as cold as a popsicle. The shape of the Earth looks like a blue-and-green marble.

Extension

Students listen to TV show theme songs or instrumentals and imagine the music as the background for a movie. Have students describe what they think the movie could be about, based on the music.

Frame This

Purpose:	ELL Technique:
To frame images of a story by creating a life-size picture to aid in visualizing details from a story	No

Materials:

- text
- 11" x 14" picture frame, with picture
- online resource Fotobabble (*optional*)

Learning Phases

I

Show a picture in a frame, and discuss how the frame holds the picture but the picture tells or captures the story of what was taking place at the time of the picture.

We

Use the outer section of an 11" × 14" frame to create a life-size talking picture frame. Have a volunteer hold the frame in front of his or her face so the "audience" can "see" the picture (the volunteer's face).

Have the student volunteer (also known as the "picture frame") begin to talk about the images that he or she recorded in his or her mind during the read-aloud. The volunteer can use facial and voice expressions to convey his or her message.

With You

After reading a leveled text with a small group, pass a frame around to capture key vocabulary. Have students share orally and capture their written responses of what was read.

By You

Have students record in their reading log an image from their mind that brings to life the fullness and rich colors of meaning from the text.

Comprehension Visualizing and Sensory Imaging

Extension

Students use an online resource such as Fotobabble (http://www.fotobabble.com) to bring story images to life and use their voice to record directly into the program their retell, key details, and interesting points to share.

Drama

Purpose:	ELL Technique:
To bring story images to life	Yes

Materials:	
• illustrated text	• props (e.g., puppets, hats, clothing, objects)

Learning Phases

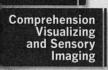

Comprehension Visualizing and Sensory Imaging

I
Read a text aloud to the class without showing any of the pictures. As they listen to you read, ask students to visualize in their mind images of what is happening in the text.

We
After a section of the text is read aloud, ask a student to use appropriate props to act out images that were in his or her mind as you read the selection. **Suggested Teacher Talk:** *Did you create a movie in your mind? If so, describe it.*

With You
Ask several students to read another section from the same text without showing illustrations to the other students. **Suggested Teacher Talk:** *How did you visualize the beginning of the text?*

Have teams come to the front of the room, perform, and try to create the images in the minds of the other students (the audience) who did not read the text.

By You
Ask the audience to discuss what they saw and determine if the drama and the images in their minds' eyes were similar or different.

Extension

Play a word guessing game, like Charades. Without using words, students act out scenes from a story while the audience tries to guess the events.

Sensory Impressions

Purpose:	ELL Technique:
To utilize senses to attend to story details	Yes

Materials:	

- *Sensory Impressions Chart* (see sensorychart.pdf)
- *Sensory Impressions Hand* (see sensoryhand.pdf)

- text
- sensory items (*optional*)

Learning Phases

I

Read a text selection that is rich in sensory details and discuss the number of times we read and are able to tap into our senses to aid in recall of important details. **Suggested Teacher Talk:** *What sensory details did the author use to help you create a picture of the story in your mind?*

We

Create sensory-filled scenarios for students to imagine. For example, ask students to close their eyes and think of the school cafeteria. Ask them to describe to a partner what they see, smell, touch, taste, and hear.

The class could also go on a nature walk to utilize their senses to describe their surroundings. Students may use the *Sensory Impressions Hand* to record one sensory item for each finger. Transfer this sensory thinking to the text.

With You

Ask students to work in groups to compare their answers and discuss any differences in their responses.

By You

Distribute the *Sensory Impressions Chart* to each student. Ask students to stop throughout their reading to write or draw their responses under the appropriate sense. **Suggested Teacher Talk:** *What sounds did you hear in your mind as you read? Record it under the picture of the ear.*

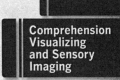

Comprehension Visualizing and Sensory Imaging

Extension

Distribute a variety of sensory items (e.g., glasses, gloves, clown nose, headphones, spoon) to students. As students listen to a read-aloud, they will reflect upon their particular sense and record appropriate sensory responses that pertain to the text being read. For example, if a student received a scented candle, his or her sense would be smell. Have students retell the story through the appropriate sense (e.g., *I could smell the cookies baking*).

Comprehension Strategy: Inferring and Drawing Conclusions

Inferring is a strategy that permits readers to merge their background knowledge with text clues to arrive at a conclusion about an underlying theme or idea. Drawing conclusions helps readers gather more information and ideas and understand the writer's point of view. According to a study by Cromley, Snyder-Hogan, and Luciw-Dubas, "Authors do not make explicit the relationships among every proposition in text. A variety of inferences—at the inter and intrasentence level—are therefore key for comprehension. Inferences typically found in reading include conclusions drawn between propositions in text, either within sentences or between adjacent sentences (bridging inferences), and conclusions drawn between prior topic knowledge and the current text (elaborative inferences)" (2010, 688).

Readers gather and question details from the text to reach a decision that makes sense. They arrive at a decision or an opinion by reasoning from known facts or evidence that seem to require that a specific conclusion be reached. This cognitive model builds "text-based representation through processes critical for semantic coherence such as pronominal reference and inferences that connects parts of text" (Johnston et al. 2008, 125). Such readers use implicit information to make a logical guess or read between the lines.

Strategic readers create unique understandings of the text, make predictions and inferences, and confirm or deny those predictions based on textual information. These readers test their developing comprehension of the text along with extending their comprehension beyond literal understandings of the printed page (Keene and Zimmermann 2007). "Inferencing is the bedrock of comprehension...it is about reading faces, reading body language, reading expressions, and reading tone, as well as reading text" (Harvey and Goudvis 2000, 105).

To support Inferring and Drawing Conclusions while reading, a set of skills is required to effectively implement this reading strategy. The synchronized application of several reading strategies results in making meaning while reading a text. The skills, additional integrated reading strategies, and their reading components found in corresponding chapters are listed on the next page.

Focus Skill(s):

- Schema

- Interpret implied information (i.e., body language, expression, tone of voice)

- Context clues

Integrated Strategies:

- Associating; Analyzing Words (Chapter 3)

- Rereading; Expressing; Wide Reading (Chapter 4)

- Previewing; Activating and Building Schema; Predicting; Questioning; Visualizing and Sensory Imaging; Determining Importance; Synthesizing (Chapter 5)

Accountable Teacher Talk for Inferring and Drawing Conclusions

Following is a list of suggested Teacher Talk that encourages readers to think strategically as they employ the Inferring and Drawing Conclusions strategy. To effectively increase levels of thinking, these suggestions incorporate Bloom's Taxonomy's higher-order questioning (Anderson and Krathwohl 2001) and Webb's Depth of Knowledge (2002).

Remembering and Understanding (Recall)

- What does it mean to "read between the lines"?

- Where are your eyes looking next? What words are you still holding in your mind but are no longer presented for you to view?

Applying (Skill/Concept)

- What is the main conclusion from _____?

Analyzing (Strategic Thinking)

- What clues did the author give that led to your conclusion? What details or evidence support your conclusion?

Evaluating and Creating (Extended Thinking)

- What would happen if _____ occurred in the text? Why do you think that would happen?

- Construct a statement that demonstrates what the text implies. Explain your thinking and search for clues within the text to support your reasoning.

Behavior Indicators for Inferring and Drawing Conclusions

As you assess students' ability to infer and draw conclusions, use the following behaviors as a guide. Do students exhibit these behaviors never, rarely, often, or always?

- ❑ Merge background knowledge with text clues

- ❑ Construct interpretations by reading between the lines

- ❑ Make judgments after considering all information presented in the text

Techniques for Inferring and Drawing Conclusions

Interpreting Text

Purpose:	ELL Technique:
To read between the lines to construct meaning	No

Materials:

- texts
- copies of text excerpt
- display options (chart paper, dry-erase boards, interactive whiteboard)
- newspaper pictures or illustrations from text
- greeting cards
- paper and art supplies
- transparency of text excerpt

Learning Phases

I

Enlarge a section of a text that supports inferring and display it with a visual enhancer (e.g., projector or interactive whiteboard), or make and distribute copies so that all students can see the text and follow along. Read aloud the passage, pausing at key sections to ask, *"So, what's really going on?"* Model how a reader answers his or her questions as he or she reads by orally answering the questions.

We

Discuss with students what you and they think is really going on. If desired, you can have students read a section silently and then stop to talk in pairs about how every part of the text takes on a deeper layer when readers make their own interpretations. **Suggested Teacher Talk:** *Why do you think that would happen? What is the story beneath the story?*

With You

Display a newspaper picture. Ask students to view it and determine what they would create as the heading for the article. Have them think of ways to write the heading to correspond with the picture without giving the reader all the information.

Have partners read each heading and determine what they think the rest of the story will be about. The goal is to encourage a reader to infer the meaning of the picture based on the heading, and entice them to read the rest of the article. You can also use greeting cards with symbolic language and discuss the real meaning of the card.

By You

Have students create their own greeting cards, using metaphors, similes, and various poetic structures.

Save the Last Word for Me

Purpose:	ELL Technique:
To construct interpretations and compare with others	Yes

Materials:	
• texts	• paper or note cards

Learning Phases

I

Select a passage, phrase, word, or sentences within the selected text that "stands out" or catches your attention. Explain to students that you have chosen a section of text that you thought was interesting. Read it to students, and explain why you selected it and what you think it means.

We

Choose a text that may elicit differing opinions or multiple interpretations to share with students. As students read the text, have them select five statements that they find interesting or would like to comment on—statements they agree or disagree with or that contradict something they thought they knew.

Ask students to write what the text said (words, phrases, or sentences) that caught their attention on the front side of a piece of paper or a note card to use for *Save the Last Word for Me* (Short et al. 1996). These can be interesting points worthy of discussion. **Suggested Teacher Talk:** *Try to read between the lines.*

With You

Have students comment and/or explain on the back of the paper or card why they selected the passage, phrase, sentence, or words. Place students into small groups for discussion.

Each student takes a turn selecting a card and reading the front of the card aloud to his or her group. All other students, in turn, respond to the statement, make comments, agree or disagree, and share what they think the quote or statement means. **Suggested Teacher Talk:** *I think this statement means_____.*

By You

The student who wrote on the front of the card gets the opportunity to turn the card over and explain to the group why he or she chose this particular quote. This gives the student whose thoughts are on the back of the card the "last word" to either alter or stand by what was written as a reflection on the phrase.

Comprehension
Inferring and
Drawing Conclusi

Talk Show

Purpose:	ELL Technique:
To reflect on and discuss the content of a book	Yes

Materials:

- text
- microphone
- T-chart
- journals

Learning Phases

Comprehension Inferring and Drawing Conclusions

I
Choose a group of three students to pretend that they are on a talk show: One student should host the show, one should pretend to be the author of a book which students have read, and one should pretend to be the reader of the book. Give students a microphone to hold when they speak.

We
Have the host open the show by giving an introduction about the book they will be discussing on the show. Have students begin with their discussion of the book. The author should make statements that imply information, and the reader should make inferences from those statements. For example, if the author states, "The main character discovered real joy," then readers might infer that the main character has been unhappy or upset about something but an event occurs that results in his or her happiness. Have the host begin to summarize the discussion with statements like, "So, what I hear you saying is ____."

With You
Have the rest of the students be the "audience" and take notes during the talk show by folding a piece of paper lengthwise to make two columns (i.e., separating the author's statements from the reader's inferences) to discuss later with partners. **Suggested Teacher Talk:** *What evidence does the author "host" provide? What does the author "host" want you to realize?*

By You
Have students reread the text and reflect on the show and how it supported their comprehension of the text.

Differentiation

Have students record in reflection journals their interpretation of the interview by reflecting on and thinking about what was said and not said (e.g., body language, tone of voice). Students who require more support can be given a paragraph frame to assist them with their writing. Students who require less support can be given an open-ended prompt.

Scenarios With T-Charts

Purpose:	ELL Technique:
To make inferences about a scenario based on evidence	No

Materials:

- text
- paper

Learning Phases

I
Use scenarios from the text from which students can practice inferring. Have students listen to these scenarios or read them to one another and decide what inferences they can draw based on the evidence in the text.

We
Have volunteers take turns stating their inferences and then noting what evidence from the scenario helped to lead them to their inferences about the section of the text. *What clues did the author give that led to your conclusion?*

With You
Have student pairs create T-charts on paper. Students should write their inferences on the left side and write the evidence, or the *why* behind their thinking, on the right side of the chart. **Suggested Teacher Talk:** *What reasoning helped you draw your conclusion?*

By You
Reread the text, having students note any changes directly on the T-chart as they listen to you read. **Suggested Teacher Talk:** *How did inferring help you understand the text?*

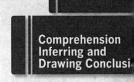
Comprehension
Inferring and
Drawing Conclusi

Extension

Create a courtroom scenario. Have students listen to the evidence presented. In the "deliberation room," have students use multiple strategies (e.g., what they visualized, connections made, questions answered) and then discuss their judgments from their points of view. Have them use their ability to gather the details and draw a conclusion. Ask them to record their conclusions and read their verdicts.

Comprehension Strategy: Determining Importance

Determining importance is a strategy that requires the reader to read closely to distinguish between what is important and what is merely interesting. "When great readers are reading this stuff that has so many ideas in it, they have to listen to that mental voice tell them which words, which sentences or paragraphs, and which ideas are important" (Keene and Zimmermann 1997, 86).

Readers are required to identify the topic and supporting details and to identify or invent their own main idea or summary statement by combining ideas across sentences. Reading requires the memory to hold and process a massive amount of information. "Readers cannot store all the information presented in a text in their minds. Sifting through information to determine the most important points ensures that working memory is not overloaded and continues to process information" (Fisher et al., 2009, 51). Sometimes, however, the reader needs to understand and remember more information than can be summed up in a brief statement. Finding the essence of the text is the key to determining what is important. The reader needs to make decisions as to what parts of a text deserve the most attention, remembering that not all the information presented is of equal value. Determining importance is critical when reading texts that emphasize learning of information. The ability to sift salient information and identify essential ideas is a prerequisite to developing insight and deciding what to remember (Harvey and Goudvis 2000, 2013; CCSS 2010). Strategic readers are able to look for text features that signal cues and for ideas that help to distinguish the important from the unimportant within the text and between fiction and nonfiction text.

To support Determining Importance while reading, a set of skills is required to effectively implement this reading strategy. The synchronized application of several reading strategies results in making meaning while reading a text. The skills, additional integrated reading strategies, and their reading components found in corresponding chapters are listed below.

Focus Skill(s):

- Identify main idea
- Identify author's purpose
- Organize information
- Connect information

Integrated Strategies:

- Synthesizing Sounds; Analyzing Sounds; Embedding (Chapter 2)
- Associating; Contextualizing (Chapter 3)
- Phrasing; Rereading; Pacing; Wide Reading (Chapter 4)
- Activating and Building Schema; Questioning; Visualizing and Sensory Imaging; Inferring and Drawing Conclusions; Summarizing; Synthesizing (Chapter 5)

Accountable Teacher Talk for Determining Importance

Following is a list of suggested Teacher Talk that encourages readers to think strategically as they employ the Determining Importance strategy. To effectively increase levels of thinking, these suggestions incorporate Bloom's Taxonomy's higher-order questioning (Anderson and Krathwohl 2001) and Webb's Depth of Knowledge (2002).

Remembering and Understanding (Recall)

- Tell me about some of the important ideas in the text.
- Show in the text what you read that was the most important idea.

Applying (Skill/Concept)

- What is the author's message in the text?

Analyzing (Strategic Thinking)

- What does the author offer as a theme or opinion from the text?

Evaluating and Creating (Extended Thinking)

- Establish criteria for determining what is important. How did you know these details were more important than other details?
- Create questions you have about the information presented. Generate evidence that the author used to support his or her case.

Behavior Indicators for Determining Importance

As you assess students' ability to determine importance, use the following behaviors as a guide. Do students exhibit these behaviors never, rarely, often, or always?

- ❑ Use supporting details from the text to clearly explain why it is important
- ❑ Determine essential information and main ideas
- ❑ Identify story elements and determine supporting key details

Techniques for Determining Importance

Picture This

Purpose:	ELL Technique:
To examine a photograph for details and determine the main purpose of the photo	Yes

Materials:

- photographs (e.g., content area, theme or unit of study)
- newspaper/magazine pictures
- plastic sleeve or picture frame
- items from family events such as photos or postcards

Learning Phases

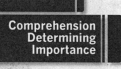
Comprehension
Determining
Importance

I — Gather several photographs and share with the class. Place pictures in a plastic sleeve, a glass picture frame, or laminate them. Circulate the photos, and ask students to describe what they think is happening in the picture(s). **Suggested Teacher Talk:** *Looking at the photograph, what do you think is the main reason this picture was taken? Why do you believe this was the main reason it was taken?*

We — Have students generate and share a headline they think would best support the picture if it were in a newspaper or a magazine. Record their generated words and details directly on the picture (e.g., use a dry-erase marker on the plastic film or lamination, or use permanent marker on the glass, which can be cleaned with rubbing alcohol).

With You — Have groups analyze the pictures and come to a consensus on the main purpose of the picture(s). Students read and compare the headline or caption that actually supports the picture from the newspaper or magazine article with students' ideas.

By You — Have students gather and share pictures, postcards, or other items to document family vacations, events, and so forth. Direct them to generate a single statement that summarizes their trip, activity, or experience based on the pictures.

Extension

Place several pictures at each table group. Ask students to discuss the pictures and put them into a story format. Students use the pictures to capture the main concept and share what they interpret, based on the pictures, what the title of the story could be and which picture they think represents the main idea of the story line.

Chapter Tours

Purpose:	ELL Technique:
To preview text and identify key nonfiction features	Yes

Materials:	
• text	• brochures
• a hat marked "Tour Guide"	• paper

Learning Phases

I

Bring in several brochures from local tourist locations or travel agents. Share how the brochure highlights key features of the location and creates a sensation for the viewer to want to visit.

We

Have students embark on a tour such as a nature tour, a school tour, or a virtual tour on the web. Have them listen to the tour guide for key words that help them connect and relate to the tour. Ask students to transfer the tour concept to a nonfiction text that they will be reading.

Have them preview the text and identify features such as photographs, labels, and key words that will help them determine what is important. **Suggested Teacher Talk:** *Look carefully at the first and last line of each paragraph. What do you notice?*

With You

Have students take turns putting on the tour guide hat and leading a small group (e.g., heterogeneous, ability) through a tour of the text students will be reading. Encourage students to make comments like a real tour guide. **Suggested Teacher Talk:** *Tell me about some of the important ideas that struck you.*

By You

Have students reread the text and reflect on how the tour guide activity supported their comprehension.

Comprehension
Determining
Importance

Differentiation

Have students create a "story/concept" travel brochure using the tour guide words. Students can become a tour guide by applying words identified in their brochure as guided imagery (adapted from Wood, Lapp, and Flood, 1992). The following is a sample of tour guide talk:

As we look over to the left, you will notice_____.

Focus your attention on_____.

Coming up now is one of the highlights of_____.

Today you will see_____.

Main Idea Wheel

Purpose:	ELL Technique:
To identify what is essential within the text	Yes

Materials:

- text
- *Main Idea Wheel: Six Spokes* (see wheelsixspokes.pdf)
- *Main Idea Wheel: Four Spokes* (see wheelfourspokes.pdf)
- items for creating spinning wheel such as pencil, brad, or paper clip (*optional*)

Learning Phases

I   Choose a familiar text and copy either *Main Idea Wheel: Six Spokes* or the *Four Spokes*. Discuss the concept of compiling important information to gather the main idea. Identify and record the important concept from a text in the center part of the wheel where students can view and observe your thinking process. Share how you think about what you have read and record important details. Ponder the details and determine from the information recorded what is essential and can be the "gist" of all the information gathered. Record the essential information on the spokes of the wheel.

We   Continue to the next section of the wheel and have students sift salient information to be recorded. Investigate with students how to read closely to determine what the author is trying to convey as essential. Continue the process until a class *Main Idea Wheel* has been completed. Lead a discussion about what various parts of information were placed on the spokes as being important. Read each of the spokes and connect them together to create a group summary based on the essential details of the text.

With You   Divide students into groups. Assign each group a different section or chapter of text to determine the essential details and record on a *Main Idea Wheel*. Students' discussions should focus on why they think it was an essential part of the story/concept.

By You   Students create their own *Main Idea Wheels* based on a text they are independently reading. Have them reflect on the ideas and statements they wrote on their spokes and on how these ideas supported their process of making meaning from the text.

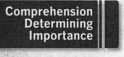

Comprehension
Determining
Importance

Extension

Students can cut out their wheels and create a puzzle effect or create spinners for the wheel by attaching them to an item like a pencil using a brad or paper clip. Students spin their wheels and share with a partner the detailed information they gathered from the text that is within that spoke of the wheel.

Highlighting the Highs

Purpose:	ELL Technique:
To identify essential information	Yes

Materials:

- texts
- overhead transparencies
- highlighters or transparency pens
- plain and colored sticky notes (*optional*)
- online resources (*optional*)

Learning Phases

I

Model the process for highlighting selective information. Use a think-aloud to model the tips for effective highlighting. See Figure 5.3 Tips for Highlighting the Highs (adapted from Ellery and Rosenboom 2010).

Figure 5.3 Tips for Highlighting the Highs

Be selective in highlighting, focusing on key ideas, new vocabulary, and ideas that you find surprising.
Highlight key words and phrases rather than whole sentences.
Use sticky notes to jot down your thoughts, questions, and concerns while reading.
Read one or two paragraphs at a time, and then highlight.
If your page appears "fluorescent," you are probably highlighting too much information.

We

Review tips and have students skim or preview a passage, focusing on text structure (e.g., bold headings, subheadings, key vocabulary) and the authors' purpose. **Suggested Teacher Talk:** *What message is the author communicating in the passage?*

With You

Project a section from the text and have students work in groups to determine and highlight essential information. **Suggested Teacher Talk:** *Highlight only necessary words and phrases. Be prepared to justify your reasoning for selecting your highlighted information.* Ask students to share their markings and the purposes for them.

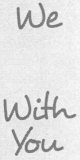

Comprehension Determining Importance

Have students reread the text and reflect on how highlighting important information guided them to a clearer understanding of the author's purpose for the text.

Extensions

- Students use sticky notes to mark sections in their text that help them to determine what information is important. On the sticky note, have students record why they selected that particular section of the text. Students may use different color sticky notes to categorize their facts. Have students highlight relationships between facts on sticky notes.

- Students can use picture notes, webbing, or two-column note taking to create a visual representation as they review their section with the class.

**Comprehension
Determining
Importance**

Comprehension Strategy: Summarizing

Summarizing is a strategy that helps the reader identify and organize the essential information found within a text. Strategic readers summarize during reading by putting together information and focusing on the key elements of what they are reading. These key elements are brief and related to important ideas, events, details, structural clues, or other information that supports the reader in bringing meaning to the text. Students continually organize these key elements throughout their reading of a text while filtering out less significant details. Research by Pearson and Duke (2002) suggests instruction on summarizing to improve students' overall comprehension of text content.

To make generalizations about a story rather than simply retelling the specifics, strategic readers select important information after reading and bring together these ideas in their own words. Retelling allows students to recall story structure and gives them guidance as they discuss the setting, theme, plot episodes, resolution of conflicts, and sequence of events (Hoyt 2008). A summary is an objective retelling and recounting of the text, succinctly reducing the passages into a simple compilation of essential facts. In order to determine important or extraneous information, readers will need to have a command of how the text is structured. Effective summarizing instruction should guide readers to "discern the inherent text structures in a text" (Marzano 2010, 83). "Text guides" are used as resources to support the ability to deconstruct, as it requires the reader to break down the main ideas that comprise the text to form a summary (Montelongo 2008).

To support Summarizing while reading, a set of skills is required to effectively implement this reading strategy. The synchronized application of several reading strategies results in making meaning while reading a text. The skills, additional integrated reading strategies, and their reading components found in corresponding chapters are listed below.

Focus Skill(s):

- Organize information
- Recognize story elements
- Deconstruct text

Integrated Strategies:

- Synthesizing Sounds; Embedding (Chapter 2)
- Associating; Contextualizing (Chapter 3)
- Rereading (Chapter 4)
- Previewing; Activating and Building Schema; Predicting; Visualizing and Sensory Imaging; Inferring and Drawing Conclusions; Determining Importance; Synthesizing (Chapter 5)

Accountable Teacher Talk for Summarizing

Following is a list of suggested Teacher Talk that encourages readers to think strategically as they employ the Summarizing strategy. To effectively increase levels of thinking, these suggestions incorporate Bloom's Taxonomy's higher-order questioning (Anderson and Krathwohl 2001) and Webb's Depth of Knowledge (2002).

Remembering and Understanding (Recall)
- What clues are within the text?
- What was the focus of the reading selection?

Applying (Skill/Concept)
- Which words helped you describe the main idea of the story?

Analyzing (Strategic Thinking)
- What is the author saying? How can you use key ideas to condense the information in this story?

Evaluating and Creating (Extended Thinking)
- What do you understand now that you did not understand before? How has your thinking changed since reading that part of the text?
- Think of all the parts in the story and put them together as if you were going to tell another person about the story. How could you say this using only a few sentences: *In brief_____. In conclusion_____. To sum it up_____? Create a summary.*

Behavior Indicators for Summarizing

As you assess students' ability to summarize, use the following behaviors as a guide. Do students exhibit these behaviors never, rarely, often, or always?

- ❏ Reconstruct the text through a retell
- ❏ Identify and organize essential information
- ❏ Examine and filter less significant details

Techniques for Summarizing

Detail/Retell

Purpose:	ELL Technique:
To recount story details in a sequential order and develop story grammar	Yes

Materials:

- *Detail/Retell Rubric* (see detailretell.pdf)
- text

- one of the following story props: gardening glove, baseball base mats, three Hula-Hoops™

Learning Phases

I

Discuss and practice ways we retell daily. **Suggested Teacher Talk:** *I am going to retell the story to you as if you never heard it before.* Remind them this is just like when they tell their friends about their weekend or vacation. When you retell a story, you are providing the details of the story so the other person can create a mental image of the story details.

Demonstrate retelling after you read a short text. Use the *Detail/Retell Rubric* as a guide to evaluate your model of a proficient retell.

We

Ask a student to begin retelling the text by only retelling the beginning of the details. Other students continue adding onto the retell until all of the details have been shared. As a group, refer to the *Detail/Retell Rubric* and evaluate the class retell for proficiency.

With You

With partners, have students tell what they did over the weekend, last night, on vacation, and so forth. Discuss how they may have used words like *first*, *next*, and *then* while they were retelling the events to their partners.

By You

Have students retell in detail orally or in written form, and have them self-check for the behavior indicators on the rubric.

Use the *Detail/Retell Rubric* as a guide for students to reflect on their ability to retell and as an evaluation tool of the students' comprehension of the text.

Comprehension
Summarizing

Extensions

- **Story Glove**—Write on a garden glove, with a permanent marker, the terms *characters* (thumb), *setting* (pointer finger), *problem* (middle finger), *events* (ring finger) and *ending* (pinky finger). Use the glove as a visual reminder of the narrative story elements for a retell. Students can trace their hand and create a retell to share by drawing or writing the story elements on the their fingers.

- **Baseball Mats**—Create or purchase a first base, a second base, and a third base, and have students stand on each base and retell in detail what happened first in the story, then what happened next in the story, and finally share how the story ended while standing on third base. You can use the home plate for students to share the information from the detail retell to "bring the retell home" by selecting key pieces of information and creating a concise summary statement.

- **Hula-Hoops™**—Place at least three different-colored Hula-Hoops™ on the floor before a read-aloud. As you are reading, stand inside a Hula-Hoop™ and move to the next hoop when there is a transition in the text. When you have finished the section, step out of the Hula-Hoops™ and ask students what was happening when you were in the first red hoop, next in the green hoop, etc. This allows students with a more spatial awareness to follow the sequence of the story and supports their Detail/Retell.

- **Table of Contents**—Have students use the table of contents as a review and an opportunity to guide them through a retell. Students read aloud the table of contents, stopping on each entry and giving the details that were within that chapter.

Summary Ball

Purpose:	ELL Technique:
To create a group summary	Yes

Materials:	
- text - beach ball - chart paper	- permanent marker - *Story Map* (see storymapping.pdf) (*optional*)

Learning Phases

I : After reading a narrative, write the words *Who*, *What*, *Where*, *When*, *Why*, and *How* on an inflated beach ball, using a permanent marker.

We : Have students toss around the ball in a small group. Ask each student who catches the ball to look to see which word is closest to his or her right thumb and to answer that question with regard to the text just read.

With You

If more than one student gets the same question, the first student can answer the question and subsequent students can elaborate on what the first student said about that topic. **Suggested Teacher Talk:** *How could you say this using only a few sentences?* Record students' responses on chart paper to provide a group story summary.

By You

Have students reread the text and reflect on the summary created. **Suggested Teacher Talk:** *How did creating a group summary support your understanding of the story we read?*

Differentiation

Copy the story map and distribute to each student. Ask students to complete the map while the story is being read and identify the characters (who they are and what the author tells about them), the setting (where and when the story takes place), the problems and events (what problems the characters are facing, whether those problems are changing throughout the story), and the solution (the conclusion, or how things work out). When the ball is tossed, students search on their story map for the information and keep track of ones contributed by the other students.

Informational Text and Narrative Pyramid

Purpose:	ELL Technique:
To organize events in a story	Yes

Materials:

- text
- *Narrative and Informational Text Pyramid* (see textpyramid.pdf)

Learning Phases

I

Choose a story students have read, and tell them that they will be constructing an eight-line *Narrative or Informational Text Pyramid* (adapted from Ellery and Rosenboom 2010; Waldo 1991) of words. **Suggested Teacher Talk:** *Think of all the parts in the story and put them together as if you were telling another person the story.*

Comprehension
Summarizing

We

Together as a class, create a pyramid to model the process as follows:

Line 1: character's name in a single word (nonfiction—one major idea)

Line 2: two words to describe that character (nonfiction—two supporting details)

Line 3: three words to portray the setting on the third line, or they can add three different locations (nonfiction—describing major idea)

Line 4: explain the problem using four descriptive words on the fourth line, or four specific conflicts occurring in the text (nonfiction—four words describing another supporting detail)

Lines 5–7: five, six, and seven will present three different events that occurred, each one utilizing the corresponding number of words for their lines (nonfiction—author's purpose and vocabulary words)

Line 8: select eight words to express the solution to the problem

With You

Have small groups construct pyramids.

By You

Have students use their pyramid to summarize the text. (nonfiction—summarize topic) **Suggested Teacher Talk:** *Using your pyramid, explain what your topic is about.*

Extension

Use the *Narrative and Informational Text Pyramid* for students to reflect on story details and record during a class Interactive read-aloud. Have them justify their sections with a partner.

Somebody/Wanted/But/So

Purpose:	ELL Technique:
To organize key information in a story and construct a graphic organizer to outline the story elements	Yes

Materials:	
• text	• Hula-Hoops™ (*optional*)
• paper	

Learning Phases

I

Model using the framework *Somebody Wanted But So* (Schmidt and Buckley 1990) to retell a life event or a movie. Write the *SWBS* framework on the board or overhead in a four-column chart. Identify and model the elements for *SWBS*, which are:

Somebody is the main character or historical figure, as you record it on the chart.

Wanted represents the plot or motivation that is occurring to the Somebody.

But stands for the conflict or challenge the Somebody faces.

So represents the outcome or resolution.

We

With students, compose a summary statement that the *SWBS* framework creates by combining the *SWBS* elements. Explain how students can use this *SWBS* framework to help them summarize any narrative text.

If they are using this technique with a longer novel, have students write a *SWBS* for each chapter or individual characters. It also helps students identify main ideas and details, recognize cause-and-effect relationships, make generalizations, and analyze points of view.

With You

In small groups, have students fold a sheet of paper into fourths and write the following headings on the four sections: *Somebody*, *Wanted*, *But*, and *So* and then summarize a narrative text that they all have read. Have them share as they record responses on their *SWBS* graphic organizer.

By You

Using a story that students have read, have students complete their individual charts by writing a statement under each section: *Somebody* (identify the character), *Wanted* (describe the character's goal or motivation), *But* (describe a conflict that impedes the character), and *So* (describe the resolution of the conflict). **Suggested Teacher Talk:** *How can you use important ideas to condense the information in this story?*

Extension

Place four Hula-Hoops™ on the classroom floor and tell students that each hoop represents one of the four headings (*Somebody*, *Wanted*, *But*, *So*). Have students stand inside the hoops after reading a story and summarize each corresponding aspect as they walk through the hoops. **Suggested Teacher Talk:** *Which details are the most and least important?*

Comprehension
Summarizing

Comprehension Strategy: Synthesizing

Synthesizing is the merging of new information with prior background knowledge to create an original idea. Strategic readers stop periodically while reading to digest what they have read and what it means before continuing. This process personalizes reading by allowing readers to form opinions and "[combine] separate pieces of knowledge to come up with knowledge that is new, at least new to the person doing the thinking" (Irwin 1991, 102). This process allows readers to make judgments that promote higher-order "elaborative" thinking. The teacher who abandons the "one right answer" approach will elicit these divergent responses (Irwin 1991).

Synthesizing usually occurs in conjunction with analysis. Both close, analytic reading, as well as synthesizing ideas across texts are essential for critical reading. Readers sift through a plethora of information, pulling out key ideas and putting these ideas together to have an overall sense of what they are reading. Students need to be able to engage with a text and synthesize information across multiple sources (CCSS 2010). This process draws together the results of developing thoughts into a conclusion to interpret, evaluate, and add information to the summary (Fisher et al. 2009). The synthesizing strategy "combines elements into a pattern not clearly there before" (Tate 2003, 6). The ability to synthesize when reading requires that readers integrate all of the comprehension strategies described previously in this chapter—which itself, actually, is synthesizing.

To support Synthesizing while reading, a set of skills is required to effectively implement this reading strategy. The synchronized application of several reading strategies results in making meaning while reading a text. The skills, additional integrated reading strategies, and their reading components found in corresponding chapters are listed below.

Focus Skill(s):

- Schema
- Organize information
- Associate information

Integrated Strategies:

- Synthesizing Sounds; Embedding (Chapter 2)
- Associating; Categorizing (Chapter 3)
- Phrasing, Expressing, and Pacing (Chapter 4)
- Activating and Building Schemas; Questioning; Visualizing and Sensory Imaging; Inferring and Drawing Conclusions; Summarizing; Determining Importance (Chapter 5)

Accountable Teacher Talk for Synthesizing

Following is a list of suggested Teacher Talk that encourages readers to think strategically as they employ the Synthesizing strategy. To effectively increase levels of thinking, these suggestions incorporate Bloom's Taxonomy's higher-order questioning (Anderson and Krathwohl 2001) and Webb's Depth of Knowledge (2002).

Remembering and Understanding (Recall)

- Try to verbalize what is happening within the text.
- What did you think about first? Now what are you thinking?

Applying (Skill/Concept)

- What do you understand now that you did not understand before? I didn't understand it when the author said _____, but now I understand that he or she _____.

Analyzing (Strategic Thinking)

- How has your thinking changed since reading that part of the text?

Evaluating and Creating (Extended Thinking)

- How could you test your theory?
- Propose an alternative to the situation.

Behavior Indicators for Synthesizing

As you assess students' ability to synthesize, use the following behaviors as a guide. Do students exhibit these behaviors never, rarely, often, or always?

- ❑ Interpret meaning of text through drama and artwork
- ❑ Combine information and form new thoughts
- ❑ Monitor and evaluate text for meaning

Techniques for Synthesizing

Creating a Play

Purpose:	ELL Technique:
To interpret students' understandings of text through drama or music	Yes

Materials:

- text
- props that correspond with text
- variety of song title selections (*optional*)

Learning Phases

I — Read a story and explain to students that they will get an opportunity to act it out. **Suggested Teacher Talk:** *Think about how you would bring the text to life.*

We — Create a list of key details students will need to incorporate into their play, and assign roles.

With You — Give students time to discuss, plan, and practice their interpretations of the text in small groups. Students can use any available props they need to recreate the story that they read.

By You — Have students discuss how their understanding of the text has changed after students perform their interpretations for the class, if it has changed at all. **Suggested Teacher Talk:** *I did not understand it when the author said _____, but now I understand that he or she meant _____.*

Differentiation

Have students select song titles that correspond with the story and then justify why they selected the titles. Provide sentence frames for students that require additional support. Sentence frames can be provided according to student readiness levels.

Mind Mapping

Purpose:	ELL Technique:
To make visual connections to words or concepts from a text to gain an overall perspective	Yes

Materials:

- text
- paper
- markers or crayons
- online resources (wisemapping.com; coggle.it; spicynodes.org) (*optional*)

Learning Phases

I — Read a text and model creating a mind map of it. Start by writing a central word or concept (or drawing a picture) in the center of a sheet of paper. **Suggested Teacher Talk:** *What words helped you figure out the main idea?*

We — Have students think of five to seven main ideas that relate to that central word or drawing; these ideas should radiate out from the center.

Create a class *Mind Map* and post in the room as a springboard for future discussions.

With You — Partners work together to create a mind map based on a text students are reading. Students may find it useful to turn their paper on the side in a landscape format for mapping. By personalizing the map with their own symbols and designs, students will construct visual and meaningful relationships between their ideas and the text.

By You — Reread the text, and have students reflect on their maps to better comprehend the text. **Suggested Teacher Talk:** *How has your thinking changed after drawing the map?*

Extension

Use online resources to create interactive Mind Maps (http://www.wisemapping.com; http://www.coggle.it; http://www.spicynodes.org).

Comprehension
Synthesizing

Rewriting a Story

Purpose:	ELL Technique:
To organize and compose thoughts from a specific point of view	No

Materials:

- text

Learning Phases

I

After reading a text, model rewriting a passage from the story in first person from any character's point of view. **Suggested Teacher Talk:** *What new ideas or information do you have after looking at the text from a different point of view?*

We

Discuss with students how some books and even movies are known to have several different endings. Compare the endings to several examples, or create the text from a different character's point of view.

With You

Invite students to share with a group any new perspectives they have gained about the character from their rewriting activity. **Suggested Teacher Talk:** *What made you think that way?*

By You

Have students rewrite an alternative ending to a text, making sure they have an effective conclusion that would make sense based on the current version.

Extension

Have students use their edited passage and revise it into a musical by turning the speaking parts into singing parts. Then, have students perform their musicals.

Say Something: Text Talk

Purpose:	ELL Technique:
To monitor thinking about text while reading	Yes

Materials:

- text

Learning Phases

I

Model reading a section from a text and stopping periodically to *Say Something* (Harste, Short, and Burke 1989) to the class about what you are reading. Use the Say Something: Text-Talk Prompts to facilitate dialogue directly related to what is being read.

Say Something: Text-Talk Prompts:

Make Prediction

Ask Questions

Clarify Something

Make a Connection

Make a Comment

We

Have the class discuss how these prompts can be beneficial in providing them with metacognitive vocabulary (automatic awareness of their own ability to comprehend and discuss text) to be able to discuss the text when reading.

Instruct students to work in groups and determine in advance the intervals at which they will stop in their reading (e.g., after a paragraph, a half-page, a whole page) to say something about the text. (The more unfamiliar or complex the text, the smaller the amounts of reading that will need to be done at a time.) **Suggested Teacher Talk:** *Try to explain what is happening in the text.*

With You

Assign students to work in pairs (e.g., homogeneous, ability grouping), and give each pair a text to read (both partners read the same text). Have the partners read to the designated place in the text and stop to take turns, making one statement about what they have just read. Students can state their reflections, a question, a fact, a connection, or an inference.

By You

Have students continue reading the texts, stopping at designated intervals to make statements to each other.

Synthesizing Target

Purpose:		ELL Technique:
To combine information and form new thoughts		Yes
Materials:		

- texts
- sticky notes
- *Synthesizing Target* (see synthesizing.pdf)

Comprehension
Synthesizing

Learning Phases

I

Model how to use the *Synthesizing Target*. Demonstrate how each ring of the circle represents a new thought, which builds from their previous ideas. **Suggested Teacher Talk:** *Try to write down what you are thinking, and continue to keep thinking about that thought as you add new thoughts.*

We

Use the *Synthesizing Target* to record a class target, having volunteers record their thoughts on sticky notes and placing them on a large target during a class interactive read-aloud.

With You

Distribute the *Synthesizing Target* to each student. Students share their targets with a partner to discuss their thought process as they were reading. **Suggested Teacher Talk:** *What did you think about first? What are you thinking now?*

By You

Reread the text and have students reflect, from the outside in, on their synthesizing targets. Students share their final thoughts and how the concept on the target supported their understanding of the text.

Extension

Students work with partners to take turns completing one of the rings of the target. After reading some of the passage in the text, they will record their first thinking in the outside circle and then pass the target to the other partner to analyze and add any additional thoughts. They will continue to read and take turns synthesizing the content. The goal is to work together to "hit the center bull's eye" as they synthesize each section.

Comprehension Wrap-Up

Comprehension is a key component of effective reading instruction. Effective comprehension instruction actively engages students in text and motivates them to use strategies and techniques. "Comprehension instruction is most effective when students integrate and flexibly use reading and thinking strategies across a wide variety of texts and in the context of challenging, engaging curriculum" (Harvey and Goudvis 2013). Such effective comprehension requires explicit and purposeful teaching. "Instruction in comprehension strategies is carried out by a classroom teacher who demonstrates, models, or guides the reader on their acquisition and use. When these procedures have been acquired, the reader becomes independent of the teacher" (NICHD 2000, 4–40).

The strategies, techniques, and Teacher Talk presented in this chapter and throughout the book support teachers in maximizing their readers' potential of becoming strategic readers.

Comprehension Synthesizing

References Cited

Adams, Marilyn J. 1990. *Beginning to Read: Thinking and Learning about Print*. Cambridge, MA: MIT Press.

———. 2011. "The Relation Between Alphabetic Basics, Word Recognition, and Reading." In *What Research Says About Reading Instruction*, 4th edition, edited by S. J. Samuels and Alan E. Farstrup, 4–24. Newark, DE: International Reading Association.

Afflerbach, Peter. 2007. *Understanding and Using Reading Assessment, K–12*. Newark, DE: International Reading Association.

———. 2010. "Assessing Reading." In *Rebuilding the Foundation, Effective Reading Instruction for 21st Century Literacy*, edited by Tim Rasinski, 293–313. Bloomington, IN: Solution Tree Press.

Akhavan, Nancy. 2007. *Accelerated Vocabulary Instruction: Strategies for Closing the Achievement Gap for All Students*. New York: Scholastic.

Allington, Richard L. 2001. *What Really Matters for Struggling Readers: Designing Research-Based Programs*. New York: Longman.

———. 2008. *Response to Intervention: Research-Based Designs*. Boston: Allyn & Bacon.

Allington, Richard L., and Sean A. Walmsley. 2007. *No Quick Fix, the RTI Edition: Rethinking Literacy Programs in America's Elementary Schools*. New York: Teachers College Press, Newark, DE: International Reading Association.

Allor, J. H., K.A. Gansle, and R. K. Denny. 2006. "The Stop and Go Phonemic Awareness Game: Providing Modeling, Practice, and Feedback." *Preventing School Failure* 50 (4): 23–30. doi:10.3200/PSFL.50.4.23

Amer, Aly. 2006. "Reflections on Bloom's Revised Taxonomy." *Electronic Journal of Research in Educational Psychology* 4 (1): 213–230.

Amtmann, Dagmar, Robert D. Abbott, and Virginia W. Berninger. 2008. "Identifying and Predicting Classes of Response to Explicit Phonological Spelling Instruction During Independent Composing." *Journal of Learning Disabilities* 41 (3): 218–234. doi:10.1177/0022219408315639

Anderson, Lorin W., and David R. Krathwohl (Eds.). 2001. *A Taxonomy for Learning, Teaching and Assessing: A Revision of Bloom's Taxonomy of Educational Objectives: Complete Edition*. New York: Longman.

Anthony, Jason, Rachel G. Aghara, Martha Dunkelberger, Teresa Anthony, Jeffrey Williams, and Zhou Zhang. 2011. "What Factors Place Children With Speech Sound Disorders at Risk for Reading Problems?" *American Journal of Speech-Language Pathology* 20 (2): 146–160.

Archer, Anita L., Mary M. Gleason, and Vicky Vachon. 2006. *REWARDS*. Longmont, CO: Sopris West.

Archer, Anita L., and Charles Hughes. 2011. *Explicit Instruction: Effective and Efficient Teaching*. New York: Guilford Publications.

Ardoin, Scott P., Laura S. Morena, Katherine S. Binder, and Tori E. Foster. 2013. "Examining the Impact of Feedback and Repeated Readings on Oral Reading Fluency: Let's Not Forget Prosody." *School Psychology Quarterly* 28 (4): 391–404.

Armbruster, Bonnie B., Fran Lehr, and Jean Osborn. 2001. *Put Reading First: The Research Building Blocks for Teaching Children to Read, Kindergarten Through Grade Three*. Washington, DC: U.S. Department of Education.

Avgerinou, Maria D., and Rune Pettersson. 2011. "Toward a Cohesive Theory of Visual Literacy." *Journal of Visual Literacy* 30 (2): 1–19.

Baldwin, R.S., Jeff C. Ford, and John E. Readence. 1981. "Teaching Word Connotations: An Alternative Strategy." *Reading World* 21 (2): 103–108.

Ball, Eileen W., and Benita A. Blachman. 1991. "Does Phoneme Awareness Training in Kindergarten Make a Difference in Early Word Recognition and Developmental Spelling?" *Reading Research Quarterly* 26 (1): 49–66.

Barger, Jeff. 2006. "Building Word Consciousness." *The Reading Teacher* 60 (3): 279–281. doi:10.1598/RT.60.3.8

Batsche, George, Judy Elliott, Janet L. Graden, Jeffrey Grimes, Joseph F. Kovaleski, David Prasse, Daniel Reschley, Judy Schrag, and W. David Tilly III. 2005. *Response to Intervention: Policy Considerations and Implementation*. Alexandria, VA: National Association of State Directors of Special Education.

Baxter, G. P., K. M. Bass, and R. Glaser. 2001. "Notebook Writing in Three Fifth-Grade Science Classrooms." *Elementary School Journal* 102: 123–140.

Bear, Donald R., Marcia Invernizzi, Shane Templeton, and Francine Johnston. 2011. *Words Their Way: Word Study for Phonics, Vocabulary, and Spelling Instruction*, 5th edition. Upper Saddle River, NJ: Prentice Hall.

Beaver, Joetta M. 2006. *Teacher Guide: Developmental Reading Assessment, Grades K–3*, 2nd edition. Parsippany, NJ: Pearson.

Beck, Isabel L., and Margaret G. McKeown. 2006. *Improving Comprehension with Questioning the Author: A Fresh and Expanded View of a Powerful Approach*. New York: Scholastic.

Beck, Isabel L., Margaret G. McKeown, Rebecca L. Hamilton, and Linda Kucan. 1997. *Questioning the Author: An Approach for Enhancing Student Engagement with Text*. Newark, DE: International Reading Association.

Beck, Isabel L., Margaret G. McKeown, and Linda Kucan. 2002. *Bringing Words to Life: Robust Vocabulary Instruction*. New York: Guilford.

———. 2008. *Creating Robust Vocabulary: Frequently Asked Questions and Extended Examples*. New York: Guilford.

Behrman, Edward H. 2006. "Teaching about Language, Power, and Text: A Review of Classroom Practices that Support Critical Literacy." *Journal of Adolescent and Adult Literacy* 49 (6): 490–498. doi:10.1598/JAAL.49.6.4

Benjamin, Rebekah G., and Paula J. Schwanenflugel. 2010. "Text Complexity and Oral Reading Prosody in Young Readers." *Reading Research Quarterly* 45 (4): 388–404.

Bishop, Ashley, and Sue Bishop. 1996. *Teaching Phonics, Phonemic Awareness, and Word Recognition*. Westminster, CA: Teacher Created Materials.

Bjork, Robert A., John Dunlosky, and Nate Kornell. 2013. "Self-Regulated Learning: Beliefs, Techniques, and Illusions." Annual Review of Psychology 64: 417-444.

Blachowicz, Camille L. Z. 1986. "Making Connections: Alternatives to the Vocabulary Notebook." *Journal of Reading* 29 (7): 643–649.

Blachowicz, Camille L. Z., and Peter J. Fisher. 2010. *Teaching Vocabulary in All Classrooms*, 4th edition. Upper Saddle River, NJ: Pearson.

Blevins, Wiley. 2001. *Building Fluency: Lessons and Strategies for Reading Success*. New York: Scholastic.

Block, Cathy Collins, Lori L. Rodgers, and Rebecca B. Johnson. 2004. *Comprehension Process Instruction: Creating Reading Success in Grades K–3*. New York: Guilford.

Bloom, Benjamin S., and David R. Krathwohl (Eds.). 1956. *Taxonomy of Educational Objectives: The Classification of Educational Goals, Handbook 1: The Cognitive Domain*. New York: David McKay.

Bolton-Gary, Cynthia. 2012. "Connecting Through Comics: Expanding Opportunities for Teaching and Learning." *US-China Education Review* B (4): 389–395. Libertyville, IL: David Publishing.

Boulware-Gooden, Regina, Suzanne Carreker, Ann Thornhill, and R. Malatesha Joshi. 2007. "Instruction of Metacognitive Strategies Enhances Reading Comprehension and Vocabulary Achievement of Third-Grade Students." *The Reading Teacher* 61 (1): 70–77.

Bowers, Peter N., John R. Kirby, and S. Hélène Deacon. 2010. "The Effects of Morphological Instruction on Literacy Skills: A Systematic Review of the Literature." *Review of Educational Research* 80 (2): 144–179.

Brassell, Danny, and Timothy Rasinski. 2008. *Comprehension that Works: Taking Students Beyond Ordinary Understanding to Deep Comprehension*. Huntington Beach, CA: Shell Education.

Bromley, Karen. 2007. "Nine Things Every Teacher Should Know About Words and Vocabulary Instruction." *Journal of Adolescent & Adult Literacy* 50 (7): 528–537. doi:10.1598/JAAL.50.7.2

Brophy, Jere. 1983. "Conceptualizing Student Motivation." *Educational Psychologist* 18: 200–215.

Brown, Rachel. 2008. "The Road Not Yet Taken: A Transactional Strategies Approach to Comprehension Instruction." *The Reading Teacher* 61 (7): 538–547. doi:10.1598/RT.61.7.3

Burmark, Lynell. 2008. "Visual Literacy: What You Get Is What You See." In *Teaching Visual Literacy: Using Comic Books, Graphic Novels, Anime, Cartoons, and More to Develop Comprehension and Thinking Skills*, edited by Douglas Fisher and Nancy Frey, 5–25. Thousand Oaks, CA: Corwin Press.

Caine, Geoffrey, and Renate N. Caine. 2007. *Natural Learning: The Basis for Raising and Sustaining High Standards of Real World Performance: Executive Summary*. Idyllwild, CA: The National Learning Research Institute. Accessed April 15, 2008, www.naturallearninginstitute.org/UPDATEDSITE/DOCUMENTS/EXECUTIVE_SUMMARY.pdf

Calkins, Lucy McCormick. 2001. *The Art of Teaching Reading*. New York: Longman.

Calkins, Lucy McCormick, 2012. *Pathways to Common Core: Accelerating Achievement*. Portsmouth, NH: Heinemann.

Cambourne, Brian. 1995. "Toward an Educationally Relevant Theory of Literacy Learning: Twenty Years of Inquiry." *The Reading Teacher* 49 (3): 182–190.

Campbell, Kenneth U. 2006. *Great Leaps*. Gainesville, FL: Diarmuid.

Campbell, Monica L., Shawnna Helf, and Nancy L. Cooke. 2008. "Effects of Adding Multisensory Components to a Supplemental Reading Program on the Decoding Skills of Treatment Resisters." *Education and Treatment of Children* 31 (3): 267–295. doi:10.1353/etc.0.0003

Castiglioni-Spalten, Maria L., and Linnea C. Ehri. 2003. "Phonemic Awareness Instruction: Contribution of Articulatory Segmentation to Novice Beginners' Reading and Spelling." *Scientific Studies of Reading* 7 (1): 25–52. doi:10.1207/S1532799XSSR0701_03

Chall, Jeanne S., and Edgar Dale. 1995. *Readability Revisited: The New Dale-Chall Readability Formula*. Cambridge, MA: Brookline Books.

Clay, Marie M. 2002. *An Observation Survey of Early Literacy Achievement*, 2nd edition. Portsmouth, NH: Heinemann.

Coffield, Frank, David Moseley, Elaine Hall, and Kathryn Ecclestone. 2004. "Learning Styles and Pedagogy in Post-16 Learning: A Systematic and Critical Review." *Learning and Skills Research*. Accessed April 15, 2009, www.lsda.org.uk/files/PDF/1543.pdf

Collins, Allan, John Seely Brown, and Susan E. Newman. 1989. "Cognitive Apprenticeship: Teaching the Crafts of Reading, Writing, and Mathematics." In *Knowing, Learning, and Instruction: Essays in Honor of Robert Glaser*, edited by Lauren B. Resnick, 453–494. Hillsdale, NJ: Erlbaum.

Collins, Norma D. 1993. *Teaching Critical Reading Through Literature*. Bloomington, IN: Clearinghouse on Reading, English, and Communication.

Common Core State Standards Initiative. 2010. Washington, DC: National Governors Association Center for Best Practices, Council of Chief State School Officers.

Conklin, Wendy. 2012. *Higher-Order Thinking Skills to Develop 21st Century Learners*. Huntington Beach, CA: Shell Education.

Conrad, Nicole J. 2008. "From Reading to Spelling and Spelling to Reading: Transfer Goes Both Ways." *Journal of Educational Psychology* 100 (4): 869–878. doi:10.1037/a0012544

Covey, Stephen R. 1989. *7 Habits of Highly Effective People*. New York: Free Press.

———. 2006. *Habit 2: Begin with the End in Mind*, CD format. New York: Free Press.

Cromley, Jennifer G., Lindsey E. Snyder-Hogan, and Ulana A. Luciw-Dubas. 2010. "Reading Comprehension of Scientific Text: A Domain-Specific Test of the Direct and Inferential Mediation Model of Reading Comprehension. *Journal of Educational Psychology* 102 (3): 687–700.

Cunningham, Anne E. 2005. "Vocabulary Growth Through Independent Reading and Reading Aloud to Children." In *Teaching and Learning Vocabulary: Bringing Research to Practice*, edited by Elfrieda H. Hiebert and Michael L. Kamil. Mahwah, NJ: Erlbaum.

Cunningham, Anne E., and Keith E. Stanovich. 1998. "Early Reading Acquisition and Its Relation to Reading Experience and Ability 10 Years Later." *Developmental Psychology* 33 (6): 934–945.

Cunningham, Patricia M. 2000. *Phonics They Use: Words for Reading and Writing*. New York: Longman.

———. 2012. *Phonics They Use: Words for Reading and Writing*, 6th edition. Parsippany, NJ: Pearson.

Cunningham, Patricia M., and Richard L. Allington. 2007. *Classrooms That Work: They Can All Read and Write*, 4th edition. Boston: Allyn & Bacon.

Dalton, Bridget, and Dana L. Grisham. 2011. "eVoc Strategies: 10 Ways to Use Technology to Build Vocabulary." *The Reading Teacher* 64 (5): 306–317.

Davis, Heather A. 2003. "Conceptualizing the Role and Influence of Student-Teacher Relationships on Children's Social and Cognitive Development." *Educational Psychologist* 38 (4): 207–234.

Deacon, S. Helene, Jenna Benere, and Adrian Pasquarella. 2013. "Reciprocal Relationship: Children's Morphological Awareness and Their Reading Accuracy across Grades 2 to 3." *Developmental Psychology* 49 (6): 1113-1126.

DeGross, Monalisa. 1994. *Donovan's Word Jar*. New York: HarperCollins.

Denton, Carolyn A., Amy E. Barth, Jack M. Fletcher, Jade Wexler, Sharon Vaughn, Paul T. Cirino, Melissa Romain, and David J. Francis. 2011. "The Relations Among Oral and Silent Reading Fluency and Comprehension in Middle School: Implications for Identification and Instruction of Students With Reading Difficulties." *Scientific Studies of Reading* 15 (2): 109–135.

Deshler, Donald D., and Jean B. Schumaker. 1988. "An Instructional Model for Teaching Students How to Learn." In *Alternative Educational Delivery Systems: Enhancing Instructional Options for All Students*, edited by Janet L. Graden, Joseph E. Zins, and Michael J. Curtis, 391–411. Washington, DC: National Association of School Psychologists.

Dewey, John. 1913. *Interest and Effort in Education*. Boston: Houghton Mifflin.

Dowhower, Sarah L. 1994. "Repeated Reading Revisited: Research Into Practice." *Reading and Writing Quarterly: Overcoming Learning Difficulties* 10 (4): 343–358.

Drieghe, Denis, Alexander Pollatsek, Adrian Staub, and Keith Rayner. 2008. "The Word Grouping Hypothesis and Eye Movements During Reading." *Journal of Experimental Psychology* 34 (6): 1552–1560.

Duffy, Gerald G., and Laura R. Roehler. 1986. *Improving Classroom Reading Instruction: A Decision-Making Approach*. New York: Random House.

Eber, Patricia A. 2007. "Assessing Student Learning: Applying Bloom's Taxonomy." *Human Service Education* 27 (1): 45–53.

Edelen-Smith, Patricia. 1997. "How Now Brown Cow: Phoneme Awareness Activities for Collaborative Classrooms." *Intervention in School and Clinic* 33 (2): 103–111. doi:10.1177/105345129703300206

Edwards, Patricia A., Jennifer D. Turner, and Kouider Mokhtari. 2008. "Balancing the Assessment of Learning and for Learning in Support of Student Literacy Achievement." *The Reading Teacher* 61 (8): 682–684.

Ellery, Valerie, and Jennifer L. Rosenboom. 2010. *Sustaining Strategic Readers: Techniques for Supporting Content Literacy in Grades 6-12*. Newark, DE: International Reading Association.

Farrington, Pat. 2007. "Using Context Clues: Children As Reading Detectives." *Literacy Today* 51: 8–9.

Fink, Rosalie, and S. Jay Samuels (Eds.). 2008. *Inspiring Reading Success: Interest and Motivation in an Age of High-Stakes Testing*. Newark, DE: International Reading Association.

Fisher, Douglas, and Nancy Frey. 2010. *Enhancing RTI: How to Ensure Success with Effective Classroom Instruction & Intervention*. Alexandria, VA: ASCD.

———. 2013. *Common Core English Language Arts in a PLC at Work, Grades 3–5*. Bloomington, IN: Solution Tree Press.

Fisher, Douglas, Nancy Frey, and Diane Lapp. 2009. *In a Reading State of Mind: Brain Research, Teacher Modeling, and Comprehension Instruction*. Newark, DE: International Reading Association.

Fitzpatrick, Jo. 1997. *Phonemic Awareness: Playing with Sounds to Strengthen Beginning Reading Skills.* Huntington Beach, CA: Creative Teaching.

Flood, James, Julie M. Jensen, Diane Lapp, and James R. Squire (Eds.). 1991. *Handbook of Research on Teaching the English Language Arts.* New York: Macmillan.

Fogarty, Robin J. 1997. *Brain-Compatible Classrooms.* Arlington Heights, IL: Skylight.

Foorman, B.R., and P. Mehta. 2002. *Definitions of Fluency: Conceptual and Methodological Challenges.* Paper presented at the Focus on Fluency Forum, San Francisco, CA.

Forbes, Salli, and Connie Briggs (Eds.). 2003. *Research in Reading Recovery* (Vol. 2). Portsmouth, NH: Heinemann.

Foster, Tori E., Scott P. Ardoin, and Katherine S. Binder. 2013. "Underlying Changes in Repeated Reading: An Eye Movement Study." *School Psychology Review* 42 (2): 140–156.

Fountas, Irene C., and Gay Su Pinnell. 1996. *Guided Reading: Good First Teaching for All Children.* Portsmouth, NH: Heinemann.

———. 1999. *Matching Books to Readers: Using Leveled Books in Guided Reading, K–3.* Portsmouth, NH: Heinemann.

———. 2012. *Genre Study: Teaching with Fiction and Nonfiction Books.* Portsmouth, NH: Heinemann.

Freeman, Marcia S. 1995. *Building a Writing Community: A Practical Guide.* Gainesville, FL: Maupin.

Fuchs, Lynn S., and Doug Fuchs. 2008. "Best Practices in Progress Monitoring Reading and Mathematics at the Elementary Grades." In *Best Practices in School Psychology V,* edited by Alex Thomas and Jeff Grimes, 2147–2164. Bethesda, MD: National Association of School Psychologists.

Fuchs, Lynn S., Doug Fuchs, Michelle K. Hosp, and Joseph R. Jenkins. 2001. "Oral Reading Fluency as an Indicator of Reading Competence: A Theoretical, Empirical, and Historical Analysis." *Scientific Studies of Reading* 5 (3): 239–256. doi:10.1207/S1532799XSSR0503_3

Gaffney, Meghan, and Darrell Morris. 2011. "Building Reading Fluency in a Learning-Disabled Middle School Reader: This Case Study Describes a Yearlong Intervention with an Eighth-Grade Reader and Explains the Intervention's Success." *Journal of Adolescent & Adult Literacy* 54 (5): 331–341.

Gary, Cynthia B. 2012. "Connecting through Comics: Expanding Opportunities for Teaching and Learning." *US-China Education Review* B4: 389–395.

Gardner, Howard. 1983. *Frames of Mind: The Theory of Multiple Intelligences.* New York: Basic.

———. 1993. *Multiple Intelligences: The Theory in Practice.* New York: Basic.

Gaskins, Irene West. 2005. *Success with Struggling Readers: The Benchmark School Approach.* New York: Guilford.

Gaskins, Irene West, Linnea C. Ehri, Cheryl Cress, Colleen O'Hara, and Katherine Donnelly. 1996. "Procedures for Word Learning: Making Discoveries about Words." *The Reading Teacher* 50 (4): 312–327.

Gentry, J. Richard. 1989. *Spell is a Four-Letter Word.* Portsmouth, NH: Heinemann.

———. 2006. *Breaking the Code: The New Science of Beginning Reading and Writing.* Portsmouth, NH: Heinemann.

Gentry, J. Richard, and Jean W. Gillet. 1992. *Teaching Kids to Spell.* Portsmouth, NH: Heinemann.

Gillet, Jean W., and M. Jane Kita. 1979. "Words, Kids, and Categories." *The Reading Teacher* 32 (5): 538–546.

Graves, Donald. 1982. *Writing: Teachers and Children at Work.* Portsmouth, NH: Heinemann.

Graves, Michael F. 2000. "A Vocabulary Program to Complement and Bolster a Middle-Grade Comprehension Program." In *Reading for Meaning: Fostering Comprehension in the Middle Grades,* edited by Barbara M. Taylor, Michael F. Graves, and Paul Van Den Broek, 116–135. Newark, DE: International Reading Association.

———. 2006. *The Vocabulary Book: Learning & Instruction.* New York: Teachers College Press.

Graves, Michael F., Connie Juel, and Bonnie B. Graves. 1998. *Teaching Reading in the 21st Century.* Englewood Cliffs, NJ: Prentice Hall.

Graves, Michael F., and Susan Watts-Taffe. 2008. "For the Love of Words: Fostering Word Consciousness in Young Readers." *The Reading Teacher* 62 (3): 185–193. doi:10.1598/RT.62.3.1

Greenwood, Scott C., and Kevin Flanigan. 2007. "Overlapping Vocabulary and Comprehension: Context Clues Complement Semantic Gradients." *The Reading Teacher* 61 (3): 249–254. doi:10.1598/RT.61.3.5

Hall, Leigh A., and Susan V. Piazza. 2008. "Critically Reading Texts: What Students Do and How Teachers Can Help." *The Reading Teacher* 62 (1): 32–41. doi:10.1598/RT.62.1.4

Hannaford, Carla. 2007. *Smart MovesL Why Learning Is Not All in Your Head, Second Edition.* Great River Books. Salt Lake City, UT.

Harackiewicz, Judith M., Amanda M. Durik, Kenneth E. Barron, Lisa Linnenbrink-Garcia, and John M. Tauer. 2008. "The Role of Achievement Goals in the Development of Interest: Reciprocal Relations Between Achievement Goals, Interests, and Performance." *Journal of Educational Psychology* 100 (1): 105–122. doi:10.1037/0022-0663.100.1.105

Harvey, Stephanie, and Anne Goudvis. 2000. *Strategies That Work: Teaching Comprehension to Enhance Understanding.* York, ME: Stenhouse.

———. 2007. *Strategies That Work: Teaching Comprehension for Understanding and Engagement,* 2nd edition. Portland, ME: Stenhouse.

————. 2013. "Comprehension at the Core." *The Reading Teacher* 66 (6): 432-439.

Harste, Jerome Charles, Kathy Gnagey Short, and Carolyn L. Burke. 1989. *Creating Classrooms for Authors: The Reading-Writing Connection*. Portsmouth, NH: Heinemann.

Hasbrouck, Jan, and Gerald A. Tindal. 2006. "Oral Reading Fluency Norms: A Valuable Assessment Tool for Reading Teachers." *The Reading Teacher* 59 (7): 636 –644.

Heckelman, Rod G. 1969. "A Neurological-Impress Method of Remedial-Reading Instruction." *Academic Therapy Quarterly* 4 (4): 277–282.

Herber, Harold L. 1984. *Teaching Reading in Content Areas*, 2nd edition. Englewood Cliffs, NJ: Prentice Hall.

Henderson, E. H. 1990. *Teaching Spelling*, 2nd Edition. Boston: Houghton Mifflin Harcourt.

Herron, Jeannine. 2008. "Why Phonics Teaching Must Change: Of Course, We Must Teach Decoding, but We Must Teach It Meaningfully." *Educational Leadership* 66 (1): 77–81.

Hiebert, Elfrieda H., 2013. *QuickReads: A Research-Based Fluency Program*. Upper Saddle River, NJ: Pearson Education.

Hiebert, Elfrieda H., P. David Pearson, Barbara M. Taylor, Virginia Richardson, and Scott G. Paris. 1998. *Every Child a Reader: Applying Reading Research to the Classroom*. Ann Arbor Center for the Improvement of Early Reading Achievement, University of Michigan School of Education.

Hilden, Katherine R., and Michael Pressley. 2007. "Self-Regulation through Transactional Strategies Instruction." *Reading and Writing Quarterly* 23 (1): 51– 75.

Hodgkinson, Harold. 2006. *The Whole Child in a Fractured World*. Accessed March 15, 2009, www.ascd.org/ASCD/pdf/fracturedworld.pdf

Holdaway, Don. 1979. *The Foundations of Literacy*. Sydney, Australia: Ashton Scholastic.

Horner, Sherri L., and Evelyn A. O'Connor. 2007. "Helping Beginning and Struggling Readers to Develop Self-Regulated Strategies: A Reading Recovery Example." *Reading and Writing Quarterly* 23 (1): 97–109.

Hornsby, David, and Lorraine Wilson. 2011. *Teaching Phonics in Context*. Australia: Pearson.

Hoyt, Linda. 1992. "Many Ways of Knowing: Using Drama, Oral Interactions, and the Visual Arts to Enhance Reading Comprehension." *The Reading Teacher* 45 (8): 580–584.

————. 2008. *Revisit, Reflect, Retell: Time-Tested Strategies for Teaching Reading Comprehension*, updated edition. Portsmouth, NH: Heinemann.

Hoyt, Linda, and Teresa Therriault. 2008. *Mastering the Mechanics: Ready-To-Use Lessons for Modeled, Guided, and Independent Editing, Grades 4–5*. New York: Scholastic.

Hyerle, David N., and Larry Alper. 2004. *Student Successes with Thinking Maps: School-Based Research, Results, and Models for Achievement Using Visual Tools*. Thousand Oaks, CA: Corwin.

International Reading Association. 1998. "Phonemic Awareness and the Teaching of Reading," Position Statement, Newark, DE.

Irwin, Judith Westphal. 1991. *Teaching Reading Comprehension Processes*, 2nd edition. Boston: Pearson.

Israel, Susan E., and Gerald G. Duffy (Eds.). 2009. *Handbook of Research on Reading Comprehension*. New York: Routledge.

Isticifi, Ilknur. 2010. "Playing with Words: A Study on Word Association Responses." *Journal of International Social Research* 3 (10): 360–368.

Jang, Hyungshim. 2008. "Supporting Students' Motivation, Engagement, and Learning During an Uninteresting Activity." *Journal of Educational Psychology* 100 (4): 798–811. doi:10.1037/a0012841

Jensen, Eric. 2000. *Different Brains, Different Learners: How to Reach the Hard to Reach*. San Diego, CA: The Brain Store.

————. 2005. *Teaching with the Brain in Mind*, 2nd edition. Alexandria, VA: Association for Supervision and Curriculum Development.

Jensen, Eric, and LeAnn Nickelsen. 2008. *Deeper Learning: 7 Powerful Strategies for In-Depth and Longer-Lasting Learning*. Thousand Oaks, CA: Corwin.

Jewitt, Carey, and Gunther R. Kress (Eds.). 2003. *Multimodal Literacy*. New York: Peter Lang.

Jiang, Yongmei. 2009. "Predicting Strategy and Listening Comprehension." *Asian Social Science* 5 (1): 93–97.

Johnson, Dale D., and P. David Pearson. 1984. *Teaching Reading Vocabulary*, 2nd edition. New York: Holt, Rinehart and Winston.

Johnston, Amber M., Marcia A. Barnes, and Alain Desrochers. 2008. "Reading Comprehension: Developmental Processes, Individual Differences, and Interventions." *Canadian Psychology* 49 (2): 125–132. doi:10.1037/0708-5591.49.2.125

Johnston, Francine, Marcia Invernizzi, Donald R. Bear, and Shane Templeton. 2009. *Words Their Way: Word Sorts for Syllables and Affixes Spellers*, 2nd edition. Boston: Pearson.

Johnston, Rhona S., Sarah McGeown, and Joyce E. Watson. 2012. "Long-Term Effects of Synthetic Versus Analytic Phonics Teaching on the Reading and Spelling Ability of 10 Year Old Boys and Girls." *Reading and Writing* 25 (6): 1365–1384.

Juel, Connie. 1988. "Learning to Read and Write: A Longitudinal Study of Fifty-Four Children from First through Fourth Grades." *Journal of Educational Psychology* 80 (4): 437–447.

Kast, Monika, Gian-Marco Baschera, Markus Gross, Lutz Jäncke, and Martin Meyer. 2011. "Computer-Based Learning of Spelling Skills in Children With and Without Dyslexia." *Annals of Dyslexia* 61 (2): 177–200.

Keene, Ellin, and Susan Zimmermann. 1997. *Mosaic of Thought: The Power of Comprehension in a Reader's Workshop*. Portsmouth, NH: Heinemann.

———. 2007. *Mosaic of Thought: The Power of Comprehension Strategy Instruction*, 2nd edition. Portsmouth, NH: Heinemann.

Kelly, Michelle J., and Nicki Clausen-Grace. 2013. *Comprehension Shouldn't Be Silent: From Strategy Instruction to Student Independence*, 2nd edition. Newark, DE: International Reading Association.

Kinniburgh, Leah, and Edward Shaw Jr. 2007. "Building Reading Fluency in Elementary Science Through Readers' Theatre." *Science Activities* 44 (1): 16–20. doi:10.3200/SATS.44.1.16-22

———. 2009. "Using Question–Answer Relationships to Build Reading Comprehension in Science." *Science Activities* 45 (4): 19–28.

Klauda, Susan Lutz, and John T. Guthrie. 2008. "Relationships of Three Components of Reading Fluency to Reading Comprehension." *Journal of Educational Psychology* 100 (2): 310–321. doi:10.1037/0022-0663.100.2.310

Knapp, Michael S. 1995. *Teaching for Meaning in High-Poverty Classrooms*. New York: Teachers College Press.

Kohn, Alfie. 1993. *Punished by Rewards: The Trouble with Gold Stars, Incentive Plans, A's, Praise, and Other Bribes*. Boston: Houghton Mifflin.

———. 2005. "Unconditional Teaching." *Educational Leadership* 63 (1): 20–24.

Krashen, Stephen. 2002. "Defending Whole Language: The Limits of Phonics Instruction and the Efficacy of Whole Language Instruction." *Reading Improvement* 39 (1): 32–42.

Kuhn, Melanie R., and Steven A. Stahl. 2003. "Fluency: A Review of Developmental and Remedial Practices." *Journal of Educational Psychology* 95 (1): 3–21.

Kunen, Seth, Ronald Cohen, and Robert Solman. 1981. "A Levels-of-Processing Analysis of Bloom's Taxonomy." *Journal of Educational Psychology* 73 (2): 202–211. doi:10.1037/0022-0663.73.2.202

Kuo, Li-jen, and Richard C. Anderson. 2006. "Morphological Awareness and Learning to Read: A Cross-Language Perspective." *Educational Psychologist* 41 (3): 161–180. doi:10.1207/s15326985ep4103_3

LaBerge, David, and S. Jay Samuels. 1974. "Toward a Theory of Automatic Information Processing in Reading." *Cognitive Psychology* 6: 293–323.

Lane, Holly B., and Stephanie Allen. 2010. "The Vocabulary-Rich Classroom: Modeling Sophisticated Word Use to Promote Word Consciousness and Vocabulary Growth." *The Reading Teacher* 63 (5): 362–370.

Langer, Judith A. 1981. "From Theory to Practice: A Prereading Plan." *Journal of Reading* 25 (2): 152–156.

Lapp, Diane, Douglas Fisher, and Nancy Frey. 2012. "Graphic Novels: What Elementary Teachers Think About Their Instructional Value." *Journal of Education* 192 (1): 23–35.

Lavoie, Richard D. 2007. *The Motivation Breakthrough: 6 Steps to Turning on the Tuned-Out Child*. New York: Touchstone.

Lenz, B. Keith. 2006. "Creating School-Wide Conditions for High-Quality Learning Strategy Classroom Instruction." *Intervention in School and Clinic* 41 (5): 261–266. doi:10.1177/10534512060410050201

Lenz, B. Keith, and Charles A. Hughes. 1990. "A Word Identification Strategy for Adolescents with Learning Disabilities." *Journal of Learning Disabilities* 23 (3): 149–158. doi:10.1177/002221949002300304

LeVasseur, Valerie Marciarille, Paul Macaruso, and Donald Shankweiler. 2008. "Promoting Gains in Reading Fluency: A Comparison of Three Approaches." *Reading and Writing* 21 (3): 205–230. doi:10.1007/s11145-007-9070-1

Levine, Mel. 2002. *A Mind at a Time*. New York: Simon & Schuster.

Lewin, Larry. 2010. "Teaching Critical Reading with Questioning Strategies." *Reading to Learn* 67 (6).

Liow, Susan J. Rickard, and Lily H.-S. Lau. 2006. "The Development of Bilingual Children's Early Spelling in English." *Journal of Educational Psychology* 98 (4): 868–878. doi:10.1037/0022-0663.98.4.868

Lipton, Laura, and Bruce Wellman. 1998. *Pathways to Understanding: Patterns and Practices in the Learning-Focused Classroom*. Guilford, VT: Pathways Publishing.

Loughran, John. 2013. *Developing a Pedagogy of Teacher Education: Understanding Teaching and Learning About Teaching*. New York, NY: Rutledge.

Lundberg, Ingvar, Jørgen Frost, and Ole-Peter Petersen. 1988. "Effects of an Extensive Program for Stimulating Phonological Awareness in Preschool Children." *Reading Research Quarterly* 23 (3): 263–284.

Lyons, Carol. 2003. *Teaching Struggling Readers: How to Use Brain-Based Research to Maximize Learning*. Portsmouth, NH: Heinemann.

Malloy, J.A., Marinak, B.A., and Gambrell, L.B. (Eds). 2010. *Essential Readings on Motivation*. Newark, DE: International Reading Association.

Manning, Maryann, and Constance Kamii. 2000. "Whole Language vs. Isolated Phonics Instruction: A Longitudinal Study in Kindergarten With Reading and Writing Tasks. *Journal of Research in Childhood Education* 15 (1): 53–65.

Many, Joyce E., Donna Lester Taylor, Yan Wang, Gertrude Tinker Sachs, and Heidi Schreiber. 2007. "An Examination of Preservice Literacy Teachers' Initial Attempts to Provide Instructional Scaffolding." *Reading Horizons* 48 (1): 19–40.

Manyak, Patrick C. 2008. "Phonemes in Use: Multiple Activities for a Critical Process." *The Reading Teacher* 61 (8): 659–662. doi:10.1598/RT.61.8.8

Marcell, B.T. 2010. Put the brakes on NASCAR reading. Educational Leadership, 67(6). Retrieved on February, 21 2014, from www.ascd.org/publications/educational-leadership/mar10/vol67/num06/num06/Put-the-Brakes-on-NaSCAR-Reading.aspx

Marzano, Robert J. 2004. *Building Background Knowledge for Academic Achievement*. Alexandria, VA: ASCD.

———. 2007. *The Art and Science of Teaching: A Comprehensive Framework for Effective Instruction*. Alexandria, VA: Association for Supervision and Curriculum Development.

———. 2010. "Teaching Inference." *Educational Leadership* 67 (7): 80–81.

———. 2010. "The Art and Science of Teaching/Summarizing to Comprehend." *Reading to Learn* 67 (6): 83–84.

Marzano, Robert J., Debra J. Pickering, and Jane E. Pollock. 2001. *Classroom Instruction that Worksand : Research-Based Strategies for Increasing Achievement*. Alexandria, VA: Association for Supervision and Curriculum Development.

Marzano, Robert J., and Julia A. Simms. 2013. *Vocabulary for the Common Core*. Bloomington, IN: Marzano Research Laboratory.

Marzollo, Jean. 2000. *I Love You: A Rebus Poem*. New York: Scholastic.

Maslow, Abraham H. 1943. "A Theory of Human Motivation." *Psychological Review* 50 (4): 370–396.

McEwan, Elaine K. 2002. *Teach Them All to Read: Catching the Kids Who Fall Through the Cracks*. Thousand Oaks, CA: Corwin.

McGinley, W. J., and P. R. Denner. 1987. "Story Impressions. A Prereading/Writing Activity." *Journal of Reading* 31 (3): 248–253.

McKeown, Margaret G. 1993. "Creating Effective Definitions for Young Word Learners." *Reading Research Quarterly* 28 (1): 16–31.

McMaster, Jennifer Catney. 1998. "'Doing' Literature: Using Drama to Build Literacy Classrooms: The Segue for a Few Struggling Readers." *The Reading Teacher* 51 (7): 574–584.

Melby-Lervåg, Monica, Solveig-Alma Halaas Lyster, and Charles Hulme. 2012. "Phonological Skills and Their Role in Learning to Read: A Meta-Analytic Review." *Psychological Bulletin* 138 (2): 322–352.

Menzies, Holly M., Jennifer N. Mahdavi, and James L. Lewis. 2008. "Early Intervention in Reading: From Research to Practice." *Remedial and Special Education* 29 (2): 67–77. doi:10.1177/0741932508315844

Merriam-Webster, s.v. "strategy," accessed January 28, 2014, http://www.merriam-webster.com/dictionary/strategy

Miller, Debbie. 2002. *Reading with Meaning: Teaching Comprehension in the Primary Grades*. York, ME: Stenhouse.

Miller, Donalyn. 2009. *The Book Whisper: Awakening the Inner Reader in Every Child*. San Francisco, CA: Jossey-Bass.

Miller, Justin, and Paula J. Schwanenflugel. 2006. "Prosody of Syntactically Complex Sentences in the Oral Reading of Young Children." *Journal of Educational Psychology* 98 (4): 839–853. doi:10.1037/0022-0663.98.4.839

Miller, Paul, and Billie Eilam. 2008. "Development in the Thematic and Containment-Relation-Oriented Organization of Word Concepts." *The Journal of Educational Research* 101 (6): 350–362. doi:10.3200/JOER.101.6.350-362

Misulis, Katherine. 1999. "Making Vocabulary Development Manageable in Content Instruction." *Contemporary Education* 70 (2): 25–29.

Moats, Louisa C., and C. Tolman. 2009. Excerpted from *Language Essentials for Teachers of Reading and Spelling (LETRS): Module 2: The Speech Sounds of English: Phonetics, Phonology, and Phoneme Awareness*. Boston: Sopris West.

Montelongo, José. 2008. "Text Guides: Scaffolding Summarization and Fortifying Reading Skills." *The International Journal of Learning* 15 (7): 289–296.

Morris, Darrell. 1992. *Case Studies in Teaching Beginning Readers: The Howard Street Tutoring Manual*. Boone, NC: Fieldstream.

Morrow, Lesley Mandel, and Diane H. Tracey. 1997. "Strategies Used for Phonics Instruction in Early Childhood Classrooms." *The Reading Teacher* 50 (8): 644–651.

Mountain, Lee. 2005. "ROOTing Out Meaning: More Morphemic Analysis for Primary Pupils." *The Reading Teacher* 58 (8): 742–749.

Moustafa, Margaret. 1997. *Beyond Traditional Phonics: Research Discoveries and Reading Instruction*. Portsmouth, NH: Heinemann.

Nagy, William E. 2003. *Teaching Vocabulary to Improve Reading Comprehension*. Newark, DE: International Reading Association.

———. 2005. "Why Vocabulary Instruction Needs to Be Long-Term and Comprehensive." In *Teaching and Learning Vocabulary: Bringing Research to Practice*, edited by Elfrieda H. Hiebert and Michael L. Kamil, 27–44. Mahwah, NJ: Lawrence Erlbaum.

Nagy, William E., Richard C. Anderson, and P. A. Herman. 1987. "Learning Word Meanings from Context During Normal Reading." *American Educational Research Journal* 24 (2): 237–278.

Nagy, William E., Irene-Anna N. Diakidoy, and Richard C. Anderson. 1991. *The Development of Knowledge of Derivational Suffixes*. Champaign, IL: Center for the Study of Reading.

Nathan, Ruth G., and Keith E. Stanovich. 1991. "The Causes and Consequences of Differences in Reading Fluency." *Theory Into Practice* 30 (3): 176–184.

National Governors Association Center for Best Practices and Council of Chief State School Officers. 2010. *Common Core State Standards for English Language Arts and Literacy in History/Social Studies, Science, and Technical Subjects*. Washington, DC: National Governors Association Center for Best Practices, Council of Chief State School Officers.

National Institute of Child Health and Human Development. 2000. *Report of the National Reading Panel. Teaching Children to Read: An Evidence-Based Assessment of the Scientific Research Literature on Reading and Its Implications for Reading Instruction*. NIH Publication No. 00-4769. Washington, DC: U.S. Government Printing Office.

Nations, Susan, and Melissa Alonso. 2014. *Primary Literacy Centers: Making Readign and Writing Stick*. Gainsville, FL: Maupin House.

Nelson, Deanna L. 2008. "A Context-Based Strategy for Teaching Vocabulary." *The English Journal* 97 (4): 33–37.

Newbury, M. 2007. "Sounds System." *Times Educational Supplement* Great Britain Issue 4753, 40–41.

Nilsen, Alleen Pace, and Don L. F. Nilsen. 2003. "Vocabulary Development: Teaching vs. Testing." *English Journal* 92 (3): 31–37. doi:10.2307/822257

Nist, S. L., and S. Olejnik. 1995. "The Role of Context and Dictionary Definitions on Varying Levels of Word Knowledge." *Reading Research Quarterly* 30 (2): 172–193.

O'Connor, Peter J., and Chris J. Jackson. 2008. "The Factor Structure and Validity of the Learning Styles Profiler (LSP)." *European Journal of Psychological Assessment* 24 (2): 117–123. doi:10.1027/1015-5759.24.2.117

O'Connor, Rollanda E., Annika White, and H. Lee Swanson. 2007. "Repeated Reading versus Continuous Reading: Influences on Reading Fluency and Comprehension." *Exceptional Children* 74 (1): 31–46.

Ogle, Donna. 1986. "K-W-L Group Instructional Strategy." In *Teaching Reading as Thinking*, edited by A. S. Palincsar, D. Ogle, B. F. Jones, and E. G. Carr, 11–17. Alexandria, VA: Association for Supervision and Curriculum Development.

———. 2000. "Make It Visual: A Picture Is Worth a Thousand Words." In *Creativity and Innovation in Content Area Teaching*, edited by Maureen McLaughlin and MaryEllen Vogt, 55–71. Norwood, MA: Christopher Gordon.

Olson, M. W., and T. C. Gee. 1991. "Content Reading Instruction in the Primary Grades: Perceptions and Strategies." *The Reading Teacher* 45 (4): 298–307.

Papadopoulos, Timothy C., Panayiota Kendeou, and George Spanoudis. 2012. "Investigating the Factor Structure and Measurement Invariance of Phonological Abilities in a Sufficiently Transparent Language." *Journal of Educational Psychology* 104 (2): 321–336.

Paris, Scott G., Barbara A. Wasik, and Julianne C. Turner. 1991. "The Development of Strategic Readers." In *Handbook of Reading Research*, Volume 2, edited by Rebecca Barr, Michael L. Kamil, Peter B. Mosenthal, and P. David Pearson, 609–640. White Plains, NY: Longman.

Parsons, Seth A. 2008. "Providing All Students ACCESS to Self-Regulated Literacy Learning." *The Reading Teacher* 61 (8): 628–635. doi:10.1598/RT.61.8.4

Paulson, Eric J. 2005. "Viewing Eye Movements During Reading Through the Lens of Chaos Theory: How Reading Is Like the Weather." *Reading Research Quarterly* 40 (3): 338–358. doi:10.1598/RRQ.40.3.3

Pearson, P. David. 2012. *The IRA Literacy Research Panel: Big Ideas, Literacy Needs, and National Priorities*. Paper presented at the meeting of the International Reading Association, Chicago, IL.

Pearson, P. David, and Nell K. Duke. 2002. "Comprehension Instruction in the Primary Grades." In *Comprehension Instruction: Research-Based Best Practices*, edited by Cathy C. Block and Michael Pressley, 247–258. New York: Guilford.

Pearson, P. David, and Margaret C. Gallagher. 1983. "The Instruction of Reading Comprehension." *Contemporary Educational Psychology* 8 (3): 317–344.

Perry, Nancy E., Lynda Hutchinson, and Carolyn Thauberger. 2007. "Mentoring Student Teachers to Design and Implement Literacy Tasks that Support Self-Regulated Reading and Writing." *Reading & Writing Quarterly* 23 (1): 27–50. doi:10.1080/10573560600837636

Pinnell, Gay Su, and Irene C. Fountas. 1998. *Word Matters: Teaching Phonics and Spelling in the Reading/Writing Classroom*. Portsmouth, NH: Heinemann.

Pinnell, Gay Su, Jack J. Pikulski, Karen K. Wixon, Jay R. Campbell, Philip P. Gough, and Alexandra S. Beatty. 1995. *Listening to Children Read Aloud Data from NAEP's Integral Reading Performance Record CIRPR at Grade 4*. Washington DC: Office of Educational Research and Improvement, U.S. Department of Education.

Pittelman, S. D., J. E. Heimlich, R. L. Berglund, and M. P. French. 1991. *Semantic Feature Analysis: Classroom Applications*. Newark, DE: International Reading Association.

Pressley, Michael. 2002. "Metacognition and Self-Regulated Comprehension." In *What Research Has to Say About Reading Instruction*, 3rd edition, edited by Alan E. Farstrup and S. Jay Samuels, 291–309. Newark, DE: International Reading Association.

Pressley, Michael, Pamela Beard El-Dinary, Irene Gaskins, Ted Schuder, Janet L. Bergman, Janice T. Almasi, and Rachel Brown. 1992. "Beyond Direct Explanation: Transactional Instruction of Reading Comprehension Strategies." *The Elementary School Journal* 92 (5): 513–555.

Pressley, Michael, Fiona Goodchild, Joan Fleet, Richard Zajchowski, and Ellis Evan. 1989. "The Challenges of Classroom Strategy Instruction." *The Elementary School Journal* 89 (3): 301–342.

Raphael, Taffy E. 1986. "Teaching Question Answer Relationships, Revisited." *The Reading Teacher* 39 (6): 516–522.

Raphael, Taffy E., Kathy Highfield, and Kathryn H. Au. 2006. *QAR Now: Question Answer Relationships*. New York: Scholastic.

Rashotte, Carol A., and Joseph K. Torgesen. 1985. "Repeated Reading and Reading Fluency in Learning Disabled Children." *Reading Research Quarterly* 20 (2): 180–188.

Rasinski, Timothy V. 1989. "Fluency for Everyone: Incorporating Fluency Instruction in the Classroom." *The Reading Teacher* 42 (9): 690–693.

———.2000. "Speed Does Matter in Reading." *The Reading Teacher* 54 (2): 146–151.

———. 2003. *The Fluent Reader: Oral Reading Strategies for Building Word Recognition, Fluency, and Comprehension*. New York: Scholastic.

———. 2004. "Creating Fluent Readers." *What Research Stays About Reading.* 61 (1): 46–51.

———. 2005. *Daily Word Ladders: Grades 4–6*. New York: Scholastic.

———. 2006. "Reading Fluency Instruction: Moving Beyond Accuracy, Automaticity, and Prosody." *The Reading Teacher* 59 (7): 704–706. doi:10.1598/RT.59.7.10

———. 2008. *Daily Word Ladders: Grades 1–2*. New York: Scholastic.

Rasinski, Timothy V., and Melissa Cheesman Smith. 2014. Vocabulary Ladders: Understanding Word Nuances. Huntington Beach, CA: Shell Education.

Rasinski, Timothy V., and Lisa A. Lenhart. 2007. "Explorations of Fluent Readers." *Reading Today* 25 (3): 18.

Rasinski, Timothy V., Kasim Yildirim, and James Nageldinger. 2012. "Building Fluency through the Phrased Text Lesson." *The Reading Teacher* 65 (4): 252–255.

Rayner, Keith. 1998. "Eye Movements in Reading and Informational Processing: 20 Years of Research." *Psychological Bulletin* 124 (3): 372–422.

Readence, John E., Thomas W. Bean, and R. Scott Baldwin. 2007. *Content Area Literacy: An Integrated Approach*, 9th edition. Dubuque, IA: Kendall/Hunt.

Redfield, Doris L., and Elaine W. Rousseau. 1981. "A Meta-Analysis of Experimental Research on Teacher Questioning Behavior." *Review of Educational Research* 51 (2): 237–245.

Reutebuch, Colleen K. 2008. "Succeed with a Response-to-Intervention Model." *Intervention in School and Clinic* 44 (2): 126–128. doi:10.1177/1053451208321598

Reynolds, Mary E., Kristie Callihan, and Erin Browning. 2003. "Effect of Instruction on the Development of Rhyming Skills in Young Children." *Contemporary Issues in Communication Science and Disorders* 30: 41–46.

Risko, Victoria J., Doris Walker-Dalhouse, Erin S. Bridges, and Ali Wilson. 2011. "Drawing on Text Features for Reading Comprehension and Composing." *The Reading Teacher* 64 (5): 376–378.

———. 1996. *Reading Clinic: Use Predictions to Help Kids Think Deeply About Books*. New York: Scholastic.

Robb, Laura. 1997. "Stretch Your Students' Reading Vocabulary." *Instructor* 106 (8): 34–36.

Robbie, Sheila, Tina Ruggierello, and Bernie Warren. 2001. *Using Drama to Bring Language to Life: Ideas, Games, and Activities for Teachers of Languages and Language Arts*. Concord, ON: Captus Press.

Roberts, Theresa A., and Anne Meiring. 2006. "Teaching Phonics in the Context of Children's Literature or Spelling: Influences on First-Grade Reading, Spelling, and Writing and Fifth-Grade Comprehension." *Journal of Educational Psychology* 98 (4): 690–713. doi:10.1037/0022-0663.98.4.690

Robinson, F. P. 1961. "Study Skills for Superior Students in Secondary School." *The Reading Teacher* 15 (1): 29–33.

Rosenthal, Julie, and Linnea C. Ehri. 2008. "The Mnemonic Value of Orthography for Vocabulary Learning." *Journal of Educational Psychology* 100 (1): 175–191.

Routman, Regie. 2000. *Conversations: Strategies for Teaching, Learning, and Evaluating*. Portsmouth, NH: Heinemann.

———. 2003. *Reading Essentials: The Specifics You Need to Teach Reading Well*. Portsmouth, NH: Heinemann.

Runge, Timothy J., and Marley W. Watkins. 2006. "The Structure of Phonological Awareness Among Kindergarten Students." *School Psychology Review* 35 (3): 370–386.

Rupley, William H., John W. Logan, and William D. Nichols. 1999. "Vocabulary Instruction in a Balanced Reading Program." *The Reading Teacher* 52 (4): 336–346.

Samuels, S. Jay. 1979. "The Method of Repeated Readings." *The Reading Teacher* 32 (4): 403–408.

———. 2002. "Reading Fluency: Its Development and Assessment." In *What Research Has to Say About Reading Instruction*, 3rd edition, edited by Alan E. Farstrup and S. Jay Samuels, 166–183. Newark, DE: International Reading Association.

Samuels, S. Jay, and Alan E. Farstrup (Eds.). 2006. *What Research Has to Say About Fluency Instruction*. Newark, DE: International Reading Association.

Schmidt, B., and Buckley, M. 1990. "Plot Relationships Chart." In *Responses to Literature: Grades K–8*, edited by James M. Macon, Diane Bewell, and MaryEllen Vogt, 7. Newark, DE: International Reading Association.

Schwartz, Robert M., and Taffy E. Raphael. 1985. "Concept of Definition: A Key to Improving Students' Vocabulary." *The Reading Teacher* 39 (2): 198–205.

Shanahan, Timothy. 2002. *A Sin of the Second Kind: The Status of Reading Fluency in America*. Paper presented at the Focus on Fluency Forum, San Francisco, CA.

Shanahan, Timothy, and Cynthia Shanahan. 2008. "Teaching Disciplinary Literacy to Adolescents: Rethinking Content-Area Literacy." *Harvard Educational Review* 78 (1): 40–59.

Sharp, Ann C., Gale M. Sinatra, and Ralph E. Reynolds. 2008. "The Development of Children's Orthographic Knowledge: A Microgenetic Perspective." *Reading Research Quarterly* 43 (3): 206–226. doi:10.1598/RRQ.43.3.1

Shaywitz, Sally E., and Bennett A. Shaywitz. 2007. "What Neuroscience Really Tells Us About Reading Instruction." *Educational Leadership* 64 (5): 74–76.

Short, Kathy G., Jerome C. Harste, and Carolyn Burke. 1996. *Creating Classrooms for Authors and Inquirers*. Portsmouth, NH: Heinemann.

Short, Rick Jay, and Ronda C. Talley. 1997. Rethinking Psychology and the Schools: Implications of Recent National Policy." *American Psychologist*. 52 (3): 234–240.

Silver, Harvey F., Richard W. Strong, and Matthew J. Perini. 2001. *Tools for Promoting Active, In-Depth Learning*, 2nd edition. Woodbridge, NJ: Thoughtful Education.

Sippola, Arne E. 1995. "K-W-L-S." *The Reading Teacher* 48 (6): 542–543.

Skinner, Ellen A., and Michael J. Belmont. 1993. "Motivation in the Classroom: Reciprocal Effects of Teacher Behavior and Student Engagement Across the School Year." *Journal of Educational Psychology* 85 (4): 571–581. doi:10.1037/0022-0663.85.4.571

Sloyer, Shirlee. 1982. *Readers Theatre: Story Dramatization in the Classroom*. Urbana, IL: National Council of Teachers of English.

Small, Marian. 2010. "Beyond One Right Answer." *Educational Leadership* 68 (1): 28–32.

Snow, Catherine E., M. Susan Burns, and Peg Griffin (Eds.). 1998. *Preventing Reading Difficulties in Young Children*. Washington, DC: National Academy Press.

Snow, Catherine, and Catherine O'Connor. 2013. "Close Reading and Far-Reaching Classroom Discussion: Fostering a Vital Connection." International Reading Association Policy Brief, Newark, DE.

Sousa, David A. (Ed.). 2010. *Mind, Brain, & Education: Neuroscience Implications for the Classroom*. Bloomington, IN: Solution Tree Press.

Spencer, Elizabeth J., C. Melanie Schuele, Kathryn M. Guillot, and Marvin W. Lee. 2011. "Phonemic Awareness Skill of Undergraduate and Graduate Students Relative to Speech-Language Pathologists and Other Educators." *Contemporary Issues in Communication Science and Disorders* 38: 109–118.

Sprenger, Marilee. 2005. *How to Teach So Students Remember*. Alexandria, VA: Association for Supervision and Curriculum Development.

Stahl, Steven A., Ann M. Duffy-Hester, and Katherine Anne Dougherty Stahl. 1998. "Everything You Wanted to Know About Phonics (But Were Afraid to Ask)." *Reading Research Quarterly* 33 (3): 338–355.

Stahl, Steven A., and William E. Nagy. 2006. *Teaching Word Meanings*. Mahwah, NJ: Erlbaum.

Stanovich, Keith E. 1986. "Matthew Effects in Reading: Some Consequences of Individual Differences in the Acquisition of Literacy." *Reading Research Quarterly* 21 (4): 360–407. doi:10.1598/RRQ.21.4.1

Stayter, Francine Z., and Richard L. Allington. 1991. "Fluency and the Understanding of Texts." *Theory Into Practice* 30 (3): 143–148.

Stiggins, Rick, and Jan Chappuis. 2008. "Enhancing Student Learning." *District Administrator* 44 (1): 42–44.

Strickland, Dorothy S. 1998. *Teaching Phonics Today: A Primer for Educators*. Newark, DE: International Reading Association.

Strickland, Dorothy S., Kathy Ganske, and Joanne K. Monroe. 2002. *Supporting Struggling Readers and Writers: Strategies for Classroom Intervention 3–6*. Newark, DE: International Reading Association.

Stull, Andrew T., and Richard E. Mayer. 2007. "Learning by Doing Verses Learning by Viewing: Three Experimental Comparisons of Learner-Generated Verses Author-Provided Graphic Organizers." *Journal of Educational Psychology* 99 (4): 808–820. doi:10.1037/0022-0663.99.4.808

Taba, Hilda. 1967. *Teacher's Handbook for Elementary Social Studies*. Reading, MA: Addison-Wesley.

Taberski, Sharon. 2000. *On Solid Ground: Strategies for Teaching Reading K–3*. Portsmouth, NH: Heinemann.

Tate, Marcia L. 2003. *Worksheets Don't Grow Dendrites: 20 Instructional Strategies That Engage the Brain*. Thousand Oaks, CA: Corwin.

———. 2010. *Worksheets Don't Grow Dendrites: 20 Instructional Strategies That Engage the Brain*, 2nd edition. Thousand Oaks, CA: Corwin.

Taylor, Barbara M. 2008. "Tier I: Effective Classroom Reading Instruction in the Elementary Grades." In *Response to Intervention: A Framework for Reading Educators*, edited by Douglas Fuchs, Lynn S. Fuchs, and Sharon Vaughn, 5–26. Newark, DE: International Reading Association.

Thompson, Mary. 2008. "Multimodal Teaching and Learning: Creating Spaces for Content Teachers." *Journal of Adolescent & Adult Literacy* 52 (2): 144–153.

Tierney, Robert J., and John E. Readence. 2005. *Reading Strategies and Practices: A Compendium*, 6th edition. Boston: Allyn & Bacon.

Tomlinson, Carol Ann, and Jay McTighe. 2006. *Integrating Differentiated Instruction & Understanding by Design: Connecting Content and Kids.* Alexandria, VA: Association for Supervision and Curriculum Development.

Tompkins, Gail E. 2000. *Teaching Writing: Balancing Process and Product.* Upper Saddle River, NJ: Prentice Hall.

———. 2001. *Literacy for the 21st Century: A Balanced Approach*, 2nd edition. Englewood Cliffs, NJ: Prentice Hall.

Torgesen, Joseph K., Carol A. Rashotte, and Ann W. Alexander. 2001. "Principles of Fluency Instruction in Reading: Relationships with Established Empirical Outcomes." In *Dyslexia, Fluency, and the Brain*, edited by Maryanne Wolf, 333–355. Timonium, MD: York.

Tovani, Cris. 2000. *I Read It, But I Don't Get It: Comprehension Strategies for Adolescent Readers.* Portland, ME: Stenhouse.

Traill, Leanna. 1995. *Highlight My Strengths: Assessment and Evaluation of Literacy Learning.* Crystal Lake, IL: Rigby.

Unsworth, Len, and Viviane Heberle. 2009. *Teaching Multimodal Literacy in English as a Foreign Language.* Oakville, CT: Brown Publishing.

Vacca, Jo Anne L., Richard T. Vacca, and Mary K. Gove. 1995. *Reading and Learning to Read*, 3rd edition. Reading, MA: Addison-Wesley.

Vacca, Jo Anne L. and Richard T. Vacca. 2008. *Content Area Reading: Literacy and Learning across the Curriculum, 9th Edition.* Boston, MA: Pearson Allyn & Bacon.

Vadasy, Patricia F., and Elizabeth A. Sanders. 2008. "Repeated Reading Intervention: Outcomes and Interactions with Readers' Skills and Classroom Instruction." *Journal of Educational Psychology* 100 (2): 272–290. doi:10.1037/0022-0663.100.2.272

Vaughn, Sharon, Sylvia Linan-Thompson, and Peggy Hickman. 2003. "Response to Instruction as a Means of Identifying Students With Reading/Learning Disabilities." *Exceptional Children* 69 (4): 391–409.

Vygotsky, L. S. 1978. *Mind in Society: The Development of Higher Psychological Processes*, edited by Michael Cole, Vera John-Steiner, Sylvia Scribner, and Ellen Souberman. Cambridge, MA: Harvard University Press.

Waldo, B. 1991. "Story Pyramid." In *Responses to Literature: Grades K–8*, edited by James M. Macon, Diane Bewell, and MaryEllen Vogt, 23–24. Newark, DE: International Reading Association.

Webb, Norman L. 1999. *Alignment of Science and Math Standards and Assessments in Four States.* Council of Chief State School Officers and National Institute for Science Education, Madison, WI: University of Wisconsin, Wisconsin Center for Education Research.

Webb, Norman L. 2002. Depth-of-Knowledge Levels for Content Areas. University of Wisconsin Center for Eductional Research.

Wiggins, Grant P., and Jay McTighe. 2005. *Understanding by Design*, 2nd edition. Upper Saddle River, NJ: Prentice Hall.

Williams, Rachel Marie-Crane. 2008. "Image, Text, and Story: Comics and Graphic Novels in the Classroom." *Art Education* 61 (6): 13–19.

Willis, Judy. 2010. "The Current Impact of Neuroscience on Teaching and Learning." In *Mind, Brain, and Education: Neuroscience Implications for the Classroom*, edited by David A. Sousa, 45–68. Bloomington, IN: Solution Tree.

Wilson, Judith K. 2012. "Brisk and Effective Fluency Instruction for Small Groups." *Intervention in School and Clinic* 47 (3): 152–157.

Wood, Audrey. 1984. *The Napping House.* New York: Harcourt Brace.

Wood, Karen D., Diane Lapp, and James Flood. 1992. *Guiding Readers through Text: A Review of Study Guides.* Newark, DE: International Reading Association.

Wylie, Richard E., and Donald D. Durell. 1970. "Teaching Vowels through Phonograms." *Elementary English* 47 (6): 787–791.

Yopp, Hallie K. 1992. "Developing Phonemic Awareness in Young Children." *The Reading Teacher* 45 (9): 696–703.

Zgonc, Y. 1999. *Phonological Awareness: The Missing Piece to Help Crack the Reading Code.* Eau Claire, WI: Otter Creek Institute.

Zigler, Edward, and Matia Finn-Stevenson. 2007. "From Research to Policy and Practice: The School of the 21st Century." *American Journal of Orthopsychiatry* 77 (2): 175–181. doi:10.1037/0002-9432.77.2.175

Zigler, Edward, Dorothy G. Singer, and Sandra J. Bishop-Josef (Eds.). 2004. *Children's Play: The Roots of Reading.* Washington, DC: Zero to Three Press.

Zimmerman, Barry J., and Dale H. Schunk (Eds.). 2013. *Self-Regulated Learning and Academic Achievement: Theoretical Perspectives.* New York: Routledge.

Zutell, J. 1998. "Word Sorting: A Developmental Spelling Approach to Word Study for Delayed Readers." *Reading and Writing Quarterly* 1 (2): 219–238.

Contents of the Digital Resource CD

Resource	Filename
Musical Rhyme Pictures	musicalrhyme.pdf
Rhyming Jar Sentences	rhymingjar.pdf
Rhyming Jar Sentences Answer Key	rhyminganswer.pdf
Draw a Rhyme Poem	drawrhymepoem.pdf
Think Sounds Pictures	thinksoundspics.pdf
Think Sounds Picture Answer Key	thinkanswer.pdf
Rimes Poster	rimesposter.pdf
Stretch-It Strips	stretchstrips.pdf
Bongo Letters and Word Cards	bongocards.pdf
Bongo Initial, Ending, and Vowel Boards	bongoinitial.pdf
Bingo/Bongo Three-Column Chart	bingobongothree.pdf
Bingo/Bongo Blank Board	bingobongoblank.pdf
Bingo/Bongo Directions	bingodirections.pdf
Syllable Rummy Directions	syllablerummy.pdf
Roll-Read-Record (3Rs) Chart	rollreadrecord.pdf
DISSECT Chart	dissectchart.pdf
Deeper DISSECTing Chart	deeperdissect.pdf
Word Ladder	wordladder.pdf
Word Detectives Badge Poster	worddetectives.pdf
Working with Words (WWW)	workingwords.pdf
Brain Trick Connection Puzzles	braintrick.pdf
Look/Say/Cover/Write/Check Bookmark	looksaybookmark.pdf
LSCWC Icons	lscwcicons.pdf
If I Can Spell Form	ificanspell.pdf
Puzzle Pieces	puzzlepiece.pdf
Reflection Connection Chart	reflectionchart.pdf
Semantic Feature Analysis Matrix	semanticfeature.pdf
What Do You Mean? List	whatdoyoumean.pdf
CCC Chart	cccchart.pdf
CCC Word Mat	cccwordmat.pdf
Clue Glue Word Cards	clueglueword.pdf
Go Figure Idiom Cards	gofigurecards.pdf
Word Relationship Web	relationshipweb.pdf
Alphabox Chart	alphaboxchart.pdf
List/Group/Label/Reflect Chart	listgroupchart.pdf
List/Group/Label Form	listgroupform.pdf
Four Corners Form	fourcornersform.pdf
Vocabulary Tree Template	vocabularytree.pdf
Rootin' Root Tree Template	rootintree.pdf
Rootin' Root Leaves Template	rootinleaves.pdf

Resource	Filename
Word Jar	wordjar.pdf
Knowledge Rating Matrix	knowledgerating.pdf
Defining Moment Feature Cards	definingmoment.pdf
Teacher Talk Phrase Strips 1	teachertalk1.pdf
Teacher Talk Phrase Strips 2	teachertalk2.pdf
Phrase Strips Choices	phrasechoices.pdf
Reading Bookmark	readingbookmark.pdf
Listen to Me Form	listentomeform.pdf
Fluency Rubric	fluencyrubric.pdf
Express Yourself Emotion Cards	expressyourself.pdf
Emotion Mat	emotionmat.pdf
Text Traits	texttraits.pdf
Text Traits Bookmark	traitbookmark.pdf
Constructing Structure Form	constructing.pdf
Connect and Reflect Puzzle Pieces	connectreflect.pdf
Anticipation/Reaction Guide	anticipation.pdf
Think Sheet	thinksheet.pdf
Two-Column Note Prediction Form	twocolumnnote.pdf
QARs	qars.pdf
Question Logs: 3Rs Form	questionlogs.pdf
SQ3R Chart	sq3r.pdf
Sensory Impressions Chart	sensorychart.pdf
Sensory Impressions Hand	sensoryhand.pdf
Main Idea Wheel: Six Spokes	wheelsixspokes.pdf
Main Idea Wheel: Four Spokes	wheelfourspokes.pdf
Detail/Retell Rubric	detailretell.pdf
Story Map	storymapping.pdf
Narrative and Informational Text Pyramid	textpyramid.pdf
Synthesizing Target	synthesizing.pdf
CAI	cai.pdf
Comprehension Assessment	compassess.pdf
Vocabulary Assessment	vocabassess.pdf
Word Study: Phonological Awareness and Phonics Assessment	wordstudyassess.pdf
Fluency Assessment	fluencyassess.pdf
Syllable Structue and Jingle Examples	syllablejingle.pdf
CCSS Standards	standards.pdf

Notes

Notes

#51185—Creating Strategic Readers 3rd Edition